PUBLIC KEY CRYPTOGRAPHY

PUBLIC KEY CRYPTOGRAPHY
Applications and Attacks

Lynn Margaret Batten

Deakin University, Melbourne, Australia

IEEE Press

IEEE Press Series on
Information & Communication
Networks Security
Stamatios Kartalopoulos, Series Editor

A John Wiley & Sons, Inc., Publication

Published by John Wiley & Sons, Inc., Hoboken, New Jersey.
Published simultaneously in Canada.

For general information on our other products and services or for technical support, please contact our
Customer Care Department within the United States at (800) 762-2974, outside the United States at (317)
572-3993 or fax (317) 572-4002.

Wiley also publishes its books in a variety of electronic formats. Some content that appears in print may not
be available in electronic formats. For more information about Wiley products, visit our web site at
www.wiley.com.

Library of Congress Cataloging-in-Publication Data:

Batten, Lynn Margaret.
  Public key cryptography : applications and attacks / Lynn Margaret Batten.
      p. cm.
  Includes bibliographical references and index.
  ISBN 978-1-118-31712-9 (cloth)
1. Public key cryptography. 2. Cryptography–Mathematics. I. Title.
  TK5102.94.B38 2012
  005.8'2–dc23

                                            2012025411

Printed in the United States of America

For Glenn

"In the margin of his copy of Arithmetica, Pierre de Fermat had jotted the words 'I have a truly marvelous demonstration of this proposition which this margin is too narrow to contain . . .' And all of a sudden she understood. The answer was disarmingly simple."

(From **The Girl Who Played with Fire** by Stieg Larsson. Translated into English from the Swedish by Reg Keeland. Maclehose Press, Quercus, London, 2009, p. 536)

CONTENTS

PREFACE

There are now many texts available giving an overview of both public key and symmetric key cryptography. The focus of this text is only the former. The objective is to give a complete description of the current major public key cryptosystems, the underlying mathematics, and the most common techniques used in attacking them.

It is assumed throughout that the reader has access to an algebraic software system such as Maple [65] or a sophisticated calculator supporting computation of large numbers and moduli. The reason for this is to emphasize the fact that, while the mathematical schemes are well designed, they supply no security unless they are implemented on sufficiently large values; thus, it is important to examine the complexity of the computations for small numbers as opposed to large ones. In each section of this book, we have provided computer-assisted examples.

The first chapters of this book cover the theory of public key systems in current use, including ElGamal, RSA, Elliptic Curve, and digital signature schemes. The underlying mathematics needed to build and study these schemes is provided as needed through the book. The latter half of the book examines attacks on these schemes via mathematical problems on which they are based fundamentally, the discrete logarithm problem and the difficulty of factoring integers.

The book is suitable for one or two semester courses for students with some discrete mathematics background including a knowledge of algorithms, computational complexity, and binary arithmetic. It is aimed at students studying cryptography in the context of information technology security and is designed to cover thoroughly the public key cryptography material needed for the writing of the CISSP exam [57]. It is equally aimed at mathematics students in the context of applications of groups and fields. Each chapter contains 40–50 problems and full solutions for the odd-numbered questions are provided in the appendix. To obtain the full solutions manual please send an email to: pressbooks@ieee.org.

LYNN MARGARET BATTEN

ACKNOWLEDGMENTS

I would like to thank Judy Chow for her considerable effort and skill in producing a LaTeX, version of this document. Bernard Colbert read and commented on several drafts, Martin Schulz assisted with Maple while Lei Pan produced elliptic curve graphics; I thank all of these people. In addition, I wish to thank Wiley representative Mary Hatcher and anonymous referees for their support and suggested improvements of the original manuscript.

LIST OF FIGURES

1

INTRODUCTION

This book is designed for use as a university text for year three, four, or honors level students. It is intended as a first approach to public key cryptography—no background in cryptography is needed. However, a basic understanding of discrete mathematics and algorithms and of the concept of computational complexity is assumed.

The major public key systems are presented in detail, both from the point of view of their design and their levels of security. Since all are based on a computationally difficult mathematical problem, the mathematics needed to construct and to analyze them is developed as needed along the way.

Each concept presented in the book comes with examples and problems, some of which can be done with limited computational capacity (a calculator for example) and some of which need major computational resources such as a mathematics-based software package or some independently written algorithms. Mathematica, Matlab, Magma [64], and Maple [65] are examples of packaged software that can be used easily to perform the necessary computations. For those who prefer open source software, see [28] where Sage is used for algorithms and examples. The book can be used without additional software resources by avoiding those problems which require them.

The software used by the author for the computationally expensive examples in this book was Maple. The solutions are presented with sufficient detail to permit an

Public Key Cryptography: Applications and Attacks, First Edition. Lynn Margaret Batten.
© 2013 by The Institute of Electrical and Electronics Engineers, Inc. Published 2013 by John Wiley & Sons, Inc.

easy translation to any other language or package. Full solutions are given to all odd-numbered problems. For those wishing to use the book at a Master's level, an emphasis on the computational complexity of the cryptographic systems and or the attacks on them would provide a solid basis for a good course including programme writing. *Emphasis on the computational complexity of attacks on public key systems provides the user with a feel for the level of security provided.*

1.1 THE MEANING OF THE WORD CRYPTOGRAPHY

In this preliminary chapter, we present some of the history of cryptography and the reasons for the development of the systems that we see in use today. There are no exercises associated with this chapter, but the interested reader can follow up any of the references and links provided.

The words *"cryptography," "cryptology,"* and *"cryptanalysis"* are commonly interchanged. However, each of them has a slightly different meaning. The common beginning "crytp" comes from the Greek $\kappa\rho\upsilon\mu\mu\varepsilon\nu\circ\zeta$ or *kruptos* for "hidden." The ending "graphy" refers to writing and so the first word in the list means "hidden writing" and generally refers to the encryption part of establishing a system for transmitting secrets. We call such an encrypted string a "cipher" or "ciphertext." Normally, when a cipher is constructed, the idea is that there will be some person or persons who can "legitimately" decipher it and so find the hidden text. In order to legitimately decipher, it is understood that a person will hold what is referred to as a "key," a means of simply and efficiently determining the original text. On the other hand, without this key, it should not be simple to deduce the hidden text.

The last word, cryptanalysis, refers to an analysis of hidden things, or ciphers, to expose what is hidden; this word generally refers to the decryption or discovery component of the system when the analyst does not have a legitimate key with which to read a cipher.

Finally, the word cryptology is made up of the two components "hidden" and "study" and refers to the study of hidden writings or secrets. This word encompasses both the establishment of encryption methods and the analysis of a cipher in order to break it without the associated key. While "cryptology" would be the correct word for a discussion including both encryption techniques and analysis of these techniques with the intent of breaking them, many people use the word "cryptography" instead.

In the next section, we cover very briefly the introduction of, and changes to, symmetric key cryptography over thousands of years. This is followed by a brief introduction to public key cryptography. Recent applications of cryptography, in addition to simply hiding data, are mentioned in Section 1.5. Section 1.6 mentions current standards in the area of cryptography and their impact.

1.2 SYMMETRIC KEY CRYPTOGRAPHY

The hiding of secrets in written and pictorial form with the intent of passing on a message to a select few has been documented over thousands of years, going far back in time to ancient Egypt [2, 36]. In many cases, it was used as a game so that the select few were able to have access to information not available to those excluded from the inner circle. However, it was also used in times of political tension and war to communicate securely, guarding secret information from the enemy.

Symmetric key systems are cryptographic systems in which decrypting is a simple method of reversing the encryption used. For example, if a message written in English is encrypted by replacing each letter with the one five places ahead in the alphabet (*a* is replaced by *f*, *b* by *g*, and so on), then to decrypt, the letters are simply moved five places back. A message written as a binary string may be encrypted by adding it to another, fixed, binary string. To decrypt, adding the fixed binary string again will produce the original message. Thus, to use a symmetric key cryptographic scheme, both the sender and the receiver use essentially the same key.

The simplicity of using the same key both to encrypt and to decrypt is off set by the difficulty of ensuring that all parties have the needed keys in a tense situation, and also when people may be widely dispersed geographically. In time of war, keys have to be physically delivered to personnel even in the remotest and most dangerous locations. In the late 1800s, the idea of a "code book" which listed which keys to be used on which dates was born. Both the transmitter and the receiver needed a copy of the same code book for this to work, but several months of communications could be based on the delivery of a single code book. (Serious users of encryption recognized the need for constantly changing the key!)

1.2.1 Impact of Technology

Despite its history of about 4000 years, cryptography only came of age in the 1800s with the invention of technologies such as the telegraph (for rapid communication over great distances) and manual rotary machines, followed in the early 1900s by electrical rotary machines [2]. David Khan, in his book *The Code Breakers* [22] explains that the electro mechanical rotary machine for cryptographic purposes was invented almost simultaneously around 1917–1919 by four different people in four different countries. None of these people became rich. One of them, the Swede *Arvid Damm*, died in 1927 and his company was taken over by another Swede, *Boris Hagelin* (1892–1983). Despite Hagelin's death, the company, Crypto AG (http://www.crypto.ch/), still operates in Zug, Switzerland. Figure 1.1 shows a machine sold by the company.

1.2.2 Confusion and Diffusion

As cryptography became less of an art form and more of a science in the 1900s, it was inevitable that at some point, someone would try to formalize the principal aims of a cryptographic system. Claude Shannon was one of the first to do so [48]. He argued that a cryptosystem designer should assume that the system may be attacked by someone who has access to it, as was indeed the case during the two world wars when machines were stolen and reverse engineered. He argued that the only point of secrecy should be the key, but that the system design should assist the security by incorporating "confusion" and "diffusion." "Confusion is intended to make the relationship between the key and

Figure 1.1. The M-209 encryption machine sold by Hagelin (from Wikipedia).

the ciphertext as complex as possible. Diffusion refers to rearranging or spreading out the bits in the message so that any redundancy in the plaintext is spread out over the ciphertext" [29]. In most symmetric key cryptosystems, confusion is provided by means of a *substitution* of some letters or symbols for others, whereas diffusion is provided by a *permutation* of the letters or symbols.

1.2.3 DES and AES

Horst Feistel (1919–1990) is believed to have been the first person to use the idea of a cipher with input broken into two parts of equal size, and iterated through several rounds in which functions and keys are applied, and right and left sides interchanged [29]. The concept is the basis for many symmetric ciphers in use today including the Data Encryption Standard (DES).

DES was the first commercially driven cryptographic product in history. By the mid-1900s, the effectiveness of cryptography for use by companies wishing to communicate in private led the U.S. government to work with IBM to develop the first fully specified cryptographic system on the open market. In 1976, the U.S. National Bureau of Standards declared it an official Federal Information Processing Standard.

In 1997, it was decided that the parameters of DES were now too small to provide the kind of protection needed, and a public, world-wide call for submissions for a new cryptosystem standard was made by the U.S. National Institute of Standards and Technology (NIST). After several years of analysis of submissions, much done by academics around the world, in 2002 a new standard, known as AES (for Advanced Encryption Standard), was chosen by NIST. While the AES does not incorporate a Feistel-type structure, such as DES, it uses substitutions and permutations along with several rounds. More details on both DES and AES can be found in [52].

Further Reading. F.L. Bauer [2]; D. Khan [22]; S. Pincock [36]; C.E. Shannon [48].

1.3 PUBLIC KEY (ASYMMETRIC) CRYPTOGRAPHY

The one major problem that held back a general uptake of cryptography for use in business circles was that of exchanging keys. While for many years, governments had established methods of managing keys, business people were not interested in employing circumspect, and perhaps even dangerous, methods of exchanging keys. In the 1960s, this became known as the "key management" problem and it was to be another decade before a viable solution was found.

1.3.1 Diffie–Hellman Key Exchange

In 1976, Whit Diffie and Martin Hellman published a paper [13] describing a method of establishing a common key in a secure manner over an insecure channel. The method is based on exponentiation and the fact that exponents can be multiplied in any order with the same result. The method is described in detail in Section 2.3. However, this scheme was useful only for establishing keys and did not actually encrypt data. The search was still on for an encryption scheme that allowed anyone to send an enciphered message to any other person, without pre-establishing keys, such that only the targeted recipient could decrypt the message.

In retrospect, the solution is amazingly simple and the first example appears to have been developed independently from two sources.

Basically, the idea is for each person to have two keys, one to encrypt and one to decrypt. The two keys would have to be bound together in some fundamental way in order for them to "invert" each other, but it should be impossible for an attacker to derive one from the other. The encryption key would be published, as in a telephone book. Only the recipient would know his/her decryption key; it would not be revealed to anyone else. This idea entirely solved the problem of exchanging keys, except for the fact that, initially, no one actually had a real way of setting up such a scheme.

1.3.2 RSA

In 1978, the first actual method for implementing such a scheme was published by Ron Rivest et al. [46] and is now widely known by the first letter of each of the authors' names as RSA. An RSA patent was filed in the United States on December 14, 1977, and approved as #4,405,829 titled "Cryptographic Communications System and Method" to the Massachusett's Institute of Technology, Rivest, Shamir, and Adelman. However, since the work had been published before the patent application, it could not be patented under European and Japanese law. (The RSA United States patent expired in 2000.) The company, RSA Data Security, was formed shortly thereafter and was granted an exclusive license on the RSA patent. In 2006, EMC Corporation (www.emc.com), a global information management and storage company, bought RSA which continues to operate as EMC's security division.

RSA security was based on the difficulty of factoring large numbers. At the time the company was established, the state-of-the-art research in factoring was not fully understood. To gauge what was known in this area, RSA Data Security put out the *RSA Factoring Challenge* in 1991 to encourage research into computational number theory and the practical difficulty of factoring large integers and the breaking of RSA keys used in cryptography. We focus on this in Chapters 7 and 8. A cash prize was offered for the successful factorization of some of the numbers posted. The smallest of them, a 100 decimal digit number called RSA-100, was factored by April 1, 1991, for a US$1000 prize. The RSA challenges ended in 2007.

In 1997, it was finally revealed that members of the British intelligence agency Government Communications Headquarters (GCHQ) had also invented essentially the same scheme early in the 1970s. See Steven Levy's book [26] for the interesting story of the parallel development.

1.3.3 ElGamal

The ElGamal cryptographic algorithm was invented a few years after the RSA scheme, developing from the PhD thesis of Taher ElGamal, which was awarded in 1984. The underlying idea on which the security is based is quite different from that of RSA. In ElGamal, the target is to determine the exponent in an equation of the form $a = b^x$, where a and b are known. The inventor did not apply for a patent on his scheme.

All known public key schemes are far more computationally intensive than symmetric key schemes. For example, a disadvantage of the ElGamal system is that the encrypted message becomes very big, about twice the size of the original message. Similarly, RSA is slower than DES by a factor of about 1000. For this reason, public key schemes are traditionally used only for small messages such as secret keys, whereas symmetric key schemes are retained for sending large messages.

Whether using a symmetric key or public key approach to encryption, the underlying mathematical formulation needs to be based on a finite system in order to ensure that infinite loops are avoided in computations. The arithmetic of such systems is developed in Chapter 2. Specifically, congruence arithmetic underpins all known cryptographic systems.

A second common feature of symmetric and asymmetric encryption is the use of both an encryption and a decryption key where data is transmitted over an insecure channel. This is illustrated in Figure 1.2.

While many public key cryptosystems have been proposed, only a few have withstood the test of time to remain in use today. In this book, we cover in detail three of those systems that have endured. RSA and ElGamal have been mentioned here. The third system we consider is based on elliptic curves and presented in Chapter 5. As mentioned

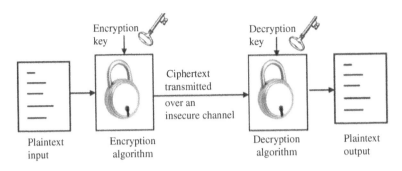

Figure 1.2. Transmitting encrypted data over an insecure channel.

in Section 5.2, the elliptic curve system is very efficient and so useful to implement on small devices.

Further Reading. W. Diffie and M. Hellman [13]; R. Rivest, A. Shamir and L. Adlemen [46]; S. Levy [26]; T. ElGamal [14].

1.4 KEY ESTABLISHMENT

The previous two sections referred to the importance of keys in cryptosystems but did not directly address the question of how to establish them. In this section, we shall only mention answers to this question that relate to public key cryptography.

In theory, anyone wishing to encrypt data can produce their own public/ private key pair based on any public key system, but in practice, people rely on a third party to provide them with keys. Out sourcing of key generation has the following benefits:

- the third party does the expensive computations;
- the third party specializes in key generation and knows the current best methods of securely and efficiently generating them;
- the third party takes on the liability for any problems arising from key failure.

However, it also has disadvantages:

- the third party knows your private key and so must be completely trust-worthy;
- the third party may be taken over by an organization which you do not trust.

However public/private key pairs are generated, trying to set up keys between two people over an insecure channel has associated problems. See the description of the "Intruder-in-the-Middle" attack in Section 6.3. (This attack is more commonly known as the "Man-in-the-Middle" attack and can be further studied in many other books on cryptography.) The concept of a "certificate" to tie a user to the key and a "certificate authority" to issue such certificates was born from trying to stop this attack. Section 13.3 of [28] gives a better discussion of these concepts.

Further Reading. The book *Protocols for Key Establishment and Authentication* by Boyd and Mathuria is a good source of further reading on this topic [4].

1.5 CRYPTOGRAPHY—MORE THAN JUST HIDING SECRETS

Along with the move from the government to the corporate sector, and the ease of use resulting from the pervasiveness of computers, a number of applications of cryptographic techniques, other than simply that for hiding data, have been developed. These have been motivated by needs of the digital age: how to confirm that a message received indeed came from the sender purported (it is quite easy to change a sender name in most e-mail systems), how to prevent a sender from claiming that they did not in fact send the message you received, and how to ensure that the message received was the one sent and had not been altered.

The most significant recent applications of cryptography are therefore for identification of senders, authentication of senders and recipients as well as the messages themselves, and digital signatures applied to messages.

1.5.1 Digital Signatures

A digital signature is a method of applying data to a message which identifies the sender of the message in the same way that a written signature on a piece of paper confirms authorship. All known public key systems have features that allow for this possibility. Digital signing is the basis of a number of the other applications mentioned earlier Chapter 6 is dedicated to this topic.

In using a public key scheme to send a signed message to Bob, Alice can simply apply her secret key to the message, essentially "encrypting" it with her decryption key. when Bob receives the message, he can verify that it was "signed" by Alice by applying Alice's public (encryption) key to it (see Figure 1.3). The result should be a readable message that makes sense to Bob. If it was not signed with Alice's private key, then

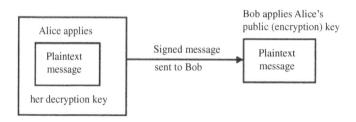

Figure 1.3. Alice signs a message for Bob.

applying her public key to it would result in nonsense, so Bob can be sure that it was signed by Alice. We discuss these procedures in more detail in Chapter 6.

1.5.2 Authentication

Parties entering into a communication over a digital pathway need to be able to identify each other. In addition, the data they transfer to each other needs to be authenticated as to origin, content, time sent, and so on. These issues all relate to an "intruder-in-the-middle" attack described in Section 6.3, where an individual places herself between two unsuspecting correspondents and reads, alters, and then passes on data between them. The integrity of data is preserved when such authentication is available.

1.5.3 Nonrepudiation

This ensures that a computer user cannot deny any actions or commitments made previously. If a dispute arises, a trusted third party can be brought in to assess the earlier communications and determine if the cryptographic protocols were in place to provide nonrepudiation.

1.6 STANDARDS

Many public key-based protocols have now become entrenched in standards. While this is good for those chosen, it means that it is difficult for any bright new idea to gain a foothold in the market place. Who chooses these standards? It is usually government or government-sponsored organizations that do so. One such organization is the National Institute of Standards and Technology, or NIST, a U.S. federal government agency that works with industry to develop and apply measurements and standards. For instance, NIST has established a standard for digital signatures, which can be found at `http://www.itl.nist.gov/fipspubs/fip186.htm`. We discuss this standard in Section 6.2. NIST is also the organization which established U.S. government standards for symmetric key and public key cryptography and hash functions (this last being the subject of Section 6.1).

Other countries have similar organizations determining standards. In Australia, the information security division of the Defence Signals Directorate determines cryptographic standards (see `http://www.dsd.gov.au/infosec/evaluation_services/epl/epl.html`). In Canada, the Standards Council of Canada is charged with recommendations on the choice of cryptographic protocol. See `http://www.scc.ca`. In the United Kingdom, it is the National Technical Authority for Information Assurance that provides this service; they can even point to products. See `http://www.cesg.gov.uk`. In the People's Republic of China, the Ministry of Public Security is responsible for protection of computer systems and the choice of cryptographic protocol to employ.

There is no international standard; each country makes its own choices. However, the Organization for Economic Co-operation and Development (OECD) issues guidelines for the use of information security systems that are often adopted by those

governments or organizations without the resources to develop them independently. See
http://www.oecd.org/document/42/0,2340,en_2649_34255_
15582250_1_1_1_1,00.html.

1.7 ATTACKS

On the one hand, many people and organizations wish to be able to communicate
information over insecure channels in such a way that only targeted receivers can read
it; on the other hand, there are many individuals and organizations who wish to gain
access to information which they would not normally receive. Examples include governments allied in war sending each other plans to combat other governments, the head
office of a large corporation distributing the plans for the next version of their product to national offices, individuals communicating instructions on transfers of money to
their banks.

In each of these cases, the communicating parties might use encryption to make
sure that an interceptor cannot read the information. In each case, there are people
waiting for an opportunity to capture, read, and possibly change the information being
transmitted.

Whenever methods are implemented to secure data, care must be taken to do so
without leaving weak components which are vulnerable to attackers. In this book, for
each method of encryption we introduce, we also consider attacks against it. However,
we restrict ourselves to the attacks against the underlying mathematical construction of
the encryption. There are countless other ways of attacking any security system ranging
from bribing or deceiving a person who is responsible for it to physically destroying
the entire communication channel with a bomb blast. Unfortunately, the attacker has the
advantage of a multitude of possible attacks many of which are not foreseen by those
who construct the encryption system.

The public key cryptosystems considered in this book are based on only two fundamental mathematical concepts known as integer factoring (see Section 4.1) and the
discrete logarithm (see Section 2.3). In Section 2.4, we consider attacks against the discrete logarithm which jeopardize key establishment and the ElGamal (Section 3.3) and
elliptic curve (Section 5.2) cryptosystems. In Section 4.3 and Chapters 7 and 8, we consider attacks based on integer factoring that affect the RSA cryptosystem. The problem
of factoring integers has been of interest to mathematicians for thousands of years and
so there is an enormous body of mathematical literature here. Thus, the techniques for
attacks based on this are now very sophisticated.

While there are many other public key cryptosystems in the literature, many of them
are still based on one of the two concepts mentioned earlier and so vulnerable to attacks
on discrete logarithms and factoring. We provide some references in the further reading
section below.

Further Reading. Chapter 8 of the *Handbook of Applied Cryptography* [29] discusses several public key cryptosystems. Like RSA, the Rabin scheme is secure only if
integer factoring cannot be done. The McEliece scheme mentioned there (Section 8.5)

has security based on the problem of decoding linear codes and the Merkle–Hellman scheme security is based on subset sums (Section 8.6); while the first of these schemes is still believed to be secure, the second has been shown to be insecure but stronger versions are known. (See Note 8.41 of [29].) The Cramer–Shoup scheme, like ElGamal, is based on the discrete logarithm. A description of the scheme and a proof of security can be found in [27]. The further reading sections in subsequent chapters also point the reader to more work on attacks.

2

CONGRUENCE EQUATIONS

In this chapter, we introduce three areas of mathematics needed for the development of the theory and implementation of the public key cryptographic systems discussed in this book. Mathematical systems of most use in developing cryptographic algorithms are finite systems, as computers are by nature finite. Thus, we deal with finite or *discrete* number systems. The three topics we cover are first congruence arithmetic, second the Euclidean algorithm, and finally, the dual concepts of exponential and logarithmic equations in the discrete setting of congruence arithmetics.

Congruence arithmetic is essentially arithmetic in discrete number systems. The standard arithmetic operations of addition, subtraction, multiplication, and division are needed. The first three of these are easy enough to define, but division is a little more complex, and not always available! The Euclidean Algorithm, presented in Section 2.2, is a very efficient method of enabling division in discrete systems. Perhaps surprisingly, this algorithm will be useful in every chapter of the book.

In Section 2.3 of this chapter, we show how to use the arithmetic of discrete systems to establish keys for securing data in transit. We then go on in Section 2.4 to show how this same congruence arithmetic can be used to attack the key establishment method.

Public Key Cryptography: Applications and Attacks, First Edition. Lynn Margaret Batten.
© 2013 by The Institute of Electrical and Electronics Engineers, Inc. Published 2013 by John Wiley & Sons, Inc.

2.1 CONGRUENCE ARITHMETIC

In many early symmetric key cryptosystems, the basis was the alphabet used in everyday writing. Thus, we might use today's English alphabet based on 26 letters. Other alphabets have different numbers of letters, and even additional symbols, but the principle is the same. In our case, we have to choose 26 numbers that will correspond to these 26 letters. We use the numbers $0, 1, 2, 3, \ldots, 25$ to correspond to a, b, c, d, and so on, respectively. The reason we begin at 0 is that we can use the zero to help introduce features such as addition, subtraction, multiplication, and, in some cases, division.

We can get an interesting system based on n letters for any n at least 2. In fact, you are probably very familiar with working in a system with the two symbols 0 and 1 in computer science where:

$$1 + 1 \equiv 0$$
$$1 + 0 \equiv 1 \equiv 0 + 1$$
$$0 + 0 \equiv 0.$$

Here, we use $\equiv$ instead of $=$ to distinguish between the operations usually used for numbers and those we apply to the set $\{0, 1\}$. In the new system, we only have the numbers 0 and 1. We can introduce a sensible, consistent addition operation on these two symbols. The result of any operation on 0 and 1 must result in one of the symbols we are using, 0 or 1.

So what is the key idea behind addition and subtraction in discrete systems based on n symbols $0, 1, 2, \ldots, n-1$? We first agree that all of these numbers (symbols) exist in the system and are different from each other. We then identify each integer m with one of these n numbers as follows: take the remainder r of m after dividing by n. It is easy to see that r must be in the set $0, 1, 2, \ldots, n-1$. We identify m with r. In fact, we write

$$m \equiv r \ modulo \ n \text{ or more briefly } m \equiv r \ (\text{mod } n)$$

and we say that m is congruent to r modulo n.

So going back to our English alphabet on 26 letters, we can write that $57 \equiv 5 \ (\text{mod } 26)$ and $-2 \equiv 24 \ (\text{mod } 26)$. The second of these is a little harder to see from our definition above. We have to get a remainder for -2 on division by 26, that is, in the range 0–25. Technically, this means we should be able to write: $-2 = 26x + r$ for some integer x, where r is in the range we want. To get r in the correct range, we can use $x = -1$.

Working in base 2, we are using congruences modulo 2: $3 \equiv 1 \equiv 5 \equiv -1 \ (\text{mod } 2)$. In 12-h clock arithmetic (base 12), we write $15 \equiv 3 \ (\text{mod } 12)$. In a system of congruences modulo 7, we have $9 \equiv 2 \equiv -5 \ (\text{mod } 7)$.

Definition 2.1 In general, $a \equiv b \ (\text{mod } n)$ precisely when $a - b$ is a multiple of n. (Here, n is assumed to be a positive integer.) In other words, this is equivalent to $a - b \equiv 0 \ (\text{mod } n)$. We use this as the working definition for the purposes of formal proofs such as those needed in propositions below. We use the notation $n|(a - b)$ to describe the fact that $a - b$ is a multiple of n, and we say that n divides $a - b$.

We can now introduce operations of addition, subtraction, and multiplication (division will be treated separately) in congruence systems. Basically, use the old familiar integer operations and then adjust the results so that they are in the correct range.

Example 2.1

$$21 + 13 \equiv \quad 34 \equiv \quad 8 \ (\mathrm{mod}\ 26).$$
$$23 - 25 \equiv \quad -2 \equiv 24 \ (\mathrm{mod}\ 26).$$
$$-15 - 19 \equiv -34 \equiv \quad 6 \ (\mathrm{mod}\ 20).$$
$$9 * 3 \equiv \quad 27 \equiv \quad 5 \ (\mathrm{mod}\ 11).$$

Before we take a look at division, we note some general properties of the above operations in congruences.

Proposition 2.1   *For all integers a and all positive integers n,*

(a) $a \equiv a \ (\mathrm{mod}\ n)$;
(b) $a \equiv 0 \ (\mathrm{mod}\ n)$ precisely when $n|a$;
(c) $a \equiv b \ (\mathrm{mod}\ n)$ if and only if $b \equiv a \ (\mathrm{mod}\ n)$;
(d) If $a \equiv b \ (\mathrm{mod}\ n)$ and $b \equiv c \ (\mathrm{mod}\ n)$ then $a \equiv c \ (\mathrm{mod}\ n)$.

We leave proof of these points as an exercise for the reader. Definition 2.1 can be used for each of them.

Proposition 2.2   *Let a, b, c, d, and n be integers, $n > 0$. Suppose that $a \equiv b$ and $c \equiv d \ (\mathrm{mod}\ n)$. Then*

(a) $a + c \equiv b + d \ (\mathrm{mod}\ n)$;
(b) $a - c \equiv b - d \ (\mathrm{mod}\ n)$;
(c) $ac \equiv bd \ (\mathrm{mod}\ n)$.

Proof. We prove the last of these and leave the others as an exercise.

We know that $n|a - b$ and $n|c - d$. Let $a - b = nk$ and $c - d = nt$ for integers k and t. Then $a = nk + b$ and $c = nt + d$. So $ac = (nk + b)(nt + d) = n^2kt + bnt + nkd + bd$. Now $n|[n^2kt + bnt + nkd = ac - bd]$. By definition, this means $ac - bd \equiv 0 \ (\mathrm{mod}\ n)$ and so $ac \equiv bd \ (\mathrm{mod}\ n)$ as required. Done!   □

Example 2.2   Solve $x + 5 \equiv 11 \ (\mathrm{mod}\ 19)$.

We can use Proposition 2.2 to add the same thing modulo 19 to each side. Choose -5 (really 14). So we get $x \equiv 6 \ (\mathrm{mod}\ 19)$, a single solution.

In integers, there is an infinite number of solutions to this: $6, -13, 25, -32, 44$, and so on.

We now turn to division and first consider some examples. Suppose

$$6 \equiv 2x \ (\mathrm{mod} \ n),$$

where we want to solve for x and we do not know what n is for the time being. The obvious approach is to notice that both 6 and 2 are divisible by 2 and so we can just remove or divide out the 2 to get $3 \equiv x \ (\mathrm{mod} \ n)$. Let us see if this is correct for some trial values of n:

$6 \equiv 2x \ (\mathrm{mod} \ 7)$ has a solution $3 \equiv x \ (\mathrm{mod} \ 7)$ and it is easy to check that this is the only solution;

$6 \equiv 2x \ (\mathrm{mod} \ 8)$ has a solution $3 \equiv x \ (\mathrm{mod} \ 8)$, but it also has the solution $x \equiv 7$ which we miss if we just divide by 2.

Thus, we need a slightly different strategy. This gets even more complex when we notice that the equation $3 \equiv 2x \ (\mathrm{mod} \ 4)$ has no solution at all. (Just check all four possible values for x and none of them works.)

These equations do not behave the way we expect linear equations to behave from our experience with real values. The different behavior arises because the modulus "n" has a common factor with one or more of the coefficients. As long as we are aware of this and take it into consideration, we will be able to obtain the correct and complete answer.

The method is as follows: rather than divide, we find the inverse of a number in the given modulus and then multiply by this inverse. We need to be clear on what an inverse is and when it exists first. So let us begin there.

Definition 2.2   *The number a in the range 1 to $n - 1$ has an inverse b modulo n if b is in the range 1 to $n - 1$ and if $ab \equiv 1 \equiv ba \ (\mathrm{mod} \ n)$.*

Since in the systems we are considering, it is always the case that $ab \equiv ba$, we need in practice only check one of these congruences.

Example 2.3   Let us see if we can find some inverses. Let $n = 10$ and choose $a = 6$. The values we obtain modulo 10 by multiplying 6 by the numbers 1–9 are given in the following table:

$6 * 1$	6
$6 * 2$	2
$6 * 3$	8
$6 * 4$	4
$6 * 5$	0
$6 * 6$	6
$6 * 7$	2
$6 * 8$	8
$6 * 9$	4

There is no 1 in the list and so 6 has no inverse modulo 10.

To understand what is happening, we need a few more facts, and we give them in the next proposition and in Section 2.1.1.

Proposition 2.3   *If a has an inverse modulo n, then this inverse is unique. Moreover, if the inverse of a is b, then the inverse of b is a.*

Proof. First, suppose that a has two inverses, b and b'. Then we must show that $b \equiv b'$ (mod n). But $ab \equiv ab' \equiv 1$ implies $a(b - b') \equiv 0$ (mod n). Multiplying both sides of this equation by b on the left: $(ba)(b - b') \equiv 1(b - b') \equiv b - b' \equiv b0 \equiv 0$ (mod n). Since $b - b'$ is in the range 0 to $n - 1$, and since n divides $b - b'$, this difference must be 0 and so $b = b'$.

It is easy simply from the definition to see that the second part of this proposition is true. ☐

Proposition 2.3 does not answer the question of when a number has an inverse modulo n. In fact, this takes us neatly into Section 2.2 of the chapter where we develop the theory behind the Euclidean Algorithm which is what we need to get our answer.

2.1.1 Computer Examples

Here are a few examples that use Maple to generate solutions. You can use any other software language to follow what is done here, or even write your own code. Any package software uses the Euclidean Algorithm to generate its solutions to questions of the following type. Notice how quickly you get the answers from the software.

1. Does 233 have an inverse modulo 2111?
   Solution.   You can write your own code to check if any of the values from 2 to 2110 give 1 when multiplied by 233. Alternatively, you can use the Maple command 233 ^(−1) mod 2111; to do this for you. The inverse is 1658.
2. Find all solutions of the equation $197x \equiv 1259$ (mod 2017).
   Solution.   You can write a program to quickly check which values modulo 2017 will work for x. Alternatively, the Maple command "solve (197*x = 1259, x) mod 2017;" will find you all values of x which satisfy, giving the answer 805. A third solution is to find the inverse of 197 (mod 2017) if it exists; it does and is 901. You can write code or the Maple command 197 ^(−1) mod 2017; will find it for you. Then $x \equiv 901*1259 \equiv 805$ (mod 2017).
3. Find integers x and y such that $65537x + 3511y = 1$.
   Solution.   The Maple command > $igcdex$(65537, 3511,"x","y"); x; y; gives output:
   1
   −1405
   26226.

This tells us that the gcd of the two numbers input is 1, and that the numbers x and y we need are $x = -1405$, $y = 26226$. The answer can be verified by substituting back: $65537*(-1405) + 3511*26226 = 1$.

Further Reading. D. Burton [6]; H. Davenport [10]; P. Garrett [17]; K.H. Rosen [47]; W. Trappe and L. Washington [52].

2.1.2 Problems

1. Prove Proposition 2.1.
2. Prove parts (a) and (b) of Proposition 2.2.
3. Which values modulo 10 have an inverse?
4. Find all solutions to the equation $7 \equiv 2x \pmod{11}$.

Computer-Assisted Problems   Throughout the book, problems under this heading are ones which need the use of a computer or sophisticated calculator to complete in a reasonable amount of time.

5. Check that the gcd of 65537 and 3511 is 1.
6. Find the inverse of 3511 modulo 65537.

2.2 THE EUCLIDEAN ALGORITHM—FINDING INVERSES

The Euclidean (or Remainder) Algorithm, (EA) is one of the most pervasive algorithms in cryptography. This is because it is both extremely useful and extremely efficient. On input of two integers, the algorithm outputs the greatest common divisor (gcd) of the two integers. The steps in the algorithm are also useful, however, and we keep them and use them to get us much more information about the input integers than just the gcd.

We begin the section with some definitions heading us in the direction of demonstrating the algorithm.

Definition 2.3   Two numbers a and b are said to be *relatively prime* if they have no common factor.

So for instance, 19 and -13 are relatively prime, whereas 6 and 8 are not.

Definition 2.4   The greatest positive integer that divides both given integers a and b is called the *greatest common divisor, or gcd, of a and b, and is referred to as* $\gcd(a, b)$.

If both a and b are 0, technically such a gcd does not exist, so we only apply the gcd concept when at least one of a and b is not zero. Also, even if both a and b are negative, the gcd will always be positive. If at least one of a and b is not zero, it is easy to see that the gcd must be unique.

As examples, $\gcd(-5, 0) = 5$ and $\gcd(197, 2017) = 1$.

In tackling congruence equations, it turns out that the most important pairs of integers are those with gcd equal to 1. Now let's see how the EA finds the greatest common divisor for us.

The Euclidean Algorithm—Motivation   This algorithm is based on long division. We begin with a motivating example:

Example 2.4   Compute $\gcd(4883, 4369)$. We begin by dividing the smaller number into the larger and determining the remainder. (This is the same as working modulo 4369!)

$$\underline{4883} = \underline{4369} * 1 + \underline{514} \text{ [So } 4883 \equiv 514 \text{ (mod 4369).]} \tag{2.1}$$

$$\underline{4369} = \underline{514} * 8 + \underline{257}. \tag{2.2}$$

$$\underline{514} = \underline{257} * 2 + 0. \tag{2.3}$$

We claim that the gcd of 4883 and 4369 is 257, the last non zero remainder. To see this, we argue as follows. Anything divides 4883 and 4369 must divide 514 by Equation (2.1). Then it divides 257 by Equation (2.2). On the other hand, by Equation (2.3), 257 divides 514, and also by Equation 2.2 divides 4369 and so by Equation (2.1) divides 4883 as well.

In the three equations, we underlined the important values needed to trace back in this last argument.

We take this example one step further. By substituting backwards from Equation (2.2), it is possible to write the gcd of 4883 and 4369 as a combination of multiples of 4883 and 4369.

$$\begin{aligned} \underline{257} &= \underline{4369} - \underline{514} * 8 \\ &= \underline{4369} - [\underline{4883} - \underline{4369} * 1] * 8 \\ &= -8 * \underline{4883} + 9 * \underline{4369}. \end{aligned}$$

In congruence notation, if we were working modulo the largest number, 4883, we can write $257 \equiv 9 * 4369 \pmod{4883}$. Thinking ahead, if the gcd had been 1 instead of 257, we would have found the inverse of 4369 modulo 4883.

The Euclidean Algorithm—Formal Presentation   Let a and b be integers with $a > b$. Then divide a by b to get

$$\begin{aligned} \underline{a} &= q_1 \underline{b} + \underline{r_1} & \text{where} \quad 0 \leq r_1 < b \\ \underline{b} &= q_2 r_1 + \underline{r_2} & \text{where} \quad 0 \leq r_2 < r_1, \\ \underline{r_1} &= q_3 r_2 + \underline{r_3} & \text{where} \quad 0 \leq r_3 < r_2 \end{aligned}$$

and so on. Note that the remainders are decreasing and so must eventually go to zero.

$$\text{Suppose } \underline{r}_{k-2} = q_k\underline{r}_{k-1} + \underline{r}_k \quad \text{where} \quad \underline{r}_k \neq 0$$
$$\text{and} \quad \underline{r}_{k-1} = q_{k+1}\underline{r}_k.$$

Thus, r_k is the gcd of a and b. The reasoning behind this last statement is the same as the argument made in Example 2.4: any number dividing both a and b must divide $\underline{r}_1$ and therefore also $\underline{r}_2$ all the way down the equations to $\underline{r}_k$. Conversely, working backwards, any number dividing $\underline{r}_k$ must divide $\underline{r}_{k-1}$ and therefore also $\underline{r}_{k-2}$ and so on, and finally must divide a and b.

Example 2.5   Consider 12345 and 11111. Write

$$\underline{12345} = \underline{11111} * 1 + \underline{1234}$$
$$\underline{11111} = \underline{1234} * 9 + \underline{5}$$
$$\underline{1234} = \underline{5} * 246 + \underline{4}$$
$$\underline{5} = \underline{4} * 1 + \underline{1}$$
$$\underline{4} = \underline{1} * 4$$

So $\gcd(12345, 11111) = 1$.

Notice that the remainders drop (usually quickly) and so you see that this algorithm will always end.

We can even write 1 as a linear combination of 12345 and 11111 by carefully tracking the underlined values as follows: $1 = \underline{5} - \underline{4} * 1 = \underline{5} - [\underline{1234} - \underline{5} * 246] * 1 = -\underline{1234} + \underline{5} * 247 = -\underline{1234} + [\underline{11111} - \underline{1234} * 9] * 247 = \underline{11111} * 247 - \underline{1234} * 2224 = \underline{11111} * 247 - [\underline{12345} - \underline{11111} * 1] * 2224 = -\underline{12345} * 2224 + \underline{11111} * 2471.$

Proposition 2.4   *Any two integers a and b, not both 0, can be written as a linear combination of integer values equal to $\gcd(a, b)$. Moreover, any linear combination of integer values of a and b must be divisible by $\gcd(a, b)$.*

Proof. We have two things to show. However, the first one follows immediately from our explanation of the formal Euclidean Algorithm and how we can use the equations in each step.

Consider the second part and some linear combination $ax + by$ of a and b, where x and y are unknown integers. Then $\gcd(a, b)$ divides both a and b and so it divides this sum.   □

Proposition 2.5   *If a and n are relatively prime, n is at least 2 and a is in the range 1 to $n - 1$, then a has an inverse modulo n; if a and n are not relatively prime, then a has no inverse modulo n.*

Proof. The first statement in this proposition says that $\gcd(a, n) = 1$. By Proposition 2.4, we can write $ax + ny = 1$ for some integers x and y. Interpreting this equation modulo

n, we get $ax' \equiv 1 \pmod{n}$ where x' is the value equivalent to x in the range 1 to $n - 1$. So x' is the inverse of a modulo n. Now look at the second statement in the proposition. Let's suppose that a does have an inverse, say b, modulo n. This means that $ab \equiv 1 \pmod{n}$. By the definition of modulus (Definition 2.1), n must divide $ab - 1$, which can be expressed as $ab - 1 = kn$ for some integer k. Rewriting this equation as $ab - kn = 1$ (although this is not really necessary), we see that the $\gcd(a, n)$ must divide 1 by Proposition 2.4. So we conclude that a and n cannot be relatively prime in this case, which is a contradiction. □

Example 2.6 Use the EA to find the inverse of 11111 modulo 12345.
We can use the work that already did in Example 2.5. First check that the two numbers are relatively prime and then use the EA to find a linear combination of them equal to 1: $1 = -12345 * 2224 + 11111 * 2471$. Now take the modulus:

$$1 \equiv 11111 * 2471 \pmod{12345}.$$

So 2471 is the inverse of 11111 modulo 12345.

Example 2.7 Solve the following equation for x : $11111x \equiv 32 \pmod{12345}$. We again check to see if the inverse of 11111 exists modulo 12345. It does, and we compute it to be 2471. Then we multiply both sides of the equation by this value: $x \equiv 32 * 2471 \equiv 5002 \pmod{12345}$, giving the answer.

In a general equation of the form $ax \equiv b \pmod{n}$, if $\gcd(a, n) = 1$, then we can see from Example 2.7 how to get at least one solution to the equation. Can there be a second one? The next proposition gives the answer to this.

Proposition 2.6 *The equation $ax \equiv b \pmod{n}$ for integers a and b, integer n at least 2 in which $\gcd(a, n) = 1$ has precisely one solution modulo n.*

Proof. We can use the EA to find the unique (Proposition 2.3) inverse of a modulo n. Multiplying by this inverse gives a solution for x. Suppose now that there are two solutions, say c and c' to this equation. Then $b \equiv ac \equiv ac' \pmod{n}$ and multiplying by the inverse of a yields $c \equiv c' \pmod{n}$, and so the solution is unique. □

Corollary 2.1 *The equation $ax \equiv b \pmod{p}$ for integers a and b, p a prime and a not divisible by p has precisely one solution.*

Proof. This follows from the proposition: since a is not divisible by p, $\gcd(a, p) = 1$. □

Many of the cryptographic systems we will be discussing work modulo a single prime number or the product of two prime numbers, and so the above corollary will be useful. Note that if we replace p by the product $p * q$ of two primes p and q in the statement of the corollary, the proof and conclusion remain true as long as a is not divisible by either prime.

When dealing with congruence equations modulo a product of primes, one strategy is to break them down into a system of equations as in the following example.

Example 2.8 Consider the equation $x \equiv 17 \pmod{22}$. Clearly, only one value (17) of x modulo 22 satisfies it. However, we note that $22 = 2 * 11$ and since $\gcd(2, 11) = 1$, we can conclude that $x - 17$ is divisible both by 2 and 11. In other words, the single equation can be written as a pair: $x \equiv 17 \pmod{2}$ and $x \equiv 17 \pmod{11}$. Separately, each of these has a solution: $x \equiv 1 \pmod{2}$ and $x \equiv 6 \pmod{11}$ and $x \equiv 17 \pmod{22}$ is a common solution to both equations.

Seeing how to get back to the single equation from the pair is not so obvious, and we introduce some theory to explain how to do this. Before proceeding, to see what kind of condition we might need, let us look at a second example: can we find a common solution to $x \equiv 2 \pmod{6}$ and $x \equiv 3 \pmod{4}$? The first equation tells us that $x - 2$ is a multiple of 6; the second equation tells us that $x - 3$ is a multiple of 4. So we can write $x = 6k + 2$ for some integer k, and also $x = 4m + 3$ for some integer m. The first equation implies that x is even, but if this is true, the second equation then implies that 3 is even, which is false. So this pair of equations has no common solution.

Theorem 2.1   The Chinese Remainder Theorem
This theorem, also known as the CRT for short, dates back to Chinese mathematician Sun Zi [20]. For integers a and b, positive integers m and n and unknown x, there is a unique common solution x modulo mn to the equations

$$\left. \begin{array}{l} x \equiv a \pmod{m} \\ x \equiv b \pmod{n} \end{array} \right\} \tag{2.4}$$

when $\gcd(m, n) = 1$.

Proof. To see this, since $\gcd(m, n) = 1$, we know by the EA that we can find values s and t such that $sm + tn = 1$.
    We now claim that the solutions of the equation $x \equiv atn + bsm \pmod{mn}$ are exactly the same as any solution to (1).
    We show first that if $x \equiv atn + bsm \pmod{mn}$ where $sm + tn = 1$, then the double congruence holds. This follows from:

$$x \equiv atn \pmod{m} \equiv a(1 - sm) \equiv a \pmod{m}$$

and

$$x \equiv bsm \pmod{n} \equiv b(1 - tn) \equiv b \pmod{n}.$$

Now we go the other way and suppose that x satisfies $x \equiv a \pmod{m}$ and $x \equiv b \pmod{n}$ and $sm + tn = 1$. Consider

$$x - (atn + bsm) \equiv a - atn \pmod{m}$$
$$\equiv a(1 - tn)$$
$$\equiv asm \equiv 0 \pmod{m}.$$

Also

$$x - (atn + bsm) \equiv b - bsm \pmod{n}$$
$$\equiv b(1 - sm)$$
$$\equiv btn \equiv 0 \pmod{n}$$

We conclude that both m and n divide $x - (atn + bsm)$ and since $\gcd(m, n) = 1$, we can write $x \equiv atn + bsm \pmod{mn}$ which is what we proposed.   □

Example 2.9   Find an integer x so that

$$3x \equiv 2 \pmod{5} \text{ and}$$
$$4x \equiv 5 \pmod{7}.$$

We first isolate x on the left using $3^{-1} \pmod{5}$ and $4^{-1} \pmod{7}$. So

$$x \equiv 2 * 3^{-1} \equiv 2 * 2 \equiv 4 \pmod{5} \text{ and}$$
$$x \equiv 5 * 4^{-1} \equiv 5 * 2 \equiv 3 \pmod{7}.$$

The CRT applies:

$$5 * (-4) + 7 * 3 = 1, \text{ so}$$
$$x = 4 * 7 * 3 + 3 * 5 * (-4)$$
$$= 24 \pmod{35} \text{ is a common solution.}$$

Checking:
$24 \equiv 4 \pmod{5}$ and $24 \equiv 3 \pmod{7}$ and both satisfy the first two equations.

In our CRT theorem, you may have noticed that there is no reason to restrict things to two equations. In fact, there is always a unique solution to such a system of any size and this can be represented theoretically by the following statement:

Notation.   The notation Z/m and Z_m are equally common for the integers modulo m.

General Chinese Remainder Theorem   There is a 1–1 correspondence between the set $Z_{m_1 m_2 \ldots m_n}$ of integers modulo $m_1 m_2 \ldots m_n$ and the set $(Z_{m_1}, Z_{m_2}, \ldots Z_{m_n})$ of m_n-tuples whenever $\gcd(m_i, m_j) = 1$ for all $i \neq j$.

The set of tuples is often also written as a cross product. For pairs, this is just (Z_m, Z_n) which is the same set as (isomorphic to) $Z_m \times Z_n$. The proof of the general case can be done by induction on n. Here, we will just show the correspondence for $n = 2$.

Theorem 2.2   *There is a 1–1 correspondence between the set Z_{mn} and (Z_m, Z_n) when* $\gcd(m, n) = 1$.

Proof. To show that there is a 1–1 function between the sets Z_{mn} and $Z_m \times Z_n$ when $\gcd(m, n) = 1$, we first of all define a function:

For $x \in Z_{mn}$, we define $f : x \rightarrow (x \pmod{m}, x \pmod{n})$. (Eg. $f : 5 \mod (3 * 4) \rightarrow (2 \pmod{3}, 1 \pmod{4})$.)

This is 1–1 if, for $x \neq y$ in Z_{mn}, we have $f(x) \neq f(y)$.

Suppose $x \neq y \pmod{mn}$ but $f(x) = f(y)$. So

$$x \pmod{m} \equiv y \pmod{m} \quad \text{and}$$
$$x \pmod{n} \equiv y \pmod{n}.$$

Thus both m and n divide $x - y$. Since $\gcd(m, n) = 1$, we conclude that mn divides $x - y$. That is, $x \equiv y \pmod{mn}$, which is false.

Now, the fact that f is $1 - 1$ and both sets Z_{mn} and $Z_m \times Z_n$ have the same (finite) size means that every element of $Z_m \times Z_n$ gets mapped to under f by <u>something in Z_{mn}</u>. $\square$

Example 2.10 If $m = 3$ and $n = 5$, the element $(2, 3)$ in $Z_3 \times Z_5$ gets mapped to by what?

We need a common solution to $x \equiv 2 \pmod{3}$ and $x \equiv 3 \pmod{5}$. Using the CRT, we first see that $1 = 5 * 2 + 3 * (-3)$ from the EA and then we can choose $x = 2 * (5 * 2) + 3 * (3 * (-3)) = -7 \equiv 8 \pmod{15}$. It is easy to verify that this is correct.

In combining solutions from each equation separately into general solutions for the system, you might think that some would reduce to the same overall solution.

The 1–1 correspondence tells us that if we have exactly a solutions to one equation and exactly b to another equation in a CRT set up, then there are exactly $a * b$ solutions to the pair of equations.

Warning: Even if $\gcd(m, n) \neq 1$, the equations

$$x \equiv a \pmod{m} \quad \text{and}$$
$$x \equiv b \pmod{n}$$

may still have a solution. The above arguments tell us nothing about this situation.

To this point, we have only considered linear equations. What we really need for use in public key cryptography is non linear congruence equations. We look at these in the next section.

2.2.1 Computer Examples

Here are a few examples which use Maple to generate solutions. You can use any other software language to follow what is done here, or even write your own code.

1. Find all solutions to $216x \equiv 66 \pmod{606}$.
   Solution. It is easy to check that (we use Maple) > gcd(216, 606); 6.
   So we cannot compute the inverse of 6 modulo 606. We could try every possible value for x, but there is a faster way as follows. Note that 66 is also divisible by 6. In this case, we can tackle the problem by arguing that if 606 divides $216x - 66$,

then 101 must divide $36x - 11$ (but we may lose some solutions to the original equation in so doing). Now $\gcd(36, 101) = 1$, so we solve $36x \equiv 11 \pmod{101}$ instead.

> solve $(36 * x = 11) \mod 101;$ 48.

This is the solution (mod 101). The solutions (mod 606) are therefore $48; 48 + 101; 48 + 202; 48 + 303; 48 + 404; 48 + 505;$ which are $48, 149, 250, 351, 452, 553$ modulo 606. All can be easily verified.

2. Find an integer such that when it is divided by 101 the remainder is 17, when it is divided by 201, the remainder is 18, and when it is divided by 301 the remainder is 19.

   Solution. This is a CRT problem. We can reformulate it as: $x \equiv 17 \pmod{101}$ and $x \equiv 18 \pmod{201}$ and $x \equiv 19 \pmod{301}$.

   Using the Maple command: > *chrem*$([17, 18, 19], [101, 201, 301]);$ produces 61122.

   You can check the answer by reducing 61122 by each of the moduli in turn. Obviously, this notation generalizes to as many equations as you want.

3. Find a common solution to the system $3x \equiv 2 \pmod{3127}$ and $4x \equiv 5 \pmod{2563}$.

   Solution. First we check $\gcd(3127, 2563)$; which yields 1. It is easy to see that $\gcd(3, 3127)$ and $\gcd(4, 2563)$ are also 1. So we are all set to use the CRT once we have multiplied by the necessary inverses. We need $3^{(-1)} \pmod{3127}$; which is 2085 and $4^{(-1)} \pmod{2563}$; which is 641. Finally, we use the CRT command in Maple:

   chrem$([2085, 641], [3127, 2563]);$ which gives the common answer 2097175. Again, this can be verified by substituting back into each equation separately.

Further Reading. D. Burton [6]; H. Davenport [10]; P. Garrett [17]; K.H. Rosen [47]; W. Trappe and L. Washington [52].

2.2.2 Problems

1. In the formal presentation of the EA, we assume that some remainder is not zero. What can you do if the very first remainder r_1 is 0?

2. Find the gcd of 3172 and 7282 using the EA. Write the gcd as a linear combination of 3172 and 7282.

3. Determine if 2563 has an inverse modulo 3127, and if it does, find it.

4. Give the precise correspondence between the elements in Z_6 and those in $Z_2 \times Z_3$ as described by the function in the proof of Theorem 2.2.

5. Solve, if possible (hint: if you run out of ideas, go back to the definition)

   (a) $x \equiv 2 \pmod{6}$ and $x \equiv 3 \pmod{4}$

   (b) $x \equiv 2 \pmod{6}$ and $x \equiv 0 \pmod{4}$.

Computer-Assisted Problems

6. Solve, if possible, $5126x \equiv 2 \pmod{6254}$.
7. Find an integer such that when it is divided by 101 the remainder is 11, when it is divided by 201, the remainder is 12, when it is divided by 301 the remainder is 13, and when it is divided by 401, the answer is 14. Confirm that your answer is correct.

2.3 DISCRETE LOGARITHMS AND DIFFIE–HELLMAN KEY EXCHANGE

Some of the most interesting cryptographic systems currently in use are based on the difficulty of solving exponential congruence equations. In the first sections of this chapter, we saw how to find solutions of linear equations, if they existed. We also saw that it was difficult to predict the number of solutions to such equations unless certain conditions were present. Now we turn to exponential congruence equations and consider the difficulty of solving them.

An equation of the form $a \equiv b^x \pmod{n}$ where a and b can be assumed to be in $\{1, 2, \ldots, n-1\}$ and x is unknown is an example of an exponential congruence equation. We want to solve this for positive integer values of x. In fact, we are asking the question: "for which positive x is a an xth power of b modulo n?"

As for exponential equations of this type with real numbers, we capture the exponent in an equation using logarithms.

Definition 2.5 Given a, b, and n, if x is the smallest positive integer such that $a \equiv b^x \pmod{n}$, then we say that x is the discrete logarithm base b of a modulo n and write $x \equiv L_b(a) \pmod{n}$.

Given integers a, b, and n, the problem of finding x such that the above equation holds is known as the discrete logarithm problem (DLP).

Example 2.11 Find all solutions to $3 \equiv 2^x \pmod{7}$. To do this, we simply try some possibilities:

$$2^0 \equiv 1$$
$$2^1 \equiv 2$$
$$2^2 \equiv 4$$
$$2^3 \equiv 1$$
$$2^4 \equiv 2$$
$$2^5 \equiv 4$$
$$2^6 \equiv 1$$
$$2^7 \equiv 2.$$

Note that no upper bound on x was given. But, we can see from the list that we are in a loop and that values of the powers will repeat. This will always happen in a congruence equation as the values obtained are limited by the modulus. In this example, we can now see that there is no solution.

We can also see that there are multiple solutions to $4 \equiv 2^x$ (mod 7); in fact, an infinite number of them. This is the reason for defining the discrete logarithm as the *smallest* positive integer solution to the exponential equation.

Readers may be familiar with the concept of logarithm for real numbers. In this case, $a \equiv b^x$ has at most one solution for x, given real numbers a and b. We can write $L_b(a) = L_b(b^x) = x$ as in the discrete case. Real and discrete logarithms have similar properties [50].

It is generally assumed that for very large values of the modulus, finding discrete logarithms is computationally infeasible. But no one actually has a proof of this! However, it is known that the modulus needs to be a large prime number and to have some additional properties in order to make an attack difficult. It can be shown that the complexity of finding x when n has d digits is about the same as that of factoring a d-digit number. We will return to the topic of factoring numbers in Chapter 8.

Considering the values obtained in Example 2.11 leads to a simple question: is it possible for the powers of b to run through all values modulo n? Indeed, all powers of 3 modulo 7 give the full list 1, 3, 2, 6, 4, 5 in that order. So for any a modulo 7, we can see that the equation $a \equiv 3^x$ (mod 7) has a solution. We give a special name to this concept in Definition 2.6.

Definition 2.6 The value a is a ***primitive root modulo the prime p*** if its powers generate all of $1, \ldots p - 1$.

It is not difficult to see that an equivalent statement is: A value a is a primitive root modulo p if the smallest positive integer l so that $a^l \equiv 1$ (mod p) is $p - 1$.

We will generalize this definition later to include non prime moduli.

Before we can prove some interesting and useful properties which assist in solving discrete logarithm problems, we need a little more theory to help us get there. Theorem 2.3 tells us something about exponential equations for prime numbers.

Theorem 2.3 Fermat's Little Theorem
If p is a prime and a an integer not a multiple of p then $a^{p-1} \equiv 1$ (mod p).

Proof. Suppose p is a prime and a is a number such that p does not divide a. We can assume $2 \leq a \leq p - 1$ since we are working modulo p. We need to evaluate a^{p-1} (mod p).

We construct a function which, at first sight, seems to have nothing to do with our problem: for each $x \in \{1, 2, \ldots p - 1\} = S$, define $f : x \to ax$ (mod p).

So f multiplies each element of S by the fixed value a and reduces it modulo p. Since $\gcd(a, p) = 1$, it follows that the inverse of a modulo p exists by Proposition 2.5, and so $ax \equiv ay$ implies that $x \equiv y$. Thus, $f(1), f(2), \ldots f(p - 1)$ are just the elements $1, 2, \ldots, p - 1$ in a different order. Therefore,

$$1 * 2 * \ldots * (p - 1) \equiv f(1) * f(2) * \ldots * f(p - 1) \ (\text{mod } p)$$
$$\equiv (a * 1) * (a * 2) * \ldots * (a * (p - 1)) \ (\text{mod } p)$$
$$\equiv a^{p-1}(1 * 2 * \ldots * p - 1) \ (\text{mod } p).$$

But p does not divide $(1 * 2 * \ldots * p - 1)$ and so this term has an inverse with which we can multiply both sides.

The result is $1 \equiv a^{p-1} \ (\text{mod } p)$ and we are done!   □

Example 2.12   Let $p = 7$. We test $2^6, 3^6, 4^6, 5^6, 6^6$ modulo 7:

$$2^6 = 64 \equiv 1 \ (\text{mod } 7)$$
$$3^6 = 729 \equiv 1 \ (\text{mod } 7)$$
$$4^6 = (2^2)^6 = 2^{12} = 2^6 \cdot 2^6 = 64^2 = 4096 \equiv 1 \ (\text{mod } 7)$$
$$5^6 = (25)^3 = 15625 \equiv 1 \ (\text{mod } 7)$$
$$6^6 = (2^6) * (3^6) \equiv 1 * 1 \equiv 1 \ (\text{mod } 7)$$

Thus, we confirm the theorem.

Fermat's Little Theorem (FLT) has some immediate consequences which are of interest to us. For instance, suppose someone gives us a (large) number and we do not know if it is a prime or not. We can use the FLT to test it. The FLT must be true for any a not a multiple of p, but since we are working modulo p, we can restrict choices for a to the set $2, \ldots p - 2$. To test to see if p is a prime, randomly choose an a in this range and compute the exponent in the theorem. If we do not get 1 as the result, then p cannot be a prime. But if we do get 1, we need to check a second value for a and so on, until we have tried them all. If any one of them fails to produce 1, then p is composite.

An obvious question now is, if we are given a number p and do not know if it is prime, and if we check all values a as above and obtain 1 in every case, must p then be prime? This would be a nice result, but unfortunately it is not true. (See Problem 9 in the problem set.)

Example 2.13   Let $p = 561$. This number is not a prime. (Factor it.) Compute a^{560} (mod 561). We choose $a = 2$ first. Note that $560 = 512 + 32 + 16$ and $2^{560} = 2^{512} \, 2^{32} \, 2^{16}$. We use a fast exponentiation method of squaring to compute the target exponent value.

$$2^8 \ = (2^4)^2 = 256$$
$$2^{16} \ = (2^8)^2 = 65536 \equiv -101 \ (\text{mod } 561)$$
$$2^{32} \ = (2^{16})^2 \equiv (-101)^2 \equiv 103 \ (\text{mod } 561)$$
$$2^{64} \ = (2^{32})^2 \equiv 511 \ (\text{mod } 561)$$
$$2^{128} = (2^{64})^2 \equiv 256 \ (\text{mod } 561)$$
$$2^{256} = (2^{128})^2 \equiv -101 \ (\text{mod } 561)$$
$$2^{560} \equiv 103 * 103 * (-101) \equiv 1 \ (\text{mod } 561).$$

The FLT held in spite of the fact that 561 is not prime. There are still many values for a to check, but we claim that none of them fails the FLT. We leave the other values for a as an exercise.

Example 2.14 Modulo a prime, the FLT can assist in making fast exponential calculations. We use it to calculate 9^{21} (mod 11) as follows. Since 11 is a prime, we can use the FLT to obtain $9^{10} \equiv 1$ (mod 11) and so $9^{21} \equiv 9^{10} * 9^{10} * 9 \equiv 9$ (mod 11).

The FLT also allows us to prove some results about primitive roots that we will need. The next two propositions describe them.

Proposition 2.7 *If a is a primitive root modulo the prime p and some exponent l of a satisfies $a^l \equiv 1$ (mod p), then $(p-1)|l$.*

Proof. To see this, use the EA to write $l = q * (p-1) + r$ where $0 \leq r < p - 1$. Then $1 \equiv a^l = a^{q*(p-1)+r} = [a^{(p-1)}]^q * a^r \equiv 1 * a^r$ (mod p) using Fermat's Theorem.

But by definition $p - 1$ is the smallest integer such that $a^{p-1} \equiv 1$ (mod p), so r must be bigger than or equal to $p - 1$, which it is not. The only option is that $r = 0$ and this proves the result. □

Proposition 2.8 *For primitive root a and values b_1 and b_2 modulo p, $L_a(b_1 b_2) = L_a(b_1) + L_a(b_2)$ (mod $p-1$).*

Proof. We have to show that if $a^x \equiv b_1 b_2$, $a^y \equiv b_1$ and $a^z \equiv b_2$ (mod p) then $x \equiv y + z$ (mod $p - 1$).

But the first three equations give us $a^x \equiv a^{y+z}$ (mod p) and so $a^{x-y-z} \equiv 1$ (mod p). Now a is a primitive root modulo p and so Proposition 2.7 tells us that $(p-1)|(x-y-z)$. It follows that $x \equiv y + z$ (mod $p - 1$) as desired. □

Corollary 2.2 *For primitive root a, value b modulo p and positive integer c, $L_a(b^c) = cL_a(b)$.*

Proof. Since $b^c = b * b * \ldots * b$ c times, this follows from Proposition 2.7. □

The properties in Proposition 2.7 and its corollary will be used several times in the following section without reference.

Example 2.15 The fact that $3 \equiv 2^8 \equiv 2^{18}$ (mod 11) implies by Proposition 2.7 that $8 \equiv 18$ (mod 10), which is true.

In cryptography, the communicating parties need to have some kind of common key with which to unlock the secret information. In general, it is assumed that secret or encrypted information is sent across insecure channels such as the Internet. In this case, it is critical that the parties involved maintain secrecy of the key. But how do they establish a common key quickly and with only insecure channels between them? One such key agreement protocol is based on the discrete logarithm problem. This protocol is a standard way of having two or more parties set up a common key over an insecure channel [13]. It was invented in 1976 during a collaboration between Whitfield Diffie and Martin Hellman and was the first practical method for establishing a shared secret over an unprotected communications channel.

Diffie–Hellman Key Exchange (DHKE)   We assume that parties A and B (often called Alice and Bob) want to exchange information secretly but are only able to communicate over insecure channels such as the Internet or telephone lines. The protocol (steps) set out here permits them to use these insecure channels to exchange information in such a way that after several communications, they share a single value known only to them and then can use this value as a key to conceal further communications.

1. In this first step, A and B agree on common parameters which do not have to be kept secret from anyone else. These are
   - a large prime q and
   - a primitive root a (mod q).

Now each user, we take A here, generates their own public key independently by

- choosing a secret integer: $x_A < q$
- and computing their **public key**: $y_A = a^{x_A}$ (mod q).

A and B now publish their respective public keys y_A and y_B wherever they like. In particular, they need to know each other's public keys and can send them to each other directly.

2. Users A and B now establish a common value as follows:
   B computes $y_A^{x_B}$ (mod q) using his private key;
   A computes $y_B^{x_A}$ (mod q) using her private key;
   But both are the same: $K_{AB} = a^{x_A x_B}$ (mod q).

Note that each party uses their own secret in generating the common value, so no one else is able to do this. Consequently, K_{AB} is known only to A and to B and can now be used as a key in encryption between Alice and Bob.

Example 2.16   Let $q = 2663$ and $a = 2$ be public, where a is a primitive root modulo 2663. Alice chooses $x_A = 1085$; Bob chooses $x_B = 1701$.

- Alice computes $2^{1085} \equiv 252$ (mod 2663);
- Bob computes $2^{1701} \equiv 1524$ (mod 2663).

Both people publish these values.

- Alice takes Bob's 1524 and uses her exponent to get
  $1524^{1085} \equiv 2103 \pmod{2663}$.
- Bob takes Alice's 252 and uses his exponent to get
  $252^{1701} \equiv 2103 \pmod{2663}$.

They can now both use $k = 2103$ as a shared secret key.

It should be clear that the security of the common key established by the DHKE protocol depends on the DLP being very hard. All an attacker has to do after all, is to capture one of the secrets, say x_A, and she has K_{AB}, since everything else is public. So it is very important that, knowing y_A, a^{x_A}, q and the equation $y_A \equiv a^{x_A} \pmod{q}$, she cannot obtain x_A computationally. Her chances are reduced by the fact that a is a primitive root, and its powers generate all possible values modulo q, so knowing y_A gives no clues.

However, there is a simple result based on the FLT that does give some information about the secret exponent.

Proposition 2.9   *If $y = a^x \pmod{q}$, a a primitive root, q a prime and $1 < x < q - 1$, then it is easy to find the parity of x (that is $x \pmod 2$):*

$$\text{If } y^{\frac{q-1}{2}} \equiv 1 \pmod{q}, \text{ then } x \text{ must be even.}$$

$$\text{If } y^{\frac{q-1}{2}} \equiv -1 \pmod{q}, \text{ then } x \text{ must be odd.}$$

Proof. First we show that if a is a primitive root modulo q, then $a^{\frac{q-1}{2}} \equiv -1 \pmod{q}$. We know by the FLT that $1 \equiv a^{q-1} \equiv \left(a^{\frac{q-1}{2}}\right)^2 \pmod{q}$. So

$$\left[1 - \left(a^{\frac{q-1}{2}}\right)^2\right] \equiv 0 \equiv \left[1 - \left(a^{\frac{q-1}{2}}\right)\right]\left[1 + \left(a^{\frac{q-1}{2}}\right)\right] \pmod{q}.$$

It follows that $a^{\frac{q-1}{2}}$ is either -1 or 1 modulo q.
Now a is a primitive root so $a^{q-1} \equiv 1$ and no smaller exponent on a can be $1 \pmod{p}$. Therefore,

$$a^{\frac{q-1}{2}} \equiv -1 \pmod{q}.$$

Returning to $y = a^x \pmod{q}$, raise both sides to the power $(q - 1)/2$ to get:

$$y^{\frac{q-1}{2}} \equiv \left(a^{\frac{q-1}{2}}\right)^x \equiv (-1)^x \pmod{q}.$$

We know y and q and so can compute:
if $y^{\frac{q-1}{2}} \equiv 1 \pmod{q}$, then x must be even;
if $y^{\frac{q-1}{2}} \equiv -1 \pmod{q}$, then x must be odd.   □

Since an attacker can easily compute this power of y, she knows the parity of the secret value, thus cutting her work to find it in half.

There are several algorithms available for computing discrete logarithms, usually assuming once again that certain conditions hold. For instance, Pohlig and Hellman [56] developed an algorithm in the case that $q-1$ has only small prime factors, say $q-1 = \prod_i q_i^{r_i}$, where the q_i are much smaller than q (of course, this needs to be said more precisely). The idea is based on the fact that if we can solve $x_i \equiv L_a(y) \pmod{q_i^{r_i}}$ for each q_i, then we can combine these equations using the Chinese Remainder Theorem to get a solution to $y = a^x \pmod{q}$. The moral of the story is do not choose such a prime q!

The best known algorithm for attacking the discrete logarithm is due to Pollard [60] and we discuss it in the Section 2.3.1.

2.3.1 Computer Examples

1. The site `http://www.math.fau.edu/Richman/carm.htm` tests the FLT for given values we can choose as input. On input of a number, which the site refers to as n, the site tests the possible values for a (they use the letter b for these values) in Theorem 2.3 of the power of a to $n-1$ modulo n. Testing $n = 9999997$ gives the following answer from the site: $b = 2$ gives 64, so 9999997 is not a prime. Testing 9999991, the answer is $b = 2, \ldots, 9999990$ all give 1. Thus, it looks like 9999991 is a prime. The Maple command *isprime*(9999991); confirms with true.

2. If some specific value for a satisfies Theorem 2.3 modulo n where n is composite, then we say that n is a *pseudoprime base a*. The site in question 1 also finds these for certain possible bases. Use the site to determine all pseudoprimes less than 1000 to base 2.
   Solution. The output is *Pseudoprimes base 2 less than 1000: 341 561 645.*

3. If a composite number n passes all the tests of Theorem 2.3, it is given a special name. It is called a *Carmichael number*. On the same site, find as many Carmichael numbers as possible.
   Solution. 561 1105 1729 2465 2821 6601 8911 10585 15841 29341 for 99999 seems to be the highest we can go.

4. Find a primitive root modulo 2663.
   Solution. First, note that 2663 is prime. The Maple enquiry isprime(2663); will tell you this, or the command ifactor(2663); will tell you it does not factor.
   You might want then to write some code to compute all powers of 2, then 3, then 5, and so on, modulo 2663 to see if you generate the whole set of numbers 1 to 2662. However, the Maple command *primroot(p)*; finds the smallest primitive root for the prime p. For $p = 2663$, you obtain the answer primitive root 5.

5. Given that 65537 is prime, use the FLT to find the inverse of 3511 (mod 65537).
   Solution. By Fermat: > 3511^65536 mod 65537; gives 1. So the inverse of 3511 is 3511^65535:
   > 3511^65535 mod 65537; is 26226.

6. Let $q = 2663$ and $a =$ be public, where a is a primitive root modulo 2663. Alice chooses a secret $x_A = 1085$; Bob chooses a secret $x_B = 1703$. Find their common key using the DHKE protocol.

Solution.

- Alice computes $2^{1085} = 252 \pmod{2663}$;
- Bob computes $2^{1703} = 770 \pmod{2663}$.

Both people publish these values. They can each then determine the common key: $252^{1703} = 770^{1085} = 2125 \pmod{2663}$.

Further Reading. P. Garrett [17]; K.H. Rosen [47]; W. Trappe and L. Washington [52].

2.3.2 Problems

1. Compute the first 12 values of $2^x \pmod{11}$ beginning with $x = 0$. What do you observe?
2. Compute a^{n-1} modulo n for all $a \pmod n$ where $n = 6$. Comment on the results in comparison with the FLT.
3. If n is even, compute $(n - 1)^{n-1} \pmod n$.
4. Use Fermat's Theorem to find the inverse of $35 \pmod{67}$.
5. Redo Example 2.13 using $a = 4$ and $a = 3$ (in that order!) and fast exponentiation.
6. Use the FLT to find $7^{184403} \pmod{101}$.
7. Find all primitive roots modulo 7.
8. Let $q = 43$ and $a = 3$ be public, where a is a primitive root modulo 43. Alice chooses $x_A = 15$; Bob chooses $x_B = 17$.

    - Alice computes $2^{15} = 2 \pmod{43}$;
    - Bob computes $2^{17} = 8 \pmod{43}$.

    Find the common key that they establish.

Computer-Assisted Problems

9. Compute 2^{340} modulo 341. Try 3^{340} modulo 341. Can you conclude anything from the FLT?
10. Compute $a^{560} \pmod{561}$ for each $a = 1, 2, 3, 4, 5, 6, 7, 8, 9, 10$ and check if the FLT is satisfied for these bases.
11. Use Proposition 2.8 to find the parity of the exponent x if 2 is a primitive root modulo the prime 2663 and $2511 = 2^x \pmod{2663}$.
12. Let $q = 2663$ and $a = 2$ be public, where a is a primitive root modulo 2663. Alice chooses $x_A = 1329$; Bob chooses $x_B = 2253$. Find the common key that they establish.

13. The security of the DHKE relies on the fact that it is difficult (computationally speaking) to derive a^{xy} even if you know all of a, a^x, and a^y all modulo a prime. For the prime 13, choose various values of a, x, and y and investigate the difficulty of finding a^{xy}.

2.4 ATTACKING THE DISCRETE LOGARITHM

In this section, we examine a simple idea of John Pollard from the mid-1970s [38, 39, 41]. It is based on a cycle-finding algorithm that attempts to find cycles in sequences. The cycle-finding algorithm used originally in Pollard's work was due to Robert Floyd, who invented it in the late 1960s [16]; however, improvements on this algorithm were found by Pollard in collaboration with Richard Brent, speeding up the time needed to find the cycle [5]. Today, it is still the best known general attack against the discrete logarithm.

We first consider cycle-finding in sequences, and then explain how this can be used to attack the discrete logarithm.

Principle of Cycle Detection   Assume we have a finite, fixed set S of numbers (such as the integers modulo 11937) and a function f which maps this set back to itself (for example, f maps every element of S to its square modulo 11937). With any initial value x_0, the sequence, $x_1 = f(x_0)$, $x_2 = f(x_1)\ldots$ maps elements of S back into S and so must eventually repeat. In this case, there must be some $i \neq j$ such that $x_i = x_j$. Once this happens, the sequence must continue by repeating the cycle of values from x_i to x_{j-1} over and over.

Example 2.17   Consider the set S of integers modulo 13. Let f be a function which maps each element x of S to $2x + 3$. If we begin with the value (randomly chosen) $x_0 = 7$, the sequence obtained is $x_1 = 4$, $x_2 = 11$, $x_3 = 12$, $x_4 = 1$, $x_5 = 5$, $x_6 = 0$, $x_7 = 3$, $x_8 = 9$, $x_9 = 8$, $x_{10} = 6$, $x_{11} = 2$, $x_{12} = 7$, $x_{13} = 4$ and we are now repeating: $x_0 = 7 = x_{12}$. So we have a cycle of length 12. Out of a possible 13 elements to cycle, this is not particularly efficient. The one value we did not obtain in the list was 10; notice that f maps 10 to itself. If we had started with 10 as our random element, we would have had a cycle immediately.

Example 2.18   We try again with a function which cubes. Consider the set S of integers modulo 37 and let f be the function that sends each element of S to its cube modulo 37. Starting with the number $x_0 = 11$, we obtain the sequence $x_1 = 36$, $x_2 = 36$, and we have already hit a single element cycle. (Since 36 is just -1 and we are cubing, clearly this just repeats.) Trying $x_0 = 5$, the sequence obtained is $x_1 = 14$, $x_2 = 6$, $x_3 = 31$, $x_4 = 6$ and we have found a two-element cycle.

Terminology   Consider a sequence of integers $x_0, x_1 = f(x_0), x_2 = f(x_1)\ldots$, where f is some function mapping the set S to itself. Suppose that the first cycle in this sequence is from x_i to x_j, $i \leq j$. Then the first values in the sequence: $x_0, x_1, \ldots x_{i-1}$ are referred

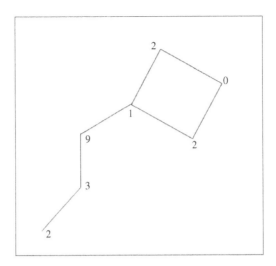

Figure 2.1. A sequence cycle.

to as the *tail of the sequence* and the *cycle length* is $j - i + 1$. We use t to refer to the number of elements in the tail (this number can be 0) and c to refer to the number of elements in the first (or smallest) cycle (this number must be at least 1).

Example 2.19 Suppose that for some modulus and seed, we generate the sequence $2, 3, 9, 1, 2, 0, 2, 1, 2, 0, 2, \ldots$ shown in Figure 2.1 that has a tail with $t = 3$ elements and a smallest cycle of size $c = 4$. It also has cycles of length 8 (1,2,0,2,1,2,0,2) and all multiples of 4. But we are only interested in the smallest cycle and the first time it occurs.

Once a sequence value falls into the cycle, it is repeated again c times later, then $2c$ times later, and so on. We can write this fact as: for $j \geq t$, $x_j = x_{j+c} = x_{j+2c}$ and in general $x_j = x_{j+kc}$ for any positive integer k.

Notice that if $c \geq t$, we get $x_c = x_{c+kc}$ and for $k = 1$, this gives $x_c = x_{2c}$. What if $c < t$? We can choose an integer n such that $nc \geq t$, and then we have, using the same argument as above, $x_{nc} = x_{2nc}$.

Robert Floyd [16] noticed this and used the idea to find the cycle. He wrote an algorithm to look for integers i with the property that $x_{2i} = x_i$. How big does i have to be? The above discussion tells us that if $c \geq t$, we only need to go as far as c. And if $c < t$, we can use the smallest n such that $nc \geq t$. Since, in either case, c must divide one of the c numbers $t, t + 1, \ldots, t + c - 1$, we will find a suitable i in this range. We have almost proved the first part of the next proposition.

Proposition 2.10 *Suppose that the sequence of integers* x_0, $x_1 = f(x_0)$, $x_2 = f(x_1) \ldots$ *where f is some function mapping the finite set S to itself has tail of length t and shortest cycle length c.*

(a) Then $x_{2i} = x_i$ for some non zero i, $t \leq i \leq t + c$.
(b) If f is sufficiently random then $t + c$ is approximately $(1.2533)\sqrt{|S|}$.

Proof. We only prove part (a). From the discussion prior to the statement of the proposition, we saw that $x_{2i} = x_i$ for some $t \leq i \leq t + c - 1$. If t is at least 1, we are done. But if $t = 0$, then i could be 0. In this case, $c \geq t$ and the discussion prior to the proposition shows that this gives $x_c = x_{2c}$ and so $t \leq i = c \leq t + c$ satisfies the requirement. The result (b) can be found in [25; pg. 55, Fact 2.37]. It is not easy to describe accurately what is meant by sufficiently random and in practice, trial and error is used to generate such a function. □

Floyd's algorithm for locating cycles now works as follows: consider the sequence generated as x_0, $x_1 = f(x_0)$, $x_2 = f(x_1)$, $x_3 = f(x_2)$, $x_4 = f(x_3)$, and so on. Consider every second one of these elements, to form the new sequence $y_0 = x_0$, $y_1 = x_2$, $y_2 = x_4$ and in general $y_i = x_{2i}$. Floyd asked, when can we find an i such that $y_i = x_{2i} = x_i$? Proposition 2.17 helps because it indicates both that there must be one, and approximately how large the upper bound on it is. The algorithm is given below [23].

Floyd's Cycle-Finding Algorithm

Set $x_i = x_0$, $y_i = x_0$, and $i = 0$.
Repeat $i = i + 1$, $x_i = f(x_{i-1})$, $y_i = f(f(y_{i-1}))$ until $x_i = y_i$.
On termination, $x = x_i$ and $y = x_{2i}$ and $x_{2i} = x_i$. This is generally referred to as a *collision* in the two sequences.

Example 2.20 Consider the sequence $x_0 = 2$, $x_{i+1} = f(x_i) = x_i^2 + 7 \pmod{31}$. We use Floyd's cycle-finding algorithm to obtain a collision.
Set $x_i = x_0 = 2$ and $y_i = x_0 = 2$ and $i = 0$. Then moving to $i = 1$, we compute pairs $x_i = f(x_{i-1})$, $y_i = f(f(y_{i-1}))$ until $x_i = y_i$: $(x_1, y_1) = (11, 4)$; $(x_2, y_2) = (4, 2)$; $(x_3, y_3) = (23, 4)$; $(x_4, y_4) = (2, 2)$. We conclude that $x_4 = x_8$.
Is this the smallest collision? In other words, is it the first one? We can check by writing out the sequence up to nine terms (starting at $i = 0$): 2, 11, 4, 23, 2, 11, 4, 23, 2, ... So x_4 is not the place the cycle starts; it begins at the 0th position. This is a sequence with no tail and cycle length 4.

Attacking the Discrete Logarithm—Pollard's Method We apply the cycle-finding algorithm to find a solution to a discrete logarithm equation of the form $a \equiv b^z \pmod{p}$, where a and b can be assumed to be in $\{1, 2, \ldots, p - 1\}$ and z is unknown. We want to solve this for positive integer values of z. We assume that p is a prime number and that b is a primitive root modulo p.
The first step is to use the cycle-finding algorithm to get an equation of the form $a^i b^j \equiv a^k b^m \pmod{p}$ for some integer exponents. To do this, we need to setup a function and a seed value. As mentioned in Proposition 2.9, if we choose a random enough function, the time it takes to actually calculate the exponents can be bounded.

Pollard [32, 33] suggested the following function:

$$f(x) = \begin{cases} bx & \text{if} \quad 0 \le x < p/3 \\ x^2 & \text{if} \quad p/3 \le x < 2p/3 \\ ax & \text{if} \quad 2p/3 \le x < p \end{cases}$$

with seed value $x_0 = 1$.

The first application of f to x gives $x_1 = f(1) = b$ since $0 \le 1 < p/3$. Now depending on where b lies in the range 0 to p, the next value x_2 will be either a power of b or a times b. Repeated applications of f will result in powers of a times powers of b, all computations done modulo p.

Floyd's cycling algorithm, therefore, tells us that we will eventually obtain $a^i b^j \equiv a^k b^m \pmod{p}$ for some non-negative integer exponents i, j, k, and m. This can be rewritten as $a^u \equiv b^v \pmod{p}$ for some integers u and v in the range 0 to $p - 1$.

Now how do we reduce the exponent on a to 1? Note that in logarithmic notation,

$$u * L_b(a) \equiv v \pmod{p - 1}. \tag{2.5}$$

If $\gcd(u, p - 1) = 1$, we immediately obtain an equation of the desired form $a \equiv b^z \pmod{p}$, where $z = vu^{-1}$. However, we may not be so lucky, in which case, we need to take some extra steps.

Let $\gcd(u, p - 1) = d \ge 1$. In Equation (2.1), d divides v. Write $u/d = r$ and $v/d = w$ (as integers). Then we can reduce Equation (2.5) to

$$r * L_b(a) \equiv w \pmod{(p - 1)/d} \tag{2.6}$$

and now invert r using the EA because it is relatively prime to $(p - 1)/d$. The result is an equation of the form

$$L_b(a) \equiv z_1 \pmod{(p - 1)/d}. \tag{2.7}$$

But we need a solution z to $L_b(a) \equiv z \pmod{p - 1}$ to have $a \equiv b^z \pmod{p}$, and we obtain it by adding multiples of $(p - 1)/d$ to z_1. The correct solution will be in the set

$$L_b(a) \equiv z_1 + k[(p - 1)/d]$$

for some $k = 0, 1, 2, \ldots, d - 1$.

Summary

To find the discrete logarithm:

1. Use the cycle-finding algorithm to get a collision.
2. Eliminate the unwanted exponent using the EA.

Since we rely on the discrete logarithm to secure communications, all of the above computations are expected to be difficult when p is large enough. Keeping this in mind, we do some examples.

Example 2.21 We use Pollard's method to solve the discrete logarithm problem: $22 \equiv 3^z \pmod{43}$ where 3 is a primitive root modulo 43 and z is unknown. We use Pollard's suggested function and seed value:

$$f(x) = \begin{cases} 3x & \text{if } 0 \leq x < 43/3 \\ x^2 & \text{if } 43/3 \leq x < 86/3 \\ 22x & \text{if } 86/3 \leq x < 43 \end{cases}$$

with seed value $x_0 = 1$. Applying Floyd's algorithm (or computing the sequence by hand since it is small), we obtain pairs: $(x_1, y_1) = (3, 9)$; $(x_2, y_2) = (9, 41)$; $(x_3, y_3) = (27, 21)$; $(x_4, y_4) = (41, 33)$; $(x_5, y_5) = (42, 19)$; $(x_6, y_6) = (21, 31)$; $(x_7, y_7) = (11, 40)$; $(x_8, y_8) = (33, 13)$; $(x_9, y_9) = (38, 41)$; $(x_{10}, y_{10}) = (19, 21)$; $(x_{11}, y_{11}) = (17, 33)$; $(x_{12}, y_{12}) = (31, 19)$; $(x_{13}, y_{13}) = (37, 31)$; $(x_{14}, y_{14}) = (40, 40)$.

We conclude that $x_{14} = x_{28}$. But what exponential equation does this give us? We compute the left-hand side based on the operations only. The sequence is 1, 3, 3^2, 3^3, $[3^3]^2$, $22 * [3^3]^2$, $22^2 * [3^3]^2$, $[22^2 * [3^3]^2]^2$, $3 * [22^2 * [3^3]^2]^2$, $22 * 3 * [22^2 * [3^3]^2]^2$, $22^2 * 3 * [22^2 * [3^3]^2]^2$, $[22^2 * 3 * [22^2 * [3^3]^2]^2]^2$, $[22^2 * 3 * [22^2 * [3^3]^2]^2]^4$, $22 * [22^2 * 3 * [22^2 * [3^3]^2]^2]^4$, $22^2[22^2 * 3 * [22^2 * [3^3]^2]^2]^4 = 3^{52} * 22^{26}$. Using the FLT, we can reduce these exponents to $3^{10} * 22^{26}$.

Continuing and using the FLT to reduce exponents along the way, we compute $x_{28} = 3^4 * 22^4$. Setting equations equal, we have $3^6 \equiv 22^{42-22} \equiv 22^{20} \pmod{43}$. From Equation (2.5), $20 * L_3(22) \equiv 6 \pmod{42}$. Unfortunately, $\gcd(20, 42)$ is not 1. However, it is 2, and 2 also divides 6, so that $10 * L_3(22) \equiv 3 \pmod{21}$ and we can invert 10 modulo 21. The inverse of 10 is 19. So $L_3(22) \equiv 3 * 19 \equiv 15 \pmod{21}$. The correct solution will, therefore, be in the set

$$L_3(22) \equiv 15 + k * 21$$

for some $k = 0$ or 1. We test both possibilities. If $L_3(22) \equiv 15$, then $3^{15} \equiv 22 \pmod{43}$, which we can compute as being correct. The other value gives $3^{36} \equiv 22 \pmod{43}$ which is not correct—this value is 21. The unknown value for z we were searching for is, therefore, 15.

The Index Calculus Attack on the Discrete Logarithm

This is another method that works quite well for computing discrete logs of any size. A bit of luck is involved.

Given a and b, we are still trying to solve $b \equiv a^x \pmod{p}$, where a is a primitive root modulo the prime p.

To limit the computation necessary, we choose a positive integer bound B and let $p_1, p_2, \ldots, p_m$ be the list of primes less than B. It would ne nice to have B small, but this will depend on the size of the modulus p in general.

Now we work on the powers of $a \pmod{p}$, a^2, a^3, and so on, trying to write them as a product of primes in our list. We keep going until we get one that works, say

$$a^k \equiv \prod p_i^{a_i} \pmod{p}.$$

Rewriting in log form with base a:

$$kL_a(a) \equiv k \equiv \sum_i a_i L_a(p_i) \pmod{p-1}.$$

This is a linear equation in the log of the m primes in the list. If we can get m independent such equations, we can solve for the values $L_a(p_i)$.

Suppose that we manage to obtain these values; we then look at numbers of the form ba^r, starting with $r = 1$, again, trying to write these in terms of the base prime list:

$$ba^r \equiv \prod_i p_i^{b_i} \pmod{p}.$$

If we can do this, we get in log form $L_a(ba^r) = L_a(\prod p_i^{b_i}) \pmod{p-1}$ So $L_a(b) = -r + \sum b_i L_a(p_i) \pmod{p-1}$.

If we know all the $L_a(p_i)$, we have found $L_a(b)$.

Note that we if we simply try to get b as a product of primes in the list, we will likely be unsuccessful. However, multiplying b by powers of a gives us a better chance of getting the right kind of equation, and it adds no complexity to the solution.

This algorithm works well for primes up to 200 digits.

Example 2.22 We use the Index Calculus method to attack the discrete logarithm $37 \equiv 2^x \pmod{131}$, 2 a primitive root modulo 131. In other words, we solve the equation for x.

We begin by choosing $B = 10$ and so the base prime set is $\{2, 3, 5, 7\}$. Computing the first few powers of 2 (mod 131), we obtain $2^1 \equiv 2$, $2^2 \equiv 2^2$, $2^3 \equiv 2^3$, simply representing the power of 2 as itself since 2 is in the base prime set. However, this just gets us the dependent equations $1 = 1$, $2 = 2$, $3 = 3$, and so on.

We need to look for higher powers of 2 that will introduce the other primes in the base set. So we keep going and pick out $2^1 \equiv 2$, $2^8 \equiv 5^3$, $2^{12} \equiv 5 * 7$, $2^{14} \equiv 3^2$, $2^{34} \equiv 3 * 5^2$ in terms of base primes. This gives log equations resulting in $1 = L_2(2)$, $8 = 3L_2(5)$, $12 = L_2(5) + L_2(7)$, $14 = 2L_2(3)$ and $34 = L_2(3) + 2L_2(5) \pmod{130}$.

Solving, we obtain: $L_2(5) \equiv 46$, $L_2(7) \equiv 96$, $L_2(3) \equiv 72$.

Now we use this to find $L_2(37)$: $37 * 2^{43} \equiv 3 * 5 * 7 \pmod{131}$ using base primes only.

So $L_2(37) \equiv -43 + L_2(3) + L_2(5) + L_2(7) \equiv 41 \pmod{130}$.

Thus $37 \equiv 2^{41} \pmod{131}$, and the fact that this is correct can be verified directly.

The Baby Step, Giant Step Attack on Discrete Logarithms

This method is very similar to the Index Calculus method in that two lists are made and a match is wanted.

Eve wants to find x such that $a^x \equiv b \pmod{p}$. She first chooses a bound $N \approx \sqrt{p-1} + 1$ so that $p - 1 \le N^2$.

Then she makes two lists: the first increases the exponent only by one each time (hence its name), while the second increases the exponent by a multiple of N each time (hence its name).

The *Baby Step* list: $a^j \pmod{p}$ for $0 \le j < N$.
The *Giant Step* list: $ba^{-Nk} \pmod{p}$ for $0 \le k < N$.

The baby step list will run through about $\sqrt{p-1}$ values modulo p several times since a is a primitive root.

The Giant step list may be a bit erratic because of multiplication by b.

As soon as Eve picks up corresponding numbers in each list (this is referred to as a table sorting problem and can take some time if p is very large) she can write $a^j \equiv ba^{-Nk} \pmod{p}$ and so $a^{j+Nk} \equiv b \pmod{p}$; thus, she has found $x = j + Nk$.

The number of steps in the algorithm is around $\sqrt{p}$ and approximately N numbers need storing.

With computer capability in 2010, the method works well for primes with up to about 1020 digits.

Example 2.23 Solve $3^x \equiv 5 \pmod{7}$. Choose $N = 4$.

Baby step list: $3^0 = 1, 3^1 = 3, 3^2 = 2, 3^3 = 6$.
Giant step list: $5 * 3^0 = 5, 5 * 3^{-4} = 3, 5 * 3^{-8} = 6, 5 * 3^{-12} = 5$.

We have two matches: $3^1 \equiv 5 * 3^{-4}$, so $3^5 \equiv 5 \pmod{7}$ and $3^3 \equiv 5 * 3^{-8}$, so $3^{11} \equiv 5 \pmod{7}$ (as expected).

There must always be a match in these two lists since any x in the range 0 to $p - 1$ can be written as $x = x_0 + x_1 N$ for some x_0 and x_1.

Example 2.24 Let $p = 131$. Choose $N = 13$.
Then if $x = 6$, we can write $6 = 6 + 0 * 13$.
If $x = 129$, we can write $129 = 12 + 9 * 13$.

2.4.1 Computer Examples

1. Find a collision for the function

$$f(x) = \begin{cases} 5x & \text{if} \quad 0 \le x < 2663/3 \\ x^2 & \text{if} \quad 2663/3 \le x < 5326/3 \\ 351x & \text{if} \quad 5326/3 \le x < 2663 \end{cases}$$

modulo 2663 with seed value $x_0 = 1$.

Solution. Writing an algorithm for this will certainly help. The fact that it is a piece-wise defined function makes this a bit harder to do, but not impossible. Here is some pseudo code:
Set $1 = x_i = x_0$, $1 = y_i = x_0$, and $i = 0$. Set

$$f(x) = \begin{cases} 5x & \text{if} \quad 0 \le x < 2663/3 \text{ modulo } 2663 \\ x^2 & \text{if} \quad 2663/3 \le x < 5326/3 \text{ modulo } 2663 \\ 351x & \text{if} \quad 5326/3 \le x < 2663 \text{ modulo } 2663. \end{cases}$$

Repeat $i = i + 1$, $x_i = f(x_{i-1})$, $y_i = f(f(y_{i-1}))$ until $x_i = y_i$.

Output (i, x_i).

We get a collision at the 32nd step: $x_{32} = 1480 \pmod{2663} = y_{32}$ meaning that $5^{7033} * 351^{1192} \equiv 5^{460927795} * 351^{78153864}$.

2. Use the work in Computer Example 1 to find a solution of $351 \equiv 5^z \pmod{2663}$ where it is known that 5 is a primitive root modulo the prime 2663.
Solution. We use the result of the last question: $5^{7033} * 351^{1192} \equiv 5^{460927795} * 351^{78153864}$ and first reduce the exponents using the FLT: $5^{1709} * 351^{1192} \equiv 5^{2495} * 351^{206}$. Now $351^{986} \equiv 5^{786}$, which can be converted to: $986L_5(351) \equiv 786 \pmod{2662}$. We now need the inverse of 986 modulo 2662: but we have a problem since these numbers are not relatively prime and so we first divide out 2: $493L_5(351) \equiv 393 \pmod{1331}$. We find the inverse of 493 modulo 1331 using the EA or by asking Maple: $493^{(-1)} \pmod{1331}$; giving 27. Therefore, $L_5(351) \equiv 27 * 393 \equiv 1294 \pmod{1331}$.
The correct solution will, therefore, be in the set

$$L_5(351) \equiv 1294 + k * 1331$$

for some $k = 0$ or 1. We test both possibilities:
$5^{1294} \pmod{2663}$; 2312
$5^{2625} \pmod{2663}$; 351. So $z = 2625$.

3. Use the Baby Step, Giant Step algorithm to find x in
$650^x = 2213 \pmod{3571}$.
Solution. We choose a bound about square root 3571: $N = 60$. And we compute the two lists adding to each list as we go, looking for a match as we build them.

Baby Step list: 1, 1122, 816, 1892, 1376, 1650, 1200, 1522, 133, 746, 2815, 1398, 1666, 887, 1619, 2476, 2450, 3405, 2801 (19th step).

Giant Step list: 2213, 1679, 2639, 1836, 2437, 2801 (5th step), 1946, 2159, 452, 351, 2619, 588, 267, 3091, 2187, 1485, 3389, 2213, 1679, 2639 (19th step).

We have a match between the 5th step of the giant list and the 19th step of the baby list. We can, therefore, write $650^{19} \equiv 2213 * 650^{-300} \pmod{3571}$ which implies that $650^{319} \equiv 2213$ and so the solution for x is 319. This can be verified directly now.

This brings us to the end of the chapter. In the next chapter we will study one of the most important public key schemes in use today—the ElGamal scheme. Its security is based on that of the discrete logarithm.

Further Reading. R.W. Floyd [16]; D.E. Knuth [23]; A.J. Menezes, P.C. van Oorschot and S.A. Vanstone [29]; J.M. Pollard [38], [39], and [41].

2.4.2 Problems

1. Give an example of a sequence with $t = 0$ and $c = 1$.
2. If you did not use a function to generate the sequence in question 1, can you find a function that will generate it?
3. Give an example of a sequence with $t = 9$ and $c = 5$.
4. If you did not use a function to generate the sequence in question 3, can you find a function that will generate it?
5. Use Floyd's cycle-finding algorithm to find two different locations with the same value in the sequence $x_0 = 3$ and $f(x_i) = 2x_i + 7$ in the system modulo 31.
6. Use the Pollard method to solve the discrete logarithm problem $7 \equiv 5^z \pmod{23}$ where 5 is a primitive root modulo 23 and z is unknown.
7. Define a "near-collision" to be a pair of elements from two sequences as in Floyd's cycle-finding algorithm which differ by at most 2. Adapt Floyd's algorithm to this case.
8. Redo Problem 5 to find a "near-collision" as defined in Problem 7.

Computer-Assisted Problems

9. Use Floyd's cycle-finding algorithm to find two different locations with the same value in the sequence $x_0 = 3$ and $f(x_i) = 2x_i^2 + 7$ in a congruence system modulo 111.
10. See the page http://www.research.att.com/~njas/sequences/index.html. This is a well-known site on integer sequences. The integers used in any given sequence there are not necessarily from a finite set. Type in a random series of integers to the search box and see if it is known by the site.

Now construct a function to map a seed value into a sequence as in Examples 2.17 and 2.18. Put the first few terms of this sequence into the search box. Does the site recognize it? Now try the sequence 1,2,1,2,1,2. What is this recognized as?

11. Use the Index Calculus method to attack the discrete logarithm $8576 \equiv 3^x$ (mod 53047), where 3 is a primitive root modulo 53047. Choose a base prime set of the primes up to 31.

12. Use the Baby Step, Giant Step algorithm to solve $8576 \equiv 3^x$ (mod 53047), where 3 is a primitive root modulo 53047. Compare the complexity of your solution with that of your solution to Problem 11.

3

THE ELGAMAL SCHEME

The ElGamal cryptography scheme is set up in a way similar to that used for the Diffie–Hellman key exchange scheme that we saw in the previous chapter. Similar to DHKE, it relies on the existence of primitive roots. While we will be working modulo a prime in this chapter, we will need a more general theory of primitive roots for non prime moduli for use in Chapter 4. Thus, we begin to develop this more general theory in the first section of this chapter and answer the question "when do primitive roots exist?"

3.1 PRIMITIVE ROOTS

In this section, we generalize the notion of primitive root for prime modulus, which we saw in Definition 2.6, to include the composite case. To do so smoothly, we first introduce some new notation regarding those elements modulo a composite number n for which an inverse modulo n exists. Recall from Chapter 2, that only those numbers which are relatively prime to n have an inverse modulo n. We give these numbers a special name.

Definition 3.1 For any positive integer n, a number between 1 and $n-1$ that is relatively prime to n is called *a unit modulo n*. We use $\phi(n)$ to denote the number of units modulo n. It is referred to as the *Euler ϕ function*, after Leonhard Euler [10].

Public Key Cryptography: Applications and Attacks, First Edition. Lynn Margaret Batten.
© 2013 by The Institute of Electrical and Electronics Engineers, Inc. Published 2013 by John Wiley & Sons, Inc.

For instance, $\phi(15) = 8$; equivalently, eight of the numbers in the range 1–14 have inverses modulo 15. For n a prime, it should be clear that $\phi(n) = n - 1$.

The Euler ϕ function has some properties that are worth noting including those in the following proposition that we give without proof.

Proposition 3.1   *Let n and r be positive integers and p represent a prime number. Then*

(a) $\phi(p^r) = \left(1 - \dfrac{1}{p}\right) p^r$

(b) $\phi(pq) = (p - 1)(q - 1)$

(c) $\phi(n) = n \displaystyle\prod_{p \mid n} \left(1 - \dfrac{1}{p}\right)$

Example 3.1 $\phi(21) = \phi(3 * 7) = 2 * 6 = 12.$
$\phi(32) = \phi(2^5) = \left(1 - \frac{1}{2}\right) 2^5 = 2^4 = 16.$

In any system modulo n, the value 1 will be a unit as it is its own inverse. We can say quite a bit more about this entire set of units modulo n as it has a nice structure. We first look at an example.

Example 3.2   We find all units in Z_{15} and determine some of the properties of this set. We know that the units are precisely those elements relatively prime to 15: 1, 2, 4, 7, 8, 11, 13, 14. As stated earlier, 1 is always a unit. However, also $n - 1 \equiv -1$ will always be its own inverse and so a unit. For a unit which is not its own inverse, of course, its inverse is also a unit and in the list; the inverse of 2 is 8; the inverse of 4 is itself; the inverse of 7 is 13. Proposition 2.3 states that inverses are unique, and so we can see that the set of values which are not their own inverses will pair up.

We can actually say much more about the structure of the set of units. The following definition helps us to do this efficiently.

Definition 3.2   A *group* is a set G with a single operation "." and the following four properties: If $a, b, c \in G$ then

(i) $a \cdot b \in G$ (the closure property)

(ii) $a \cdot (b \cdot c) = (a \cdot b) \cdot c$ (the associative property)

(iii) G has an identity 1 such that
      $1 \cdot a = a \cdot 1 = a$ for every a in G (the identity property)

(iv) for every a in G, there is a b in G such that $ab = ba = 1$ (the inverse property).

Does property (i) hold for the units in Example 3.2? For instance, both 4 and 7 are units, so is $4 * 7 = 13$ a unit? Yes, it is. In fact, we are able to prove:

Theorem 3.1 *In Z_n, $n \geq 1$, the set of all elements relatively prime to n forms a group under multiplication $*$. This group has $\phi(n)$ elements.*

Proof. Property (ii) holds in any modulus system, so we do not need to say anything further. For property (i), given a and b units, we have to show that $a * b$ is a unit. We can do this by showing its inverse. But its inverse is just $b^{-1} * a^{-1}$ since $(b^{-1} * a^{-1}) * (a * b) = b^{-1} * (a^{-1} * a) * b = b^{-1} * b = 1$. We know that properties (iii) and (iv) hold because of Proposition 2.5.   □

Definition 3.3   We refer to the group structure of Theorem 3.1 as the *group of units* modulo n.

As a consequence of Theorem 3.1, we can say that the set of all non zero elements modulo p a prime forms a group.

Notation
Z_n^* is used for the group of units of Z_n.
     We are now at the point where we can define a primitive root for the case of a general modulus system and state when they exist.

Definition 3.4   The value a is a *primitive root* modulo the positive integer n if its powers generate the entire group of units modulo n.

It is not difficult to see that this definition includes the special case when n is a prime given in Definition 2.6. This earlier definition was able to reformulate the definition for prime moduli in terms of an exponential congruence. In fact, there is an equivalent statement in the general case. To generate the entire group using its powers, it must be the case, by Theorem 3.1, that there are $\phi(n)$ distinct powers of a.
     This leads to an alternate definition for 3.4:

Definition 3.5   The value a is a *primitive root* modulo the positive integer n if the smallest positive integer l so that $a^l \equiv 1 \pmod{n}$ is $\phi(n)$.

The next result tells us when we can expect to have primitive roots.

Theorem 3.2   The Primitive Root Theorem
Z/n, $n > 1$ has a primitive root if and only if n is of the form $2^a p^b$ where p is an odd prime, $0 \leq a \leq 1$, and $b \geq 0$, or if $n = 4$.

We do not prove this statement, but an interested reader can find a proof in [17; pg 230]. Note that if n is prime, there is always a primitive root.

Example 3.3   Since $p = 3$ meets the criterion of Theorem 3.1, we should be able to find a primitive root of the group of units $\{1, 2\}$. The only reasonable option is 2 and indeed, $2^2 \equiv 1 \pmod{3}$ so the powers of 2 generate the units in the group.

Example 3.4   Consider Z_{15} that, according to Theorem 3.1, has no primitive root. We can test each value to verify this: $2^2 = 4, 2^3 = 8, 2^4 = 1$ so 2 does not generate all units for instance. We leave the other verifications as an exercise.

Theorem 3.1 does not tell us how many primitive roots there are, nor how to find them. To get some partial answers to these questions we introduce a little additional notation.

Definition 3.6   Let $a \in Z$ and $n \in N$ with $\gcd(a, n) = 1$. Then the *order of a modulo n* is the smallest positive integer e such that $a^e = 1 \pmod{n}$.
We write $e = ord_n(a)$ in this case.

It follows that another way of defining a primitive root a using *ord* notation is to write that $ord_n(a) = \phi(n)$.
A good question now is does the order of a above always exist? In the case that n is prime, the FLT gives the answer. At least one positive integer, $n - 1$, works, and so there must be a smallest one that does. But what if n is composite? We look at some examples.

Example 3.5

    (a) Find $ord_{11}(3)$.
        We have $3^2 = 9, 3^3 = 5, 3^4 = 4, 3^5 = 1$. So $ord_{11}(3) = 5$ and it follows that 3 is not a primitive root modulo 11.
    (b) Find $ord_{37}(2)$.
        We have $2^5 = 32 = -5, 2^6 = 27, 2^7 = 17 \ldots$ (fill in the gaps)$\ldots 2^{36} = 1$. So $ord_{37}(2) = 36$ and we have shown that 2 is a primitive root modulo 37.
    (c) Find $ord_6(3)$.
        We take all powers of 3 modulo 6: $3^1 = 3, 3^2 = 3, 3^3 = 3$ and so on. So $ord_6(3)$ does not exist.

With a little thought, if $a^e \equiv 1 \pmod{n}$, then $a * a^{e-1} \equiv 1 \pmod{n}$ and so a must have an inverse modulo n. Thus, the order can only exist if $\gcd(a, n) = 1$. But is this condition sufficient? The answer is yes, but we shall not see why until we meet Euler's theorem in Chapter 4.

There is no easy way to find a primitive root, but once you find one, we can show how to find the rest:

Proposition 3.2   *If a is a primitive root modulo n and $a^l \equiv 1 \pmod{n}$, then $\phi(n)$ divides l.*

Proof. By definition, we know that $\phi(n)$ is smaller than or equal to l. Let us assume that $\phi(n)$ does not divide l.

Use the EA to write $l = q * \phi(n) + r$ where $0 < r < \phi(n)$. Now $1 \equiv a^l = a^{q*\phi(n)+r} = [a^{\phi(n)}]^q * a^r \equiv 1 * a^r \pmod{n}$. Now r is smaller than $\phi(n)$ and $a^r \equiv 1 \pmod{n}$, which is a contradiction. $\qquad\square$

In fact, the proof of the previous proposition can easily be seen to extend to prove the following. We leave the proof as an exercise.

Proposition 3.3 *If g is an element of Z_n and if $ord_n(g) = s$ and $g^l \equiv 1 \pmod{n}$, then $s|l$.*

Proposition 3.4 *If g is an element of Z_n, then $g^d \equiv 1 \pmod{n}$ if and only if $ord_n(g)|d$.*

Proof. There are two directions to prove. First, note that if $g^d \equiv 1$, we may assume that $d \geq 2$ (since everything divides 0 and $ord_n(1) = 1$), from which it follows that $g * g^{d-1} \equiv 1 \pmod{n}$ and so g has an inverse modulo n and is, therefore, relatively prime to n. By Proposition 3.3, $ord_n(g)|d$.

Now suppose that $ord_n(g)|d$. It then follows from the definition of $ord_n(g)$ that $g^d \equiv 1 \pmod{n}$. $\qquad\square$

Proposition 3.5 *If a is a primitive root modulo n, then so is a^e for any e relatively prime to $ord_n(a) = \phi(n)$.*

Proof. It suffices to show that if a is a primitive root modulo n, then $\{a^e, a^{2e}, \ldots, a^{e\phi(n)}\}$ runs through all numbers modulo n and relatively prime to n. Suppose $a^{ie} \equiv a^{je} \pmod{n}$ for some $i \neq j$ in the set. We can suppose $i > j$. Then $a^{e(i-j)} \equiv 1 \pmod{n}$. By Proposition 3.3, $\phi(n)$ divides $e(i - j)$. However, $\phi(n)$ is relatively prime to e, and so $\phi(n)$ divides $i - j$. But $0 < i - j < \phi(n)$, so this is a contradiction. $\qquad\square$

Example 3.6 Given that the value 5 is a primitive root modulo 18, the possible values of e from the last proposition are 1 and 5. Thus, 5 raised to each of these powers is a primitive root modulo 18: 5 and 11.

Proposition 3.6 *If Z/n has a primitive root a, then it has $\phi(\phi(n))$ of them and each primitive root has the form a^e for any e relatively prime to $ord_n(a) = \phi(n)$.*

Proof. Any primitive root is in the list generated by powers of a, and so looks like a^e for some e. By *Proposition 3.5*, every a^e for $\gcd(e, \phi(n)) = 1$ is a primitive root. But there are $\phi(\phi(n))$ such values for e, completing the proof. $\qquad\square$

Example 3.7 We saw in Example 3.5 that $ord_{37}(2) = 36$. By Proposition 3.5, all other primitive roots are of the form 2^e where $\gcd(e, \phi(37)) = 1$. Now $\phi(37) = 36$ and values for e are $\{1, 5, 7, 11, 13, 17, 19, 23, 25, 29, 31, 35\}$. So there are 12 primitive roots modulo 37.

Before moving to the next section, we complete this one by adding a result on the number of solutions to certain equations.

Proposition 3.7 *There are precisely t distinct roots to the equation $x^t \equiv 1 \pmod{n}$, where n has a primitive root a and $t|\phi(n)$.*

Proof. Let $s = \dfrac{\phi(n)}{t}$. Then $(a^s)^t \equiv a^{\phi(n)} \equiv 1$. Also, $(a^{2s})^t \equiv (a^{3s})^t \equiv \ldots (a^{ts})^t \equiv 1$. So we have potentially t distinct roots $a^s, a^{2s}, \ldots a^{ts} = a^{\phi(n)}$. If $a^{si} = a^{sj}$ for some $t \geq j > i > 0$, then $a^{s(j-i)} \equiv 1 \pmod{\phi(n)}$ and by Proposition 3.3, $\phi(n)$ divides $s(j-i)$. But this last value is less than $s*t = \phi(n)$ and greater than 0, which is impossible. So we have at least t distinct roots.

Now suppose that there is another solution $x = a^m$ where we may assume that $1 \leq m \leq \phi(n)$. Since $x^{mt} \equiv 1 \pmod{n}$, then $\phi(n) = s*t$ divides $m*t$. Thus, $s|m$. Write $m = s*j$ where $1 \leq j \leq t$. Then we already have this solution in the above list. So there are precisely t solutions. □

Example 3.8 We find all solutions of $x^3 \equiv 1 \pmod{7}$. By Proposition 3.7, there are 3 solutions to $x^3 \equiv 1 \pmod{7}$, since Z_7 has a primitive root and since $3|(6 \equiv \phi(7))$. We can find all solutions directly by testing each value in the set, or, we can take a primitive root, say 3, in which case, 3^3, $(3^2)^3$ and $(3^3)^3$ should all be solutions.

Proposition 3.8 *There are precisely t distinct roots to the equation $x^t \equiv c \pmod{n}$, c not 0, if there is at least one solution and if n has a primitive root and $t|\phi(n)$.*

Proof. Let $x = a$ be one solution. Then we can write $x^t \equiv a^t \pmod{n}$, from which we obtain $(xa^{-1})^t \equiv 1 \pmod{n}$. This last equation has precisely t solutions by Proposition 3.5. Let these be c_1 to c_t. Then ac_1 to ac_t are the t solutions to the original equation. □

The proof of Proposition 3.6 also gives us the method of finding all solutions once we have one. In Chapter 4, we will see some results that indicate how to find (at least) one solution.

3.1.1 Computer Examples

1. Consider $n = 18 = 2 * 3^2$ that, by Proposition 3.4, has $\phi(\phi(18))$ primitive roots. $\phi(18) = 6$ and $\phi(6) = 2$.
   A primitive root must be relatively prime to 18 and so can only be 5, 7, 11, 13, or 17. Checking powers with Maple, we see that only 5 and 11 are primitive roots. Using Proposition 3.3, it follows that 5^5 must be 11 modulo 18, and 11^5 must be 5 modulo 18. This is easy to verify.
2. We find all primitive roots modulo 37 using the information of Example 3.7. They are $2, 2^5, 2^7, 2^{11}, 2^{13}, 2^{17}, 2^{19}, 2^{23}, 2^{25}, 2^{29}, 2^{31}$, and $2^{35} \pmod{37}$ that are 2, 32, 17, 13, 15, 18, 35, 5, 20, 24, 22, and 19.

3. Given that 3 is a primitive root of $Z/31121$, use Proposition 3.2 to find all primitive roots.

Solution. According to the proposition, we need to find all numbers relatively prime to $\phi(31121) = 31120$ (since 31121 is prime) $= 2^4 * 5 *$ 389, where 389 is prime. We can count how many of these are relatively prime to 31120 (i.e., $\phi(31120)$), using part (c) of Proposition 3.1. This number is $31120 * (1 - 1/2)(1 - 1/5) * (1 - 1/389) = 12416$. We can also list them all directly simply by checking each number in turn: $\{1, 3, 7, 9, 11, 13, 17, 19, 21, 23, 27, 29, 31, 33, 37 \ldots\}$. This is rather a long list, so as long as we have the idea now, we proceed. There are 12416 primitive roots and they are obtained by raising 3 to the values in the previous list, obtaining $\{3, 27, 2187, 19683, 21542, \ldots\}$.

3.1.2 Problems

1. List the numbers that have inverses (a) modulo 16 and (b) modulo 25.
2. Show directly (by checking all the properties) that the set of units modulo 16 forms a group.
3. Complete Example 3.4.
4. Find $ord_{18}(5)$.
5. Show that:
   (a) 3 is not a primitive root modulo 13;
   (b) 3 is a primitive root modulo 7.
6. Find all primitive roots modulo 6.
7. Prove Proposition 3.3.
8. Use Proposition 3.4 to find all solutions of $x^{121} \equiv 1 \pmod{2663}$. [Hint: see Computer Example 2 of Section 2.4.1 to obtain a primitive root for 2663.]
9. Let G be a group with operation $*$ and H a subset of G. H is a *subgroup* of G if it satisfies the four group properties. Find all eight subgroups of the group Z_{30}^* under multiplication.

Computer-Assisted Problems

10. Find all primitive roots modulo 29.
11. Given the primitive root 11 modulo 29, verify that all powers 11^e for e relatively prime to $\phi(29)$ produces the same list obtained in question 10.
12. Find $ord_{55}(37)$.

3.2 THE ELGAMAL SCHEME

ElGamal is just one of a number of public key cryptographic schemes available to secure your data. Why have more than one public key scheme?

- some work faster than others, depending on the hardware or software in which they are implemented;
- having several different schemes keeps attackers busy and away from a single target;
- it is always good to look for better schemes.

Taher ElGamal developed the encryption scheme that we present in this chapter as part of his PhD thesis in the 1980s. The scheme was first published in [14].

We can break any cryptographic scheme into three components: key generation, encryption, and decryption. We present these separately for ElGamal.

Key Generation

Each user chooses a large prime p and primitive root α (mod p). These two values form part of the user's public key.

Each user chooses a (secret) random a in $[2, p - 2]$ and computes α^a (mod p). The user's *public key* is (p, a, α^a) and *private key* is a.

Suppose that two parties, Alice and Bob now want to use this scheme. Bob may have a message that he wants to send to Alice. To be usable, this message has to be in the form of a number modulo the agreed prime p. This can be done using a scheme such as that mentioned in Section 2.1 in which each letter of the alphabet becomes a number between 0 and 25. If necessary, numbers can be added to include punctuation and spaces. We consider these options in some of the exercises, but here simply assume that the message to be sent is a number modulo p.

Encryption

Bob generates the message m modulo p that he wants to send to Alice.
He obtains Alice's public key (p, α, α^a).
He chooses $b \in [2, p - 2]$ randomly.
He computes α^b and $m(\alpha^a)^b$ (mod p).
He sends $c = (\alpha^b, m\alpha^{ab})$ to Alice.

Decryption

Alice receives α^b and $m\alpha^{ab}$. (The order is important.)
To recover m, she computes $(\alpha^b)^{-a} \equiv (\alpha^b)^{p-1-a}$ (mod p)
and computes $(\alpha^b)^{-a}m\alpha^{ab} \equiv \alpha^{-ab}\alpha^{ab}m \equiv m$ (mod p).

Notice that to compute $(\alpha^b)^{-a} \equiv (\alpha^b)^{p-1-a}$ (mod p), Alice avoids having to find an inverse using the fact that $\alpha^{\phi(p)} \equiv \alpha^{p-1} \equiv 1$ (mod p), which is true by the FLT.

Example 3.9 Bob wants to send $m = 2132$ to Alice encrypted using the ElGamal scheme. The common parameters for their scheme are prime $p = 3359$ and primitive root $\alpha = 11$.

Alice has chosen a secret value $a = 5$ and published $(3359, 11, 11^5 \equiv 3178 \pmod{3359})$.

Bob downloads Alice's public key triple from the database containing it.

Then Bob chooses his secret $b = 69$ and computes $\alpha^b \equiv 11^{69} \equiv 193 \pmod{p}$.

He also computes $m(\alpha^a)^b = 2132 * (3178)^{69} \equiv 2719 \pmod{3359}$ giving him the ciphertext pair $c = (193, 2719)$ that he sends to Alice. (Notice that the order is important.)

To decrypt, Alice computes $(\alpha^b)^{p-1-a} = 193^{3353} \equiv 2243 \pmod{3359}$ and then $2243 * 2719 \equiv 2132 \pmod{p}$ and so she has the message.

The reason for choosing a secret in $[2, p - 2]$ rather than in $[1, p - 1]$ is to avoid giving away the secret: if 1 were chosen for a, then $\alpha^a = \alpha$ revealing $a = 1$; if $p - 1$ were chosen for a, then $\alpha^a = \alpha^{p-1} = 1$ again revealing a.

In fact, choosing α as a primitive root is not essential. But a "good" choice for α will avoid giving away the secret key. A "good" choice for α is a value whose powers cover a large part of Z_p, so that, computationally, it is infeasible to find a from α and α^a as described in the Discrete Logarithm Problem explained in Section 2.3.

3.2.1 Computer Examples

1. Tony selects the prime $p = 2357$ and a primitive root $g = 2 \pmod{2357}$. Tony also chooses the private key $a = 1751$ and computes $g^a \pmod{p}$, which is $2^{1751} \pmod{2357} \equiv 1185$. So Tony's public key is $(p = 2357; g = 2; g^a = 1185)$.

   To encrypt a message $m = 2035$ to send to Tony, Shalu selects a random integer $k = 1520$ and computes $u = 2^{1520} \pmod{2357} \equiv 1430$ and $v = 2035 * 1185^{1520} \pmod{2357} \equiv 697$. Shalu sends the pair $(1430, 697)$ to Tony.

   We show how Tony decrypts the message. Tony computes $u^{p-1-a} = 1430^{605} \pmod{2357} \equiv 872$; and recovers m by computing $m = 872 * 697 \equiv 2035 \pmod{2357}$.

2. Tanya needs to securely send the message: "I will mark this weekend" to her colleague Jo. How could you make this message into a number that can be used in an ElGamal scheme?
   Solution. There are several ways to do it. For example, we can take each letter and associate it with a number from 0 to 25 starting with a and ending with z. We cannot add the result as it will not be possible to separate out the letters again when we decrypt; so we want to maintain a distinction between each letter. Thus, it would be better to use two digits per letter and assign 00 to a, 01 to b, and so on. Also, we can ignore spaces in this message as it will be easy to read the intended message without putting the spaces back. Applying this method, the message becomes $m = 0822081111200171019070818220404100413 03$.

To use this number in an ElGamal scheme, we now need a prime larger than m. It is certainly possible to find one; but for a much larger message, this task becomes difficult. What we can do when we have a large message and want to reduce the computational costs of working in a very large modular system, is to break the message down into equal size parts. We will do this to demonstrate how it works. We choose message blocks of size 4 and so take 10 messages $m_1 = 0822, m_2 = 0811, m_3 = 1112, m_4 = 0017, m_5 = 1019,$ $m_6 = 0708, m_7 = 1822, m_8 = 0404, m_9 = 1004,$ and $m_{10} = 1303$. (Note that if we had only two digits in the last message, we could have added two random digits or simply 00 to "pad" it out).

Now we just need a prime number larger than any of the possible messages; we take $p = 3109$. We need a public parameter primitive root modulo 3109 also, and we use $\alpha = 6$. Tanya checks Jo's public key that is $6^{11} \equiv 270 \pmod{3109}$.

Now Tanya chooses her secret. We will see in the next section why it is not a good idea for her to use the same secret for each of the messages: if she does reuse the secret, then anyone capturing one of the messages and seeing the ciphertext, can determine the remaining messages. However, let us assume that Tanya uses the same secret 10 for each message here. (See Problem 1 of Section 3.2.3.) She computes $6^{10*11} \equiv 45^{11} \equiv 1243 \pmod{3109}$ and sends to Jo $(6^{10} \equiv 45; \quad m_1 * 1243, m_2 * 1243, \ldots, m_{10} * 1243) = (45; 822 * 1243, 811 * 1243, 1112 * 1243, 17 * 1243, 1019 * 1243, 708 * 1243, 1822 * 1243, 404 * 1243, 1004 * 1243, 1303 * 1243 \pmod{3109}) = (45; 1994, 757, \ldots, 2949)$.

To decipher, Jo computes $(45)^{-11} \equiv (45)^{3109-1-11} \equiv 2071 \pmod{3109}$ and computes $2071m\alpha^{ab} \equiv \alpha^{-ab} * \alpha^{ab}m \equiv m \pmod{3109}$ for each of the 10 messages, obtaining 822 (which is adjusted to 0822), 811 (adjusted to 0811), and so on.

Computer Example 2 in Section 3.2.1 raises an interesting point. Suppose that we have a very long document that we want to encrypt. It may be a thesis, a will, or a document describing a new invention. We would have to break it into many small pieces, even with a very large prime, and then encrypt each one using a different private key. This is far from practical. In practice, public key cryptographic systems such as ElGamal are used to send "small" messages—ones that fit into a modulus system or can do so by being divided up into only a few blocks.

To encrypt very big messages, it is much cheaper and easier to use private, or symmetric, key cryptography. The single drawback—but it is a major one—of symmetric key cryptography is that both the users must know the keys (usually just one key that they share). So how do people at great distances from each other, with only insecure, untrusted communications channels at their disposal, set up common keys to use? In Section 2.3, we described how the DHKE is set up precisely for this purpose. But even a public key scheme such as ElGamal can be used to do this: the message that Bob sends to Alice is the key that both will be able to use henceforth in symmetric key schemes.

Further Reading. Good descriptions of the ElGamal scheme can be found in [35], [28], and [31]. Some good references on symmetric key schemes can be found in [29], [52], and [35].

3.2.2 Problems

1. Alice uses an ElGamal scheme based on the prime 43 and primitive root 3. She chooses 7 as her private key. She then computes a public key as $3^7 \equiv 37 \pmod{43}$ and publishes the triple (43, 3, 37). Bob wants to send the message $m = 14$ to Alice. He picks a secret exponent 26 modulo 43. What does he send to Alice? Explain how Alice decrypts it.

2. Bob uses the same scheme and secret as in question 1 to send the new message 27 to Alice. Compute what he sends to Alice and how Alice decrypts to find the message.

3. Gary wants to send Amad the message "Meet at 7" and do so securely. Amad has a published ElGamal scheme triple $(37, 5, 5^9 \equiv 6 \pmod{37})$. Explain how Gary could convert his message into a number that could be used in Amad's scheme and determine the encrypted message that Amad would receive. Show how Amad would decrypt.

4. Jose wants to set up an ElGamal scheme but does not have access to computer software with which he can determine a primitive root. He takes the number 2 and checks to see how much of $Z/53$ can be generated from it. In your opinion, would 2 be suitable as a substitute for a primitive root?

5. Serdar notices that he has a chance of finding the private key of a user who publishes an ElGamal public key based on a small prime. He checks a site with ElGamal public keys and sees that Adi has published (43, 3, 37). He chooses the message 14 and uses it to generate the ciphertext (15, 31). How quickly can Serdar find Adi's secret key by hand or with a calculator?

Computer-Assisted Problems

6. Redo Computer Example 2 of Section 3.2.1 where Tanya has chosen 10 different keys for the 10 messages m_1, m_2 and so on, of 10, 20, 30, 40, 50, 60, 70, 80, 90, 100, respectively.

7. You have selected the prime $p = 2357$ and a primitive root $g = 2 \pmod{2357}$ and you now choose the private key $a = 312$. Your published triple is, therefore, $(p = 2357; g = 2; 2^{312} = 1256 \pmod{2357})$. You receive the following pair from Frida: (512,1234). Decrypt Frida's message.

8. Serdar has just acquired access to a fast computer and now tries finding the private key of a user who publishes an ElGamal public key based on a big prime. He checks a site with ElGamal public keys and sees that Adi has published $(1125899839733759, g, g^a)$. He chooses a message m and uses it to generate the ciphertext (g^b, mg^{ab}), where b is his secret. How quickly can Serdar find

Adi's secret key if his computer can calculate $x^a \pmod{1125899839733759}$ in a millisecond?

9. ASCII, the American Standard Code for Information Interchange (see `http://www.asciitable.com/` for instance), is a code that gives the numerical representation of characters available on your computer. The standard set of 127 characters can all be written in binary blocks of 7 bits, from 0000000 to 1111111. This is convenient for use in a public key system where messages, in binary, are multiples of 8 bits in length. Suppose you have a 56 bit-based encryption system. What message blocks would you use as input to an ElGamal scheme if your plaintext message was "replayed."

3.3 SECURITY OF THE ELGAMAL SCHEME

Once Alice has established and published her scheme (p, α, α^a), she is committed to keeping her secret a until she changes her parameters on the site. Just as it is inconvenient to change telephone numbers frequently, Alice may not want to annoy her friends and business colleagues by changing her keys often. However, Bob can choose a different secret b each time he sends a message to Alice, as Alice does not need any public information from Bob other than what he sends to her. But let us consider the question, is it safe for Bob to reuse his secret?

Reusing secret keys

Suppose Bob has sent two different message m_1 and m_2 to Alice using the same secret b.

Let us suppose that an attacker, Oscar, works with Alice and has seen m_1. Oscar is now keen to obtain m_2 without Alice knowing.

We assume that Oscar has $c_1 = (\alpha^b, m_1 \alpha^{ab})$ and m_1 and α, and also has $c_2 = (\alpha^b, m_2 \alpha^{ab})$.

Oscar can now generate m_2 using the above pieces:

$$m_2 = (m_2 \alpha^{ab})(m_1)(m_1 \alpha^{ab})^{-1}.$$

Conclusion: Bob should change his secret each time.

In cryptography, it is often difficult to provide a definitive mathematical-like proof that a scheme is secure. An approach that is frequently used is to show that the security of one scheme is equivalent to the security of another in the sense that if one can be broken, then so can the other. We give a formal proof in the next theorem that the security of the ElGamal cryptographic scheme is equivalent to the security of the Diffie–Hellman Key Exchange protocol.

Theorem 3.3   *Breaking the ElGamal scheme is equivalent to breaking the Diffie–Hellman Key Exchange protocol.*

Proof. Assume first that Oscar can break the DHKE protocol. So there is a fixed prime p, and primitive root α.

If Oscar has α^a and α^b (mod p), we assume that Oscar can compute α^{ab} (mod p).

So in ElGamal, Oscar wants to get m from $c = (\alpha^b, m\alpha^{ab})$, where Oscar knows Alice's public key (p, α, α^a). But with α^a and α^b, Oscar can get α^{ab} by assumption, and then get $m = (m\alpha^{ab})(\alpha^{ab})^{-1}$.

In the other direction, we suppose that Oscar can get m just knowing Alice's public key (p, α, α^a) and $c = (\alpha^b, m\alpha^{ab})$.

So can he compute α^{ab} since he knows α^a and α^b?

But if Oscar can get m, he easily gets $\alpha^{ab} = (m^{-1})m\alpha^{ab}$.

And we have shown the security equivalence of the two schemes. □

We noted in Section 2.3 that the security of the DHKE was based on that of the discrete logarithm problem: finding the exponent given the base and the result of exponentiation. It should be clear that ElGamal also depends on this. The secrets reside in the exponent and need to be unrecoverable despite major computational effort. To avoid a brute force attack (simply computing all powers of α modulo p) in determining the exponent the prime needs to be large. A length of at least 1024 bits is standard in 2011. Prime-finding algorithms are available to assist in choosing suitable p, and the reader is referred to Chapter 7 for information on this subject.

Where is the ElGamal scheme used in everyday life? Taher ElGamal himself is credited with inventing SSL, the secure socket layer application which he released through Netscape in 1995 [44, 49]. The ElGamal scheme described earlier, along with its variants are now embedded in many applications for browsers, providing secure means of communicating over the Internet. The Internet Engineering Task Force (http://www.ietf.org/) monitors developments in this field and its website is a good source of information about current uses. PGP Corporation uses ElGamal to set up keys in its software developers kit. PGP, of course, is the provider of Pretty Good Privacy software to ensure the security of e-mail communications over the Internet. [PGP Software Developer Kit Cryptographic Module FIPS 140-2 Security Policy, Document Version 3.2.1, Revised 12/18/2008. PGP Corporation. Available at http://csrc.nist.gov/groups/STM/cmvp/documents/140-1/140sp/140sp1101.pdf; http://www.pgp.com/].

3.3.1 Computer Examples

1. For the same ElGamal setup with $\alpha = 2$ and $p = 103$, Bob reuses his secret key b on two messages to Alice: $m_1 = 32$ and m_2. Eve knows the system parameters and has seen the first set of data received by Alice and has been able to get $m_1 = 32$ from her. Show how Eve now illegally obtains m_2.
   Solution. Eve knows $c_1 = (2^b, 32 * 2^{ab})$ and $m_1 = 32$ and $\alpha = 2$, and we can assume she also has $c_2 = (2^b, m_2 2^{ab})$ as this was sent over an insecure channel. She does not know secret keys a (Alice's key) or b. All she needs to do now is compute $m_2 = (m_2 2^{ab})(32)(32 * 2^{ab})^{-1}$.

2. Assume in question 1 that $c_1 = (2^{54}, 15)$ and $c_2 = (2^{54}, 32)$. Find m_2.
   Solution. We compute m_2 as in the formula of Example 1: $m_2 = (32)(32)(15)^{-1} = 82$.

Further Reading. The DHKE, and so also the ElGamal scheme, is susceptible to an intruder-in-the-middle attack [7]. We discuss this in Section 6.3. In Chapter 8 of [27], Mao considers the security weakness of the basic ElGamal scheme; Paar and Pelzl [35] consider actions and passive attacks on the scheme in Section 8.5.4 of their book.

3.3.2 Problems

1. In questions 1 and 2 of Section 3.2.2, Alice uses an ElGamal scheme based on the prime 43 and primitive root 3. She chooses 7 as her private key. She then computes a public key as $3^7 \equiv 37 \pmod{43}$ and publishes the triple $(43, 3, 37)$. Bob then sends two messages $m_1 = 14$ and $m_2 = 27$ to Alice using the same secret exponent 26. The attacker, Eve, works with Alice and has seen m_1 and she has seen $c_2 = (\alpha^b, m_2\alpha^{ab})$ arrive. She is now keen to obtain m_2 without Alice knowing. Show how Eve determines the second message from Bob.

2. Suppose that Oscar can break the DHKE protocol. In other words, if Oscar has α^a and $\alpha^b \pmod{p}$, then Oscar can compute $\alpha^{ab} \pmod{p}$. Chantal has published her ElGamal public key $(p, \alpha, \alpha^a) = (89, 7, 7^{30})$ and Stefan uses it to send her the encrypted message $c = (7^{42}, m7^{30*42})$, which Oscar intercepts. Show how Oscar finds the message.

3. Adam is given the task of setting up an ElGamal scheme but does not have time to find a primitive root of the prime $p = 89$ that he has chosen. He guesses that 2 will likely work fine in the scheme. Adam's boss is suspicious that Adam is a sloppy worker and has not set up the scheme correctly. He wants to do a quick check that the value 2 is really a primitive root and computes $2^9 \equiv 67 \pmod{89}$. He then uses Proposition 2.8 to test. Show how he does this.

Computer-Assisted Problems

4. For the same ElGamal setup with $\alpha = 10$ and $p = 97$, Bob reuses his secret key b on two messages: $m_1 = 78$ and m_2. Eve knows the system parameters and has seen both sets of data received by Alice $c_1 = (10^b, 78 * 10^{ab}) = (10^{31}, 78 * 10^{31*29}) \equiv (74, 53)$ and $c_2 = (10^b, 50 * 10^{ab}) = (10^{31}, 50 * 10^{31*29}) \equiv (74, 29)$ and has been able to get $m_1 = 78$ from her. Show how Eve now illegally obtains m_2.

5. Suppose that Oscar can break the DHKE protocol. In other words, if Oscar has α^a and $\alpha^b \pmod{p}$, then Oscar can compute $\alpha^{ab} \pmod{p}$. Chantal has published her ElGamal public key $(p, \alpha, \alpha^a) = (89, 7, 47)$ and Lei uses it to send her the encrypted message $c = (69, 18)$, which Oscar intercepts. Show how Oscar finds the message given that $7^{ab} \pmod{89} = 40$.

4

THE RSA SCHEME

RSA was invented by Ron Rivest, Adi Shamir, and Leonard Adleman, after whom it is named, in the 1970s [46]. This scheme relies on the difficulty of factoring integers, a problem that appears to be quite different from that of solving discrete logarithms. However, we will see in later chapters that some of the techniques used to attack factoring can also be used against the discrete logarithm.

We begin the chapter with some background needed to define the RSA cryptosystem. This also allows us to generalize the FLT to the non prime modulus case, a result which, as we shall soon see, is very useful.

4.1 EULER'S THEOREM

Since an RSA modulus will be defined to be a product of two primes, it is useful to know a bit more about primes. For instance, we all "know" that if someone gives us a number, we can factor it into a product of primes. This fact is called the *"Fundamental Theorem of Arithmetic"* or the *"Unique Factorization Theorem"* [8] and we prove it below.

It says even more: you can only do this factorization in one way! So if we all try to factor 6936 we would all get the same answer $6936 = 2^3 * 3 * 17^2$.

Public Key Cryptography: Applications and Attacks, First Edition. Lynn Margaret Batten.
© 2013 by The Institute of Electrical and Electronics Engineers, Inc. Published 2013 by John Wiley & Sons, Inc.

(Notice that the order of the factors does not matter, but we can agree to write the primes in increasing order of magnitude, which makes it easier to compare answers.)

The fact that we can factor uniquely means that a legitimate decryptor using a system based on integer factorization will not have any trouble finding the correct plaintext: there will only be one choice. The following proposition helps in proving the Unique Factorization Theorem.

Proposition 4.1   *If p is a prime and p|ab, a product of two integers, then either p|a or p|b.*

Proof. Suppose p does not divide a (otherwise we are finished). Since p is prime, $\gcd(a, p) = 1$. By the Euclidean Algorithm, we can write $ax + py = 1$ for some integers x and y. Multiply through by b : $abx + pby = b$.

But $p|ab$ is given, and $p|pby$ so $p|(abx + pby = b)$. We have shown that p must divide either a or b.   □

Corollary 4.1   *It follows easily that if a prime divides a product of several numbers, it must divide one of the numbers.*

Theorem 4.1   Unique Factorization Theorem
Any integer greater than 1 can be factored into a product of primes in a unique way, up to order of the primes.

Proof. We first show that it is always possible to factor any integer greater than 1 in at least one way as a product of primes. Suppose there is a *smallest* positive integer n which does not factor as a product of primes. So it is not a prime itself. It must be composite, and we can write it as $n = ab$, where $1 < a < n$ and $1 < b < n$. Since n is the smallest bad number, a and b must factor nicely into primes. So then $n = ab$ is a product of primes, which is a contradiction. Thus, our assumption was false, and *every* integer must factor as a product of primes.

Uniqueness: If $n = p_1^{a_1} p_2^{a_2} \cdots p_s^{a_s} = q_1^{b_1} q_2^{b_2} \cdots q_t^{b_t}$, where all p_i and q_i are primes, in particular, p_1 must divide the product of all the q_i's by the Corollary to Proposition 4.1, and so it must be a q_i. So we can drop p_1 off both sides and continue this way. Since we can make this argument in both directions, the primes on each side must have been the same.   □

In Theorem 3.1, we showed that in $Z_n, n \geq 1$, the set of all elements relatively prime to n forms a group under multiplication. This group has $\phi(n)$ elements, where ϕ is the Euler phi function.

At this point, we are ready to give a generalization of the FLT, which is due to Euler.

Theorem 4.2   Euler's Theorem
If $\gcd(a, n) = 1$, then $a^{\phi(n)} \equiv 1 \pmod{n}$.

Proof. Let $G = \{g_1, \ldots g_t\}$ be the set of all invertible elements modulo n (the group of units modulo n). The proof is similar to that of the FLT.

For any $x \in G$, we define a function $f_x : g \to xg$ for every $g \in G$. Note that xg is in G since $(xg)^{-1} = g^{-1}x^{-1}$.

We claim that f_x is $1 - 1$. To show this, let $g_1 \neq g_2$ in G, but suppose $f_x(g_1) = f_x(g_2)$. In other words, $xg_1 = xg_2$. But now $x^{-1}(xg_1) = x^{-1}(xg_2)$ implies $g_1 = g_2$, which is a contradiction.

Since the sets G and $xG = \{xg_1, \ldots, xg_t\}$ have the same size, and they contain the same elements in a different order, we can write

$g_1 \cdot g_2 \cdot \ldots \cdot g_t = (xg_1) \cdot (xg_2) \cdot \ldots \cdot (xg_t) \pmod{n}$, or
$g_1 \cdot g_2 \cdot \ldots \cdot g_t = x^t g_1 \cdot g_2 \ldots g_t \pmod{n}$ and so $1 \equiv x^t \pmod{n}$.

But of course, t is $\phi(n)$ and we are done!   □

Note that the "relative primeness" is only needed in the proof at the point where the factors are divided out.

Example 4.1   Check that $x^{\phi(15)} = x^8 \equiv 1 \pmod{15}$ for every x such that $\gcd(x, 15) = 1$ and $x \in \{0, 1, \ldots, 14\}$.

Choices for x are 1, 2, 4, 7, 8, 11, 13, 14.

For $x = 1$, this is easy.

For $x = 2$, $2^4 \equiv 1 \pmod{15}$ and so $2^8 \equiv (2^4)^2 \equiv 1$ also. We leave the reader to check the other values.

In Chapter 2, we saw that the FLT was useful in making fast calculations in modular arithmetic. The same is true of Euler's theorem.

Example 4.2   We find the last three digits of 7^{803}.

To obtain the last three digits of any number, we can evaluate it modulo 1000 (for the last four digits, modulo 10,000, and so on).

We know by Euler's theorem, and since $\gcd(7, 1000) = 1$, that $7^{\phi(1000)} \equiv 1 \pmod{1000}$. This will cut our work down. Let us compute $\phi(1000) = \phi(2^3 * 5^7) = 1000 \left(1 - \dfrac{1}{2}\right)\left(1 - \dfrac{1}{5}\right) = 400$.

So,

$$7^{400} \equiv 1 \pmod{1000}.$$

Thus, $7^{803} = 7^{400} * 7^{400} * 7^3 \equiv 343 \pmod{1000}$. The last three digits of 7^{803} are 343.

Example 4.3   Compute $2^{43210} \pmod{101}$.

Solution.   Since 101 is a prime (verify!), we can apply either the FLT or Euler's theorem. Both give $2^{100} \equiv 1 \pmod{101}$. So $(2^{100})^{432} \equiv 1 \pmod{101}$.
Thus, $2^{43210} \equiv 2^{10} \pmod{101} \equiv 14$.

Example 4.4   Compute 11^{402} (mod 100).

Solution.   Since 100 is composite, we use Euler. Since $\gcd(11, 100) = 1$, we have
$11^{\phi(100)} \equiv 1 \equiv 11^{40}$ (mod 100).
So $(11^{40})^{10} \equiv 11^{400} \equiv 1$ (mod 100) and therefore $11^{402} \equiv 11^2 \equiv 21$ (mod 100).

In each of the examples, we are working with $\phi(n)$ in the exponent. This is a critical observation that we will use many times as it is the basis of the RSA system. We state it as a proposition.

Proposition 4.2   *If $x \equiv y$ (mod $\phi(n)$) then $a^x \equiv a^y$ (mod n) for any integers a, x, y, n, and $n \geq 1$ with $\gcd(a, n) = 1$.*

Proof. If $x \equiv y$ (mod $\phi(n)$) we can write $x = y + \phi(n)k$ for some integer k. Then $a^x \equiv a^{y+\phi(n)k} \equiv a^y(a^{\phi(n)})^k \equiv a^y$ (mod n) by Euler.   □

The converse of Proposition 4.2 is not true, but there is a result similar to it, which is true. This is given in Proposition 4.3.

Proposition 4.3   *If $a^x \equiv a^y$ (mod n) and $\mathrm{ord}_n(a) = e$, then $x \equiv y$ (mod e) for any integers a, x, y, n, and $n \geq 1$ with $\gcd(a, n) = 1$.*

Proof. We can suppose that $x > y$ and rewrite the first equation to get $a^{x-y} \equiv 1$ (mod n). Thus $x - y \geq e$. Use the EA to write $x - y = e * k + r$, where $0 \leq r < e$. It follows that $1 \equiv a^{x-y} \equiv a^{e*k+r} \equiv (a^e)^k * a^r \equiv a^r$ (mod n). But this is a contradiction to the definition of order unless $r = 0$. The result we wanted follows immediately.   □

Corollary 4.2   *If a is a primitive root modulo n and $a^x \equiv a^y$ (mod n) for integers x and y and $n \geq 1$, then $x \equiv y$ (mod $\phi(n)$).*

4.1.1 Computer Examples

1. Find the last five digits of $3^{1234567}$.
   Solution.   We use Maple to get $3^{1234567}$ mod $100000; 40587$.
2. Let $n = 43129$, $x = 3921$, and $y = 42897$. Check that $x \equiv y$ (mod $\phi(n)$) and that, therefore (Proposition 4.3), $2976^{3921} \equiv 2976^{42897}$ (mod 43129).
   Solution.   The first check needs $\phi(n)$, which can easily be obtained by factoring $n = 17 * 43 * 59$ (use the *ifactor* command in Maple or some other method of factoring). So $\phi(n) = 16 * 42 * 58 = 38976$. This divides (in fact is equal to) $42897 - 3921$, and so the first congruence is true. The second congruence follows from Proposition 4.3 if $\gcd(2976, 43129) = 1$. We have already factored n, and it is sufficient to check that none of the primes 17, 43, 59 divides 2976. This is true, and so the second congruence holds.

Further Reading. Proofs of the Unique Factorization Theorem can be found in many books on elementary number theory including [6] and [10]. Euler's Theorem may also be found in some elementary books on number theory such as [12; pp. 11–12].

4.1.2 Problems

1. Let $n = 391 = 17 * 23$. Show that 2^{n-1} is not congruent to 1 (mod n). Find an exponent j such that $2^j \equiv 1$ (mod n).
2. Find an example where the converse of Proposition 4.2 does not hold.
3. Give an example that illustrates Corollary 4.2.

Computer-Assisted Problems

4. Find the last seven digits of $6^{12345678}$.
5. Confirm Euler's theorem by checking that $1573^{299520} \equiv 1$ (mod 314183).

4.2 THE RSA ALGORITHM

RSA is the best known and most widely used public key scheme. It is based on exponentiation in a congruence system over the integers modulo a product of two primes. It uses large integers (e.g., 1024 bits) and its security is based on the fact that factoring large numbers is difficult (computationally expensive). For instance, factoring n using a standard factoring algorithm takes $\mathcal{O}(e^{\log n \log \log n})$ operations.

In key generation, each person sets up their own private and public key pair as in ElGamal.

Key Generation

Each user generates a public/private key pair by:

- selecting two large primes at random, p and q;
- computing the system modulus $n = p * q$;
- selecting at random the encryption key e
  - where $1 < e < \phi(n)$, $\gcd(e, \phi(n)) = 1$ (note $\phi(n) = (p-1)(q-1)$);
- solving the following equation to find decryption key d
  - $e * d = 1$ (mod $\phi(n)$) and $0 \le d \le n$.

Then each user publishes their public encryption key: $PU = \{e, n\}$ and keeps secret the decryption key: $PR = \{d, p, q\}$.

Suppose that two parties, Alice, and Bob now want to use this scheme. Alice may have a message she wants to send to Bob. To be usable, this message has to be in the form of a number acceptable by Bob's modulus system. This can be handled in the same way as for the ElGamal scheme. In particular, the message m must be smaller than the modulus n so Alice breaks it into blocks if needed.

Encryption

To encrypt a message m, Alice:

- obtains the public key of Bob $PU = \{e, n\}$;
- computes: $c = m^e \pmod{n}$, where $0 \le m < n$

and sends c to Bob.

Decryption

To decrypt the ciphertext c, Bob:

- uses his private key $PR = \{d, p, q\}$;
- and computes $m = c^d \pmod{n}$.

In the decryption stage, Bob only needs to use d. Recall that, to compute d, he needs to have p and q. But once he has set up his public key, he can throw away p and q as d is sufficient to retrieve messages. This may be useful in situations where storing the secret primes is a problem. They do not need to be kept.

We glossed over the last step of the decryption, not explaining why the simple action of taking c to the dth power gives m back. We take a closer look at this now.

Because $e * d = 1 \pmod{\phi(n)}$, we can write $e * d = 1 + k * \phi(n)$ for some integer k. Hence $c^d \equiv m^{e*d} \equiv m^{1+k*\phi(n)} \equiv m^1 * (m^{\phi(n)})^k \equiv m^1 * (1)^k$ (by Euler's theorem) $\equiv m^1 \equiv m \pmod{n}$.

Example 4.5   Ruth sets up her public key system by first choosing two prime numbers, $p = 17$ and $q = 11$. Her $n = 187$ and $\phi(n) = 16 * 10 = 160$. She needs an e such that $\gcd(e, 160) = 1$ and chooses $e = 7$.

Now she has to find d, the inverse of e modulo $\phi(n)$. She notices that $23 * 7 = 161 = 10 * 160 + 1$ (or uses the EA to get this), and so $d = 23$. She publishes $\{7, 187\}$ and keeps $\{23, 11, 17\}$ secret.

Example 4.6   Ali intercepts the message $c = 106$ that Lief sends to Ruth using her public key scheme setup in Example 4.5. What are Ali's chances of decrypting the message using a brute-force attack of trying all possibilities?

All Ali has to do is test every value of $0 \le m < 187$ by raising it to the power 7 and comparing with the captured message 106. If using a calculator to compute the modulus, this takes on average 10 seconds per choice of m, then the answer can be obtained in at most 1870 seconds or about 32 min. In fact, the message was 13, so this would be found in about 2 min using this slow method.

Example 4.6 underlines the importance of choosing large prime values in the set up phase.

Example 4.7 Ruth also receives the message from Lief sent in Example 4.6. She decrypts it with her decryption key $d = 23$. She computes $m \equiv 106^{23} \equiv 13 \pmod{187}$.

As in the ElGamal scheme, RSA needs to rely on speedy encryption by exponentiation. We saw how to do this in Chapter 2 using a squaring and multiplying algorithm. For instance, to compute $3^{129} \pmod{23 * 41 = 943}$, rewrite as $3^{128} * 3$ and obtain the first value by repeated squaring: $370 * 3 \equiv 167 \pmod{943}$.

Obviously, the smaller the encryption exponent e, the faster encryption will be. Choices of $e = 3$ or $e = 17$ are common. Clearly, e will not be 2, as the value of $(p - 1)(q - 1)$ will always be even. We will see in the next section that small values of d, the decryption exponent, can be problematic, however, as they are susceptible to attacks.

The RSA scheme is widely used in electronic commerce applications for buying items online, and in automated teller machines (ATMs). Some of its products can be seen at `http://www.rsa.com/`. For many years, the RSA organization challenged the cryptographic community to break its latest "challenge" a decryption problem based on the latest RSA key size. See Figure 4.1; this challenge was solved in December 2003. [E. Weisstein. RSA-576 Factored. MathWorld Headline News, Dec. 5, 2003; Factored by: J. Franke, T. Kleinjung, P. Montgomery, H. te Riele, F. Bahr and NFSNET.].

Press Release:

- *Tuesday, April 27, 2004*

- *Mathematicians From Around the World Collaborate to Solve Latest RSA Factoring Challenge*

- *Contest provides practical gauge of current cryptographic research and encourages development of higher standards of security for organizations*

- *BEDFORD, Mass. RSA Laboratories, the research center of RSA Security Inc. (NASDAQ: RSAS) today announced that a team from the Scientific Computing Institute and the Pure Mathematics Institute in Germany, along with the National Research Institute for Mathematics and solved the RSA-576 Factoring Challenge. The worldwide team of eight solved the challenge using approximately 100 workstations in a little more than 3 months, and earned a cash prize of $10,000 from RSA Security for their efforts.*

- *RSA-576 is a smaller-scale example of the types of cryptographic keys that are recommended to secure Internet and wireless transactions. Typical keys are at least 1024 bits (310 decimal digits); RSA-576 is 576 bits (174 decimal digits). Larger numbers are considered to provide significantly greater security. The next challenge number in the series is RSA-640.*

Figure 4.1. The RSA challenge.

2011 official recommended length for the RSA modulus is about 2048 bits, or equivalently about 600 digits. We can estimate the number available using the following well-known result.

Theorem 4.3 Prime Number Theorem. [8]
Let $\pi(x)$ be the number of primes in the range 2 to x. Then $\pi(x)$ is approximately $x/\ln(x)$.

For example, the number of 100-digit primes would be about

$$\pi(10^{100}) - \pi(10^{99}) \approx \frac{10^{100}}{\ln 10^{100}} - \frac{10^{99}}{\ln 10^{99}}$$

Using Maple, this comes out to approximately $3.9 * 10^{97}$, so there are lots available.

How would you try to factor a 150-digit number? It may be a prime, and therefore not factorable at all. Since brute-force trial prime division takes too long for most people, you would not be able to determine this in a reasonable amount of time. We saw in Chapter 2 that the FLT can be used as a test for primality. It will easily catch a composite number masquerading as a prime. But it may not be able to confirm definitively if a prime is indeed prime. We will see various factoring techniques in Chapter 8.

4.2.1 The RSA Parameters

Consider the public values n and e, and the secret values d, p, and q, where $p * q = n$ and d and e are inverses modulo $\phi(n)$. Consider what happens if we can bribe Oscar to give us some of the secret information. With $\phi(n)$ we can find the inverse of e. So, for RSA to be secure, it should be difficult to obtain $\phi(n)$ even knowing n. But computing $\phi(n)$ directly involves knowing what factors n has which is connected with factoring n. We already know that having p and q also gets us $\phi(n)$ and therefore also the decryption key. And obviously, having one of the primes, along with knowing n, gets us the other prime. So, if Oscar is not available and if it is computationally infeasible to factor n, RSA should be safe. However, this is not quite true, and we will see various types of attacks in the next section.

In Proposition 4.4, we show a simple way of factoring n if we know $\phi(n)$.

Proposition 4.4   *Given that n is a product of two primes, then knowing $\phi(n)$ is sufficient to factor n and recover the two primes.*

Proof. Let the two unknown primes be p and q. Then

$$n - \phi(n) + 1 = n - (p-1)(q-1) + 1 = n - pq + p + q - 1 + 1 = p + q.$$

Also, assuming $p > q$, then

$$p - q = \sqrt{(p-q)^2} = \sqrt{p^2 + q^2 + 2pq - 4pq} = \sqrt{(p+q)^2 - 4n}.$$

So from n and $\phi(n)$, we get $p+q$ and then from n and $p+q$, we get $p-q$. Then we can solve for p and q:

$$p = \tfrac{1}{2}\{(p+q)+(p-q)\}$$
$$q = \tfrac{1}{2}\{(p+q)-(p-q)\}.$$

$\square$

Example 4.8 Suppose $n = 16{,}867$ and $\phi(n) = 16{,}600$ are known. Then $p+q = 16{,}867 - 16{,}600 + 1 = 268$. So $p-q = \sqrt{(268)^2 - 67{,}468} = 66$.

This gives us

$$p = \tfrac{1}{2}[268 + 66] = 167 \quad \text{and}$$
$$q = \tfrac{1}{2}[268 - 66] = 101.$$

4.2.2 Computer Examples

1. Erik's public key is $n = 823091$ and $e = 17$. (a) Suno sends Erik the message 809 (Hi) encrypted with Erik's public key. What does Erik receive? (b) Show how Erik decrypts the message.
   Solution.
   (a) Using a Maple command, we request 809^{17} (mod 823091). Erik receives 596912.
   (b) Erik has to use his decryption key, which is the inverse of 17 modulo $\varphi(823091)$. In practice, the modulus would be too large for anyone to compute this directly—that is, by counting the values relatively prime to 823091. However, since Erik knows the two prime components, he can easily compute it. In this case, we ask Maple to compute it directly: $\varphi(823091)$ and get the answer 821184. We then ask Maple for the inverse of 17 modulo 821184: 17^{-1} (mod 821184). The answer is 48305. Erik now decrypts by calculating (we use Maple again) 596912^{48305} (mod 823091). The answer is 809.

2. Audrey's friend Leo says he will send the message one if he is meeting her at noon, and two if not. He also tells Audrey that he will transform text to digits using the correspondence $a = 01, b = 02$, and so on. Leo uses Audrey's RSA public key to encrypt with $n = 712446816787$ and $e = 7129$. Audrey receives the encrypted message 2751916280. What was the plaintext?
   Solution. Since RSA takes as input integers base 10, we first convert the messages into numbers using the method Leo chose. Thus, one is 151405 and two is 202315. Encrypt each of the two messages and see which one it is:
   - 151405^{7129} mod 712446816787; 51667061689
   - 202315^{7129} mod 712446816787; 2751916280.

   Therefore, the plaintext was "two."

3. Joel receives a message from Nevine just before Nevine leaves on hol-
idays. Nevine has used Joel's public key to encrypt: $e := 457$ and $n = 2628773266896335954087$.

Joel's private key is $d = 1553104555909567360609$ and his primes are $p = 76543692179$, $q = 343434343453$.

The received ciphertext is 2304329328016936947195 where Joel knows
that it was derived from a message based on an alphabetic transformation $a = 01$, $b = 02$, and so on. Joel tries to decrypt and read it, but it makes no sense. He
then checks the transmission data and suspects that the last digit of the ciphertext
was dropped. Determine the missing digit and decrypt the message.

Solution. We try all possibilities for the last digit until we get a meaningful
message. To do this, we append a 0 to the received text and then add 0, 1, 2, ...
and decrypt.

Let $c := 23043293280169369471950$.

Now calculate the possible texts trying to decrypt the various possibilities as
we go. Note that any containing two-digit blocks larger than 26 will be incorrect
ones which cannot be changed back to letters:

- $(c + 0)^d \mod n$;
  417411604663$1355447474$ which cannot be correct.
- $(c + 1)^d \mod n$;
  $85797102664$19129803917 which cannot be correct.
- $(c + 2)^d \mod n$;
  1913091205 which we must check.
- This one can be changed back to letters either using the num2text(%); command
  in Maple, or directly taking pairs $19 \rightarrow s$, $13 \rightarrow m$, and so on until we obtain
  smile.

Therefore, the missing digit was 2 and the plaintext was "smile." (Technically,
we should continue to see if any others worked, but it is unlikely.)

Further Reading. RSA is a much-studied public key cryptosystem and material
or it can be found in almost any recent book on cryptography. Recommended references
include [17, 19, 27–29, 31, 35, 49, 52].

4.2.3 Problems

1. Joshua sets up an RSA scheme by choosing the primes 47 and 71. He chooses
   encryption key 79. What decryption key does he compute?

2. An RSA cipher is set up with modulus 210757 and encryption key 3. Encrypt
   the plaintext 12345.

3. Emmanuel wants to set up his own RSA public key and chooses two primes 229
   and 277. He then chooses the encryption key 74. Explain what is wrong with his
   choice.

4. Emmanuel has another chance to set up a scheme. He chooses the same primes
   as in question 3: 229 and 277, and this time is careful to choose an encryption

key which is relatively prime to $\varphi(229 * 277) = 62928$. He chooses 77. He posts his parameters (77, 63433). Then he receives the encrypted message 727 from Bai. What is the plaintext version of this message?

5. An knows that Asha has set up an RSA scheme with $n = 1050589$ and $\varphi(n) = 1048540$. Show how An can now factor n.

Computer-Assisted Problems

6. Erika receives the message 78777 that was encrypted with her own public RSA key (7214, 30069476293). What is the message plaintext?

7. Approximately, how many primes of 200 digits are there? How does this compare with the number of 100-digit primes?

8. Alice publishes the public key numbers $e = 79$ and $n = 3337$. Bob wants to send Alice the message **hide**. He converts the message into a number using an alphabetic transformation modulo 26 ($a = 00$, $b = 01$, etc.). Then he breaks this number string into smaller blocks, which are usable for the given modulus and encrypts. What is the encrypted message, in text form, that Bob sends to Alice?

4.3 RSA SECURITY

Both the RSA and the ElGamal schemes are based on exponential equations in a modulus. However, in ElGamal, the owner's secret is embedded in the exponent while the base and result are both known. In the RSA scheme, the exponent is public and it is the base (the message) that is the target of an attacker. So in this section, we assume that we are trying to obtain the message m from the equation $c = m^e \pmod{n}$, where $0 \le m < n$ and we know c, e, and n, but do not have the decryption key d.

If we were able to take the eth root across the equation, this would give us one or more potential solutions for m. Although e cannot be 2 (recall why this is true), we begin this section by looking at some of the theory of square roots in congruence equations.

First note that not all quadratic equations have roots modulo a prime. For instance, $x^2 \equiv 3 \pmod{6}$ has no solution. [Verify this!] However, in a cryptographic setting, we can often assume that the user began by choosing x (a message) and then computing a power of it, so we know that there is at least one solution.

Interestingly, primes do not all act in the same way when it comes to finding square roots. Primes congruent to 3 (mod 4) (e.g., 3, 7, 11, 19) are good in the sense that there is a nice formula for computing the roots if they exist. We give this formula in the next proposition. Primes congruent to 1 (mod 4) (e.g., 5, 13, 17) are more difficult in the sense that there is no known formula for telling if roots exist nor how to find them if they do.

Proposition 4.5 *Let $p \equiv 3 \pmod{4}$ be prime and y be an integer.*

1. *If y has a square root* mod p, *then its square roots are* $\pm y^{\frac{p+1}{4}}$ (mod p).

2. *If y has no square root* mod p, *then* $-y$ *has square roots* $\pm y^{\frac{p+1}{4}}$ (mod p).

Proof. If $y \equiv 0$ (mod p), then y has square root 0 and we are finished.

Suppose y is not congruent to 0 modulo p. We can then use Fermat's theorem to obtain $y^{p-1} \equiv 1$ (mod p). Therefore, $y^{p+1} \equiv y^2 y^{p-1} \equiv y^2$ (mod p).

We can factor into

$$\left(y^{\frac{p+1}{2}} + y\right)\left(y^{\frac{p+1}{2}} - y\right) \equiv 0 \pmod{p}.$$

Thus, $y = \pm y^{\frac{p+1}{2}}$ are solutions since one of the terms on the left must be divisible by p.

If $y \equiv y^{\frac{p+1}{2}}$, the fact that $4 | p + 1$ gives us the square roots $\pm y^{\frac{p+1}{4}}$

Otherwise, $-y \equiv y^{\frac{p+1}{2}}$ and so $-y$ has these square roots.   □

Definition 4.1   If $p \equiv 3$ (mod 4) is prime and y has a square root modulo p, then $y^{(p+1/4)}$ is called the *principal square root* of y.

Example 4.9   We find the square roots of 5 (mod 11), or, if it does not have one, of -5 (mod 11). Using Proposition 4.8, we first note that 11 is a prime congruent to 3 (mod 4). If 5 has square roots, they would be $\pm 5^3$ (mod 11), or ± 4. We can check these: $(\pm 4)^2 \equiv 5$ (mod 11), which are correct.

Example 4.10   We work the same example for 2 (mod 11). Then $\pm 2^3 \equiv \pm 8$ are potential square roots. Squaring gives 9, however, rather than 2. So 2 has no square roots. But $9 \equiv -2$ (mod 11) and so we have square roots for $-2 : \pm 8$.

We now consider square roots in which the modulus is a composite number, as in the RSA scheme. Suppose we want to solve $x^2 \equiv a$ (mod mn) where $\gcd(m, n) = 1$. Using the CRT, we can instead solve

$$x^2 \equiv a \pmod{m} \quad \text{and} \quad x^2 \equiv a \pmod{n}.$$

Example 4.11   Find solutions of $x^2 \equiv 4$ (mod 21) other than $x \equiv \pm 2$.

Solution.   Since $21 = 3 * 7$ and $\gcd(3, 7) = 1$, we try finding simultaneous solutions to $x^2 \equiv 4$ (mod 3) and $x^2 \equiv 4$ (mod 7).

Note that 3 and 7 are primes congruent to 3 modulo 4. So we can use Proposition 4.8. Thus if 4 is a square, then the solution is

$$x \equiv 4^{\frac{p+1}{4}} \pmod{p}.$$

So we consider $x \equiv 4^1 \equiv 1$ (mod 3) and $x \equiv 4^2 \equiv 2$ (mod 7).

By the EA, we can write $3 * (-2) + 7 * 1 = 1$.

Using the CRT, $x = 2 * (-6) + 1 * 7 = -5 \equiv 16$ (mod 21).

Let us verify if this is a solution:

$$16^2 \equiv 4 \ (\text{mod} \ 21) \qquad \text{YES!}$$

So, in addition to ± 2, $x = 16$ and -16 are both solutions to the original equation.

Now we consider the case where the exponent is general. The next theorem gives us an existence result.

Theorem 4.4   *If p is a prime and $\gcd(p-1, n) = 1$, then every y has an nth root modulo p.*

That is, for any y, $x^n \equiv y \ (\text{mod} \ p)$ always has a solution for x.

Proof. We just have to check that $(y^r)^n \equiv y \ (\text{mod} \ p)$ where r is the inverse of n modulo $p - 1$. There were no assumptions on y, so p might divide it, in which case, the equation is trivially satisfied. So suppose p does not divide y. We now take the exponent rn and write it as $rn = 1 + k(p-1)$ for some k, which we can do using the EA. Then, using the FLT,

$$(y^r)^n \equiv y^{1+k(p-1)} \equiv y(y^{k(p-1)}) \equiv y(y^{(p-1)})^k \equiv y * 1 \equiv y.$$

$\square$

Corollary 4.3   *If p is a prime, $\gcd(p-1, n) = 1$ and r is the inverse of n modulo $p - 1$, then $x = y^r$ is a solution of $x^n \equiv y \ (\text{mod} \ p)$.*

Example 4.12   We apply the theorem to the values $p = 7$ and $n = 5$ and check that every y (i.e., 1, 2, 3, 4, 5, 6) has a fifth root modulo 7. Note that $\gcd(5, 6) = 1$. We need the multiplicative inverse of 5 $(\text{mod} \ 6)$, which is 5. Now for each y, a fifth root $(\text{mod} \ 7)$ is y^5. For $y = 1$, this is just y. For $y = 2$, it is 4. For $y = 3$, it is 5, and so on.

Example 4.13   Let $p = 9967$ and $n = 13$. We use Corollary 4.3 to find a solution to $x^{13} \equiv 212 \ (\text{mod} \ 9967)$. We need r, the inverse of 13 modulo 9966. The EA gives us $1 = 5 * 9966 - 13 * 3833$ and so $r = -3833 = 6133$. So $212^{6133} \ (\text{mod} \ 9967)$ is a solution to the equation.

MAPLE check: $(212^{6133})^{13} \ (\text{mod} \ 9967)$; 212.

In case $\gcd(p-1, n) = n$, an nth root might be found using a slightly different result about n and $(p-1)/n$.

Theorem 4.5   *If p is a prime with $p \equiv 1 \ (\text{mod} \ n)$ and $\gcd(n, (p-1)/n) = 1$, and if y is an nth power modulo p, then $x = y^r$ is an nth root of $x^n \equiv y \ (\text{mod} \ p)$, where r is the inverse of n modulo $(p-1)/n$.*

We do not provide a proof of this result. Unlike the previous theorem, this one does not guarantee an nth root.

Example 4.14 We choose $p = 103$ and $n = 17$ and ask if 5 is an nth power modulo 103. The necessary conditions of Theorem 4.5 hold. We determine the inverse of 17 (mod 6), or in other words, the inverse of 5. This is 5. Now let us see if $x = 5^5 \equiv 35$ (mod 103) is an nth root: $35^{17} \equiv 47$ (mod 103), so no, we did not obtain a 17th root of 5. In fact, there cannot be one, as we will see by the next result.

Theorem 4.6 EULER's Criterion
Let p be a prime, $p \equiv 1$ (mod n). Let $\gcd(y, p) = 1$. Then y is an nth power (mod p) if and only if

$$y^{\frac{p-1}{n}} \equiv 1 \ (\text{mod } p).$$

Proof. "If and only if" means we have to prove necessity and sufficiency implications in both directions.

A. First suppose that y is an nth power. So there is an x with $y \equiv x^n$ (mod p). Let's check $y^{\frac{p-1}{n}} \equiv (x^n)^{\frac{p-1}{n}} \equiv x^{p-1} \equiv 1$ (mod p) using the FLT. Done!

B. Now suppose $y^{\frac{p-1}{n}} \equiv 1$ (mod p). By the Primitive Root Theorem, Theorem 3.2, we know that there is a primitive root g modulo p which generates every element in the system including y: Let $y = g^l$ (mod p) for some exponent l.
   Thus $y^{\frac{p-1}{n}} = g^{l(p-1)/n} \equiv 1$ (mod p).

Invoking Proposition 3.4, $\phi(p) = p - 1$ must divide $l(p - 1)/n$. Stated slightly differently, this means that $l(p - 1)/n$ is a multiple of $p - 1$, and so l/n is an integer. In this case, we can write $l = kn$. Now $y = g^l = g^{kn} = (g^k)^n$ (mod p) and so the "x" we are looking for is g^k!
   We have thus finished the proof.   □

We can actually get more out of this proof when $n = 2$, the square case:

Corollary 4.2 The Square Case
Let p be an odd prime and $\gcd(y, p) = 1$. Then
$y^{\frac{p-1}{2}} \equiv 1$ (mod p)   *if y is a square (mod p), and*
$y^{\frac{p-1}{2}} \equiv -1$ (mod p)   *if y is a nonsquare (mod p).*

Proof. The first part follows immediately from the previous theorem. We need to do a little more work to get the second part . . .
   We know by the FLT that $y^{p-1} \equiv 1$ (mod p). This can be rewritten as

$$\left(y^{\frac{p-1}{2}} - 1\right)\left(y^{\frac{p-1}{2}} + 1\right) \equiv 0 \ (\text{mod } p).$$

Thus, p must divide one of the factors on the left. By assumption, and Theorem 4.6, it does not divide the first one! So it must divide the second one, and we can rewrite this as

$$y^{\frac{p-1}{2}} \equiv -1 \pmod{p}.$$

$\square$

We look at some examples.

Example 4.15 Show that 69 is not a square modulo 101. Here $n = 2$, $y = 69$, and $p = 101$. Note that $\gcd(69, 101) = 1$. Compute $69^{50} \equiv 100 \pmod{101}$. So by Euler's criterion, 69 is not a square.

Example 4.16 Show that 2 is a cube modulo 109. So $n = 3$, $y = 2$ and $p = 109$. Note that $\gcd(2, 109) = 1$.
Compute $2^{36} \equiv 1 \pmod{108}$. So by Euler's criterion, 2 is a cube.

A completely different type of attack can be made on RSA if the decryption exponent of an RSA scheme is relatively small. We state the result in Proposition 4.6 but do not give a proof.

Proposition 4.6 [55] *Suppose p and q are primes with $q < p < 2q$. Let $n = pq$ and $1 = d$, $e < \phi(n)$ satisfy $de \equiv 1 \mod ((p-1)(q-1))$. If $d < n^{1/4}/3$, then d can be calculated in polynomial time about $\log(n)$.*
This low exponent attack can be avoided if the user first chooses a sufficiently large d and then computes e.

Finally, we consider the following question: in an RSA scheme, how can we be sure that an RSA equation $c = m^e \pmod{n}$ has a single solution for m? We answer this with the following proposition.

Proposition 4.7 *Any equation of the form $m^e \equiv c \pmod{n}$, where $\gcd(e, \phi(n)) = 1$, which has an invertible solution m modulo n has only one solution.*

Proof. Suppose there are two solutions, m_1 and m_2. Then $m_1^e \equiv c$ and $m_2^e \equiv c \pmod{n}$. Suppose that m_2 is an invertible solution. Dividing the equations using the inverse of m_2 gives $m_1^e(m_2^{-1})^e = (m_1 m_2^{-1})^e = 1 \pmod{n}$.
Let $ord_n(m_1 m_2^{-1}) = s$. Then by Proposition 3.3, s divides e. But Euler's Theorem says $(m_1 m_2^{-1})^{\phi(n)} \equiv 1 \pmod{n}$ and so also, s divides $\phi(n)$. So s must be 1 and $m_1 = m_2$. Done! $\square$

Under what circumstances would we have a non invertible solution to $m^e \equiv c \pmod{n}$? If n is an RSA modulus, for example, $n = pq$, p and q both large primes, a message m might inadvertently be chosen as a multiple of p or of q. In this case, not only is the message not invertible, but if the sender checks $\gcd(m, n)$, they will have factored n.

Although most of the results in this section assume that the modulus is a prime, we are, of course, really interested in the case where the modulus is a product of two primes. The examples in the next section show how we can combine the Chinese Remainder Theorem with the results on primes to obtain solutions for RSA-type equations.

As indicated in Section 1.3, public key schemes are used to encrypt data of relatively small size (such as keys) while symmetric key schemes are used for large data sets. The essential difference between the two types is that all known public key cryptographic protocols require many multiplications, whereas symmetric key schemes are based on permutations and substitutions, which are inexpensive for a computer to handle. The book by Paar and Pelzl [35; pp. 197] estimates the cost of a typical RSA decryption and encryption for a 2048 bit modulus: "Today, a typical decryption operation on a 2 GHz CPU takes around 10ms ... the throughput is about ... 204,800 bits/s if one uses RSA for encryption of large amounts of data. This is quite slow compared to the speed of many of today's networks."

4.3.1 Computer Examples

1. Find all square roots of the number 1522756 (mod 2325781).

   Solution.   We first notice that 2325781 is not a prime, but that it factors as $523 * 4447$. We use Proposition 4.8 to find separate solutions to each prime factor and then recombine using the CRT. First, check if the conditions of the proposition hold: $523 \equiv 3$ and $4447 \equiv 3$ (mod 4), so we can use the proposition for each value.

   $1522756 \equiv 303$ (mod 523) and $303^{(524/4)} \equiv 335$ (mod 523).
   $1522756 = 1882$ (mod 4447) and $1882^{(4448/4)} \equiv 1234$ (mod 4447).

   We should check if $\pm$ these values are actually solutions. 335^2 (mod 523) is 303 and 1234^2 (mod 4447) is 1882, so we have found the square roots.

   We now combine these using the CRT. Maple commands:
   > *chrem*([335, 1234], [523, 4447]);
   437040
   > *chrem*([−335, 1234], [523, 4447]);
   1234
   > *chrem*([335, −1234], [523, 4447]);
   2324547
   > *chrem*([−335, −1234], [523, 4447]);
   1888741
   These are the four square roots.

2. Mary, Bai, and Raef all use RSA to set up transmission of important documents for their company XSell. To simplify their in-house computations, they all choose the same encryption exponent $e = 3$, but different, and pairwise relatively prime, moduli n_1, n_2, and n_3. One day, their new client Suneeta sends them each the same message m using their respective public keys.

Eve, who works in the computer centre at XSell, intercepts the ciphertexts c_1, c_2, and c_3.

(a) Show that Eve can find m.

(b) Moreover, if $n_1 = 4254673$, $n_2 = 5186239$, $n_3 = 8510561$ and Eve intercepts the following ciphertexts, respectively, $c_1 = 2910512$, $c_2 = 1200265$, $c_3 = 8382011$, determine the message that Eve intercepts.

Solution. Let m be the message. Eve knows m^3 (mod n_1), (mod n_2), and (mod n_3). By the Chinese Remainder Theorem, she knows m^3 (mod $n_1 * n_2 * n_3$). Since $m < n_1, n_2, n_3$ separately, then $m^3 < n_1 * n_2 * n_3$. Therefore, Eve knows m^3 as a number, not as a modulus. Taking the cube root, she can obtain m using Corollary 4.3, for example.

For part (b), we follow the steps outlined above using Maple commands.

$> w := chrem([2910512, 1200265, 8382011], [4254673, 5186239, 8510561]);$
9342949468551140783
$> \%^{(1/3)};$
$9342949468551140783^{(1/3)}$
$> simplify(\%);$
805121215
$> num2text(\%);$
"hello"

3. (a) Does Corollary 4.3 apply to $p = 1000039$ and $n = 7$? Compute the multiplicative inverse of 7 (mod 1000038).
Solution.   Yes, since 7 does not divide 1000038. The inverse of n is 714313.

(b) Using (a), find a 7th root of 32. Check your answer.
Solution. $> 32^{714313}$ mod 1000039; 711431.
To check, $> 711431^7$ mod 1000039; 32.

4. Use Proposition 3.8 to find all solutions to the equation $x^{14} \equiv 3$ (mod 50429).
Solution.   Note that the modulus is the product of the two primes 211 and 239. However, this is not an RSA type scheme as the exponent 14 divides $\varphi(211 * 239) = 49980$, which is a condition of Proposition 3.8. However, in order to be able to apply Proposition 3.8, we also need a primitive root for the system. Theorem 3.2 tells us that it does not exist. But if we take the usual approach to solving an equation with composite modulus, the CRT, we can break the equation into two with prime moduli in which each has a primitive root. So consider $x^{14} \equiv 3$ (mod 211) and $x^{14} \equiv 3$ (mod 239). Note again that in each case, 14 divides $\varphi(211)$ and $\varphi(239)$. (This will not usually be the case!) If we can find at least one solution for each equation, then primitive roots will give us all solutions and we can recombine using the CRT to find solutions to the original equation. However, applying Euler's criterion, we can check that neither equation separately has a solution. This gives us no solution to the original equation. Checking for solutions using the Maple command, we obtain
$$msolve(a^{14} = 3, 50429);$$
(no output = no solutions).

Further Reading. Some books with a good discussion on the security of RSA are [18, 19, 27, 31]. Paar and Pelzl [35] point out that in practice RSA must be used with a padding scheme to ensure security. Section 7.7 of their book gives a good description of how this works; see also Problem 4 of Section 4.4.2. Many attacks on RSA are aimed at factoring the modulus. Chapter 8 has a good discussion of factoring attacks.

4.3.2 Problems

1. Find the principal square root of $x^2 \equiv 40$ (mod 83) if possible.
2. Find the square roots of 26055 (mod 34807) if they exist.
3. Explain why Theorem 4.4 does not apply to Example 4.14.
4. Explain why Euler's Criterion indicates that 5 is not a 17th power modulo 103.
5. Is 5 an 11th power modulo 103? If so, find its 11th root.
6. Let $p = 10069$. What does Euler's criterion (Theorem 4.6) say about solutions to $31 \equiv x^n$ (mod p) where (i) $n = 235$; (ii) $n = 839$?
7. Examine the case $e = 2$ for the results in this section on square roots.
8. Find all square roots of 7 modulo 143.
9. Find an example of a square root problem with an RSA modulus $n = pq$ in which one equation modulo p does have solutions while the other, modulo q, does not. What is the overall solution to the original system in this case?

Computer-Assisted Problems

10. Find a cube root of 2 modulo 101.
11. Find the square roots of 48382 or its negative modulo 83987.
12. Use Proposition 4.9 to find the principal square root of 2 modulo 1000039 and check it using a calculator or the modulus square root function in some software. (Maple's *msqrt* function for example.)
13. Determine as many solutions as possible for m of the equation $m^5 \equiv 5$ (mod 527). [Note Theorem 4.5.]

4.4 IMPLEMENTING RSA

There are several ways of implementing the RSA algorithm. Since the RSA modulus is a product of relatively prime numbers, the Chinese Remainder Theorem (Section 2.2) is commonly used to perform both the encryption and the decryption. Of course, the factors of n need to be known in both cases.

RSA encryption using the CRT can be described as follows ([29; p. 613]). We assume that n is a product of the two primes p and q. To encrypt m using the encryption exponent e, let

$$m_p \equiv m^e \text{ (mod } p) \text{ and } m_q \equiv m^e \text{ (mod } q).$$

We are looking for the unique solution to

$$x \equiv m^e \ (\text{mod} \ pq).$$

The solution to Theorem 2.1 tells us how to do this. We first determine integers s and t such that $sp + tq = 1$. (This uses the EA.) Then, let $x = m_q sp + m_p tq \ (\text{mod} \ pq)$. Working modulo p, $tq \equiv 1$ and $x \equiv m_p tq \equiv m^e * 1 \equiv m^e \ (\text{mod} \ p)$. Similarly, $x \equiv m^e \ (\text{mod} \ q)$. Thus, $x \equiv m^e \ (\text{mod} \ pq)$ is the desired encryption of m.

Computing the decryption of x works in exactly the same way, and it is left as an exercise.

Example 4.17   We use the CRT method to encrypt $m = 37$ modulo $n = 17 * 19 = 323$ using the exponent 5. Following the terminology of the general case,

$$m_p = 37^5 \ (\text{mod} \ 17) \equiv 3^5 \equiv 5 \quad \text{and}$$
$$m_q = 37^5 \ (\text{mod} \ 19) \equiv (-1)^5 \equiv 18.$$

Using the Euclidean Algorithm, we can write $1 = (-8) * 19 + 9 * 17$. Therefore, our encryption solution modulo n should be $x = 18 * 9 * 17 + 5 * (-8) * 19 \ (\text{mod} \ 323)$. This is $x \equiv 56$ modulo 323.

It can also be verified directly that $37^5 \ (\text{mod} \ 323)$ is equal to 56.

As we have described, RSA can be manipulated in a number of ways. One of these is illustrated in the next example.

Example 4.18   Jo tells his friend Lou that he will send him a message, encrypted using Lou's RSA parameters $n = 799$ and $e = 19$, stating the amount he would like Lou to give him for his old ipod. Jo takes the number 45 and computes $45^{19} \ (\text{mod} \ 799) \equiv 702$ and asks his Aunt Lynn to e-mail this value to Lou. Jo's Aunt Lynn thinks that Jo should be able to get twice as much for it. So instead of sending 702 to Lou, she sends him $2^{19} * 702 \equiv 414 \ (\text{mod} \ 799)$. When Lou decrypts this, he sees that Jo is offering to sell his ipod for $414^{155} \equiv 90$ dollars.

This example demonstrates how to change a message by any multiple while it remains encrypted. Letting $c \equiv m^e \ (\text{mod} \ n)$, to change m to $r * m$, simply use $r^e * c$; the receiver then applies d to obtain $(r^e * c)^d = r^{ed} * c^d = r * m$.

One way to avoid this manipulation is to embed some random structure into the plaintext before it is encrypted. A universally accepted way of doing this is called *padding*, which is now part of public key standard PKCS#1. We refer the reader to Problem 5 of Section 4.4.2 to find out more about this standard. In padding, a message is broken into smaller parts and data is added to each part to extend it to a fixed size. Each part is then encrypted separately. To decrypt, the above process needs to be reversed in order to reconstitute the original message. (Investigating RSA padding further is a good project topic.)

The high cost of exponentiation means that large data sets are encrypted using symmetric key schemes, which are computationally much cheaper, while public key schemes are reserved for small quantities of data such as key strings. Nevertheless, cryptosystem designers are always on the lookout for new, efficient, public key schemes. This is especially important for the future as data transmission moves from large computing platforms to portable hand-held devices. The most efficient, well tested, public key cryptosystem is the elliptic curve system which we explore in Chapter 15.

Formal comparisons of the efficiencies of the elliptic curve system with other public key cryptosystems have been undertaken by a number of authors. The first such comprehensive analysis was probably that of Lenstra and Verheul in 2001 [25]; in this article, the authors establish a common parameter setting on which a reasonable comparison of symmetric, RSA, ElGamal and elliptic curve schemes is made based on key size, encryption of the same data set, and an expectation of 20 years of security. While the elliptic curve scheme needs a larger key than a symmetric key scheme, it is much smaller than the key size needed for RSA or ElGamal in [25] (see their Table 1). Wander et al. [54] compare RSA and elliptic curves on small wireless devices. They determined that with a given amount of energy, elliptic curve cryptography based on a key size of 160 bits was able to perform four times the key exchange operations of RSA with a 1024-bit key.

4.4.1 Computer Examples

1. The modulus $n = 97 * 151 * 251$ (a product of three prime numbers) was used to encrypt m with encryption modulus $e = 17$. The result was 2,197. Decrypt 2197 using the CRT method to find m.
   Solution. We can make use of the Maple *chrem* command here. However, first we need the decryption exponent $d = 17^{-1} \mod (96 * 150 * 250) = 1482353$. Then we ask Maple for the common solution to

$x \equiv 2197^{1482353} \pmod{97}$

$x \equiv 2197^{1482353} \pmod{151}$ and

$x \equiv 2197^{1482353} \pmod{251}$.

Reducing each right-hand side in the applicable modulus and using the FLT gives

$x \equiv 63^{17} \equiv 34 \pmod{97}$

$x \equiv 83^{53} \equiv 101 \pmod{151}$

$x \equiv 189^{103} \equiv 181 \pmod{251}$.

Now *chrem* *([34, 101, 181], [97, 151, 251])* yields the answer 2721272. We can confirm that this is the correct answer by checking that $2721272^{17} \equiv 2197 \pmod{n}$.

Further Reading. Montgomery multiplication [33] is still the most efficient known algorithm for computing modular exponentiation due to its use of addition and division by powers of 2. Integer divisions are eliminated. Continued use of RSA, and all public key systems, rests on the ability to implement the algorithm efficiently while maintaining security. The use of cryptography on small, portable electronic devices is helping to generate pressure targeting efficiency. The paper by Verma and Garg [53] explains some of the variations of RSA which have been introduced to reduce computation and hence increase efficiency. See also [51].

4.4.2 Problems

1. $c = m^e \pmod{pq}$ is the encrypted form of m using the RSA scheme. Describe the method of decrypting c using the CRT, given d, the decryption exponent.
2. Use the CRT method for RSA encryption to encrypt $m = 29$ modulo 323 using the exponent 7.
3. Use the CRT method for RSA decryption to decrypt $c = 31$ modulo 323 using the decryption exponent 11.

Computer-Assisted Problems

4. Go to `http://www.rsa.com/rsalabs/node.asp?id=2125` and find the PDF document or PKCS#1v2.1. How long must the padding string PS in step 2 of Section 7.2.1 be in this standard?
5. Ben wants to order 150 new writing books for the staff in his office but Anna knows that there is only enough money in the budget to pay for 50. When Ben sends her the encrypted version 601 of the order for 150 using the parameters of the Internet site ALL YOUR OFFICE SUPPLIES ($n = 799$ and $e = 39$), explain what she actually sends to the Internet site to reduce the order to 50.
6. Use the CRT method for RSA encryption to encrypt $m = 2111$ modulo ($97 * 151 * 251$) using the exponent 11111.

5

ELLIPTIC CURVE CRYPTOGRAPHY

In this chapter, we examine a cryptographic system, which is widely used in portable devices. It is based on a geometric system called "elliptic curves." We will first see how elliptic curves work, and then, in the next section, use them to build cryptographic systems.

Elliptic curves have been studied for many years. In the eighteenth century, it was natural to ask about the arc length of an ellipse (by then the Earth's orbit was known to be an ellipse as were trajectories followed by other planets). This question led to the study of integrals involving $\sqrt{f(x)}$, where $f(x)$ is a polynomial of degree 3 or 4. We know now that such integrals cannot be described in terms of familiar functions that we teach in calculus. They came to be known as elliptic integrals. For some reason, it is often easier to work with the inverse of such an integral (calculus students are reminded of $sin^{-1}x$). The inverses of elliptic integrals were called elliptic curves. In the mid-1980s, researchers were able to use elliptic curves in a range of applications including primality testing and integer factorization and in defining public key cryptosystems that are close analogs of the RSA and ElGamal schemes.

Public Key Cryptography: Applications and Attacks, First Edition. Lynn Margaret Batten.
© 2013 by The Institute of Electrical and Electronics Engineers, Inc. Published 2013 by John Wiley & Sons, Inc.

5.1 ELLIPTIC CURVES AND ELLIPTIC CURVE GROUPS

5.1.1 What is an Elliptic Curve?

An elliptic curve is the set of points that satisfy an elliptic curve equation in two variables where one variable appears as a cubic and the other as a quadratic, and the coefficients are numbers from a set of elements known as a field. We give a formal definition of elliptic curve after defining a field.

We formally define a field below, but essentially, it is a set equipped with two operations just as the integers and real numbers have plus and times defined on them. Under both operations, we need an identity, in the same way as we have one for groups (see Section 3.1, Definition 3.2), and these identities are referred to as 0 (under the addition operation) and 1 (under the multiplicative operation). Under addition, the set forms a (commutative) group, and under multiplication, all the elements except for 0 also form a (commutative) group. So all additive inverses exist, and except for 0, all multiplicative inverses also exist. We add an additional condition bringing the two operations together—this is called the distributive property.

Definition 5.1   A *field* is a set F with two operations $+$ and $*$ such that the following properties hold.

   (i) Under $+$, F forms a group; we use 0 for its identity.
   (ii) Under $*$, $F\backslash\{0\}$ forms a group; we use 1 for its identity.
   (iii) Both groups above are *commutative*, that is, $a + b = b + a$ and $a * b = b * a$ for all a and b in F.
   (iv) $a * (b + c) = a * b + a * c$ for all a, b, and c in F. (This is the ***distributive*** property.)

Example 5.1   The real numbers and the complex numbers with real coefficients are both examples of fields. Every system Z_p for p a prime is also a field. However, Z_n for n composite is never a field.

Example 5.2   Each choice of coefficients yields a different elliptic curve. For example, the equation $y^2 = x^3 - 4x + 0.67$ with real coefficients is elliptic and its graph is shown in Figure 5.1.

Throughout the study of elliptic curves and their cryptosystems, we shall assume that the field used is of the form Z_p, p a large prime. Despite this assumption, the figures in this section will be those of real-valued elliptic curves as it is much easier to interpret the operations on them than with graphs of elliptic curves over finite fields. All the elliptic curve graphs appearing in this section appear in a tutorial on elliptic curves, found at http://www.certicom.com/index.php/10-introduction, provided by the company Certicom, which uses elliptic curve cryptography in its products.

If we assume that the prime over which we are working is not 3, it is possible to reduce the equation to a better form. Since many of our applications will be modulo large

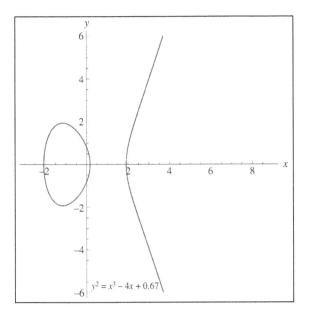

Figure 5.1. An elliptic curve with real coefficients

primes for cryptosystems, we assume that this is the case and so define an elliptic curve as follows:

Definition 5.2 An *elliptic curve* is the set of solutions (x, y) to the equation $y^2 = x^3 + ax + b$, where $x, y, a,$ and b are from a finite field over a prime other than 3.

Example 5.3 The points on $y^2 = x^3 + 2x + 3$, where x, y are from Z_7 are $(0, \sqrt{3})$, $(1, \sqrt{6})$, $(2, \sqrt{1})$, $(3, \sqrt{1})$, $(4, \sqrt{5})$, $(5, \sqrt{5})$, and $(6, 0)$. Proposition 4.8 states what the square roots will be, since $7 \equiv 3 \pmod 4$. But only $1, 2,$ and 4 have square roots (check the squares). So the curve has the points $(2, 1), (2, 6), (3, 1), (3, 6),$ and $(6, 0)$.

Example 5.3 shows that we can list the points on the elliptic curve over Z_p by substituting the values $0, 1, 2, 3 \ldots p - 1$ for x and determining the corresponding values for y. We can only get a value for y if the right-hand side has a square root, and this will happen about half the time. However, when we do get a square root, we usually get two and so we expect about p points on the curve. The graph of such a curve will not have the smooth appearance of Figure 5.1, but will simply be a set of points.

Definition 5.3 The *discriminant* of the elliptic curve over Z_p, $p > 3$, is defined as $4a^3 + 27b^2$.

If $x^3 + ax + b$ contains no repeated factors, or equivalently, if the discriminant $4a^3 + 27b^2$ is not 0, then the elliptic curve $y^2 = x^3 + ax + b$ can be used to form a group.

An elliptic curve group over real numbers or a finite field consists of the points on the corresponding elliptic curve, together with a special point O called the "point at infinity." Definition 3.2 states what a group is. So what we now do is explain what the operation on the group elements will be, introduce the "point at infinity," and then consider the four group conditions.

5.1.2 Operations on Points

We make an elliptic curve into a group by defining the *addition* of two points. We do this geometrically.

First of All We Need the Negative of a Point.

Definition 5.4   The *negative of a point* $P = (x, y)$ is its reflection in the x-axis: the point $-P$ is $(x, -y)$.

Notice that for each point P on an elliptic curve, the point $-P$ is also on the curve (because of the y^2).

Example 5.4   The point $P(2, 6)$ is on the elliptic curve $y^2 = x^3 + 2x + 3$ over Z_7. Then the point $-P$ is the point with co-ordinates $(2, -6) = (2, 1)$; note that it is also on the curve.

Adding Distinct Points.
The points P and Q will be added to get a third point R. Notice that a nonvertical line, which is not a tangent, meets the curve at three points in the real coefficient case (see Figure 5.2). This is also true when the field is finite. We use the next proposition to lead to our definition of addition.

Proposition 5.1   *If $P = (x_P, y_P)$ and $Q = (x_Q, y_Q)$ are distinct points of an elliptic curve modulo the prime p such that P is not $-Q$, then $-R = (x_R, -y_R)$, where $s = (y_P - y_Q)/(x_P - x_Q) \pmod{p}$ and $x_R = s^2 - x_P - x_Q \pmod{p}$ and $y_R = -y_P + s(x_P - x_R) \pmod{p}$, is the third point on the curve made by the line PQ.*

Proof. We show that the co-ordinates of $-R$ satisfy both the equation of the line PQ and the equation of the elliptic curve. Let the equation of the line PQ be $y = sx + c$, where c is to be determined. Note that s is not zero since P is neither Q nor $-Q$. Since P is on this line, we have $y_P = sx_P + c$ and so $c = y_P - sx_P$. Thus, the line's equation is $y = sx + y_P - sx_P$. Substituting x_R for x on the right-hand side, we obtain $sx_R + y_P - sx_P$ that is equal to $-y_R$ and so $-R$ is on PQ.
     Let the equation of the elliptic curve be $y^2 = x^3 + ax + b$. We first obtain a and b by using the points P and Q : $a = s(y_P + y_Q) - (x_P^2 + x_P x_Q + x_Q^2)$ and $b = y_P^2 - x_P^3 - sx_P(y_P + y_Q) + x_P(x_P^2 + x_P x_Q + x_Q^2)$. We then consider the two sides of the elliptic curve equation, substituting the co-ordinates of $-R$ on each side. The left-hand side becomes $y_R^2 = (-y_P +$

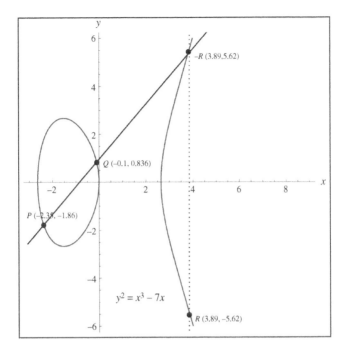

Figure 5.2. Adding two distinct points

$s(x_P - x_R))^2 = (-y_P + [(y_P - y_Q)/(x_P - x_Q)] * (x_P - (s^2 - x_P - x_Q))^2$. The right-hand side becomes $x_R^3 + ax_R + b = (s^2 - x_P - x_Q)^3 + [s(y_P + y_Q) - (x_P^2 + x_Px_Q + x_Q^2)](s^2 - x_P - x_Q) + y_P^2 - x_P^3 - sx_P(y_P + y_Q) + x_P(x_P^2 + x_Px_Q + x_Q^2)$. Using $s = (y_P - y_Q)/(x_P - x_Q)$ on both sides, multiplying both sides out and reducing terms, we reach equality. So the point $-R$ is in fact on both the line and the elliptic curve.   □

Definition 5.5   If $P = (x_P, y_P)$ and $Q = (x_Q, y_Q)$ are distinct points of an elliptic curve modulo the prime p such that P is not $-Q$, then we *define* $P + Q = R = (x_R, y_R)$ *where* $s = (y_P - y_Q)/(x_P - x_Q) \pmod{p}$ *and* $x_R = s^2 - x_P - x_Q \pmod{p}$ *and* $y_R = -y_P + s(x_P - x_R) \pmod{p}$.

Definition 5.5 makes sense in view of Proposition 5.1 as this shows that $-R$ is on the curve, and so R is also on the curve. The fact that the line PQ meets the curve in exactly one more point $-R$ of the curve, implies that under the addition operation, closure holds. Note that s is the slope of the line through P and Q (see Figure 5.3). The line through P and $-P$ is a vertical line, which does not intersect the elliptic curve at a third point; thus, the points P and $-P$ cannot be added as in Definition 5.5. It is for this reason that the elliptic curve group includes the point at infinity O.

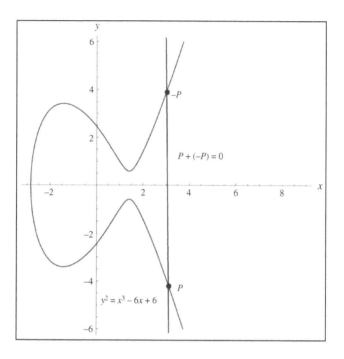

Figure 5.3. Adding a point to its negative

5.1.3 Adding a Point to Its Negative

Definition 5.6 By definition, $P + (-P) = O$ for every point P. The line through the distinct points P and $-P$ is vertical.

As a result of this equation, $P + O = P$ in the elliptic curve group. O is called the *additive identity* of the elliptic curve group; all elliptic curves have an additive identity.

Example 5.5 We first, check that $(8, 9)$, $(9, 4)$ are points of the elliptic curve $y^2 = x^3 + 4x + 5$ over Z_{13}. This is the case because $9^2 \equiv 8^3 + 4*8 + 5 \equiv 3$ and $4^2 \equiv 9^3 + 4*9 + 5 \equiv 3 \pmod{13}$.

Now we add the two points together. Note that one is not the negative of the other. Also s, the slope, is 8 : $(8, 9) + (9, 4) = (8^2 - 8 - 9, -9 + 8(8 - 8)) = (8, 4)$. (Check, by substituting, that this point is on the curve.)

5.1.4 Adding a Point to Itself

To add a point P to itself, a tangent line to the curve is drawn at the point P. If y_P is not 0, then the tangent line intersects the elliptic curve at exactly one other point, $-R$.

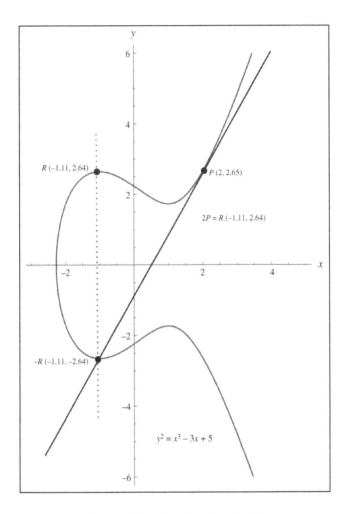

Figure 5.4. Doubling the point P

The point $-R$ is reflected in the x-axis to R. This operation is called doubling the point P (Figure 5.4); in this case, the law for doubling a point on an elliptic curve group is defined by: $P + P = 2P = R$. So $3P = 2P + P$, and so on.

Consider the case $y_P = 0$. Differentiating implicitly the equation $y^2 = x^3 + ax + b$ gives $2yy' = 3x^2 + a$. The derivative y' exists if and only if y is not 0. Here, the tangent at P is always vertical.

Definition 5.7 Provided that y_P is not 0, $2P = R$ where

$$s = (3x_P^2 + a)/(2y_P) \pmod{p},$$

$$x_R = s^2 - 2x_P \pmod{p},$$

and

$$y_R = -y_P + s(x_P - x_R) \pmod{p},$$

where s is the slope of the tangent through P and a is the coefficient of x in the elliptic curve equation.

Definition 5.8   If a point P is such that $y_P = 0$, then the tangent line to the elliptic curve at P is vertical and does not intersect the elliptic curve at any other point. By definition, $2P = O$ for such a point.

If we wanted to find $3P$ in this situation, we can add $2P$ and P that is $O + P = P$. Thus, $3P = P, 4P = O, 5P = P, 6P = O, 7P = P$, and so on. See Figure 5.5 for this case.

Example 5.6   We find $2(8, 9)$ where the point $(8, 9)$ is on the elliptic curve $y^2 = x^3 + 4x + 5$ over Z_{13}. The interpretation of $2(8, 9)$, when $(8, 9)$ is a point, is the sum of the point with itself. Since the second co-ordinate is not zero, Definition 5.7 applies. The slope $s = (3x_P^2 + a)/(2y_P) \equiv (3 * 64 + 4)/18 \equiv 7 * 9^{-1} \equiv 8 \pmod{13}$. The point we want is therefore $(9,9)$.

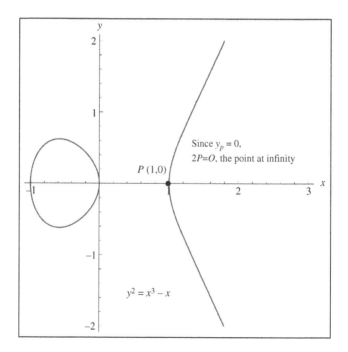

Figure 5.5.   Doubling a point with tangent infinity

Example 5.7   We find $2(12, 0)$, where the point $(12, 0)$ is on the elliptic curve $y^2 = x^3 + 4x + 5$ over Z_{13}. In this case, Definition 5.8 applies. The sum is the point O at infinity.

Theorem 5.1   *The set of points with addition and point at infinity O defined as above, on an elliptic curve $y^2 = x^3 + ax + b$ over a field where $4a^3 + 27b^2$ is not 0, forms a group.*

Proof. We have seen how to add any two points in the set and so the closure operation is well defined. The identity is the point at infinity O. Additive inverses have all been defined. The final condition is that of associativity. This is difficult to show because of the number of cases involved. We would need to consider $P + Q + R$ when all three points are different or when some two are the same, and when all three are the same. We leave the reader to check some of the cases or look up the details in [17; p. 452]. Finally, we point out that the fact that the discriminant is not zero means that points on the curve are well defined as they are all distinct.   □

A graph of these points is given in Figure 5.6.

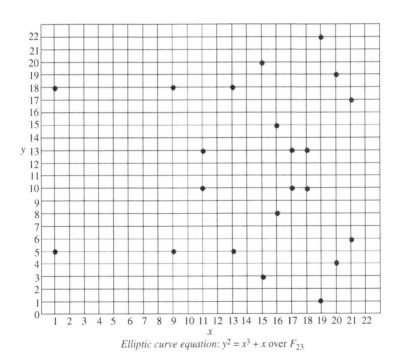

Elliptic curve equation: $y^2 = x^3 + x$ over F_{23}

Figure 5.6.   The graph of a finite elliptic curve

Definition 5.9 An *elliptic curve group* is the set of points of an elliptic curve of the form $y^2 = x^3 + ax + b$ over a field where $4a^3 + 27b^2$ is not 0.

Example 5.8 The points of the elliptic curve $y^2 = x^3 + x$ over the field Z_{23} form an elliptic curve group. The 23 points that satisfy this equation are
(0, 0), (1, 5), (1, 18), (9, 5), (9, 18), (11, 10), (11, 13), (13, 5), (13, 18), (15, 3), (15, 20), (16, 8), (16, 15), (17, 10), (17, 13), (18, 10), (18, 13), (19, 1), (19, 22), (20, 4), (20, 19), (21, 6), (21, 17).

5.1.5 Computer Examples

1. Find all points on the elliptic curve $y^2 = x^3 + 39x + 72$ over Z_{101}.
   Solution. We can do this the same way we did Example 5.3, by substituting all possible values for x and then checking which y^2 values have a corresponding square root y. However, with 101 possible values for x, the use of an algorithm is a good idea. We do this here with Maple:

```
>ell := proc()
  local i, j, x, y;
  for x from 0 to 100 do
        i := x^3 + 39 * x + 72  mod  101;
        for y to 100 do
                j := y^2 mod 101; if i = j then print ([x, y])
                end if
        end do
  end do
  end proc
>ell();
```

The 106 points on the curve are

[3, 32],	[3, 69],	[6, 44],	[6, 57],	[7, 48],	[7, 53],	[8, 47],	[8, 54],
[11, 32],	[11, 69],	[13, 7],	[13, 94],	[16, 34],	[16, 67],	[19, 20],	[19, 81],
[20, 41],	[20, 60],	[21, 31],	[21, 70],	[22, 8],	[22, 93],	[23, 39],	[23, 62],
[26, 49],	[26, 52],	[28, 47],	[28, 54],	[31, 41],	[31, 60],	[34, 10],	[34, 91],
[36, 37],	[36, 64],	[37, 31],	[37, 70],	[38, 13],	[38, 88],	[39, 3],	[39, 98],
[43, 31],	[43, 70],	[46, 11],	[46, 90],	[47, 48],	[47, 53],	[48, 27],	[48, 74],
[50, 41],	[50, 60],	[51, 33],	[51, 68],	[52, 46],	[52, 55],	[53, 18],	[53, 83],
[55, 15],	[55, 86],	[58, 30],	[58, 71],	[59, 46],	[59, 55],	[63, 50],	[63, 51],
[64, 30],	[64, 71],	[65, 47],	[65, 54],	[66, 26],	[66, 75],	[68, 4],	[68, 97],
[70, 33],	[70, 68],	[71, 9],	[71, 92],	[72, 2],	[72, 99],	[73, 37],	[73, 64],
[76, 6],	[76, 95],	[77, 19],	[77, 82],	[78, 21],	[78, 80],	[79, 22],	[79, 79],
[80, 30],	[80, 71],	[81, 33],	[81, 68],	[82, 42],	[82, 59],	[87, 32],	[87, 69],
[88, 14],	[88, 87],	[91, 46],	[91, 55],	[93, 37],	[93, 64],	[97, 16],	[97, 85],
[99, 17],	[99, 84].						

2. Find all points on the elliptic curve $y^2 = x^3 + 99x + 123$ over Z_{127} for which the tangent is vertical.

   Solution. We approach this question in the same way as we did with Example 1. However, in this case, we are only concerned with those points on the curve for which $y = 0$. We adapt the above algorithm:

   Do: from $x = 0$ to 126,

   evaluate $a = x^3 + 99x + 123$ (mod 127)

   if for some x, a exists and is zero, output $(x, 0)$

   otherwise, continue

   End

   Alternatively,

   ```
   sqrt127zero := proc()
   proc()
       local a, b, x, y;
       for x from 0 to 126 do
           a := x^3 + 99 * x + 123,  mod  127;
           if a = 0 then
                   for y to 126 do
                       b := y^2,  mod  127: if b = 0 then print ([x, y])
                       end if
                   end do
           end do
   end proc
   sqrt127zero();
   ```

   Thus, there are no points with y value 0.

3. Compute the difference $(5,9)-(1,1)$ on the curve $y^2 = x^3 - 11x + 11$ (mod 593899).

   Solution. The negative of $(1,1)$ is $(1,-1)$. Therefore, we compute a sum using a Maple command:

   addell([5,9],[1,-1],-11,11,593899);

   [148475, 222715] is the difference of the given points.

Further Reading. The elliptic curve tutorial in [58] is the best place to see basic examples of elliptic curves and elliptic curve operations over the real numbers. See also [18, 28, 35].

5.1.6 Problems

1. Check all the conditions of Definition 5.1 for the set Z_5.
2. Explain what conditions of Definition 5.1 fail in the system Z_6.
3. Is the point $(7, 5)$ on the elliptic curve $y^2 = x^3 + 19x + 6$ over Z_{23}?
4. Find all points on the elliptic curve $y^2 = x^3 + 4x + 5$ over Z_{13}.
5. Given that $P = (22, 693)$ is a point on the elliptic curve $y^2 = x^3 + 322x + 964$ over Z_{1123}, compute $-P$ and $2P$ and confirm that both are on this curve.

6. Consider the curve $y^2 = x^3 + 2x + 8$ over Z_{11}. Is $4a^3 + 27b^2$ equal to 0?

7. Draw the elliptic curve of Example 5.3.

8. Show that if the elliptic curve $y^2 = x^3 + ax + b$ does not have three distinct roots, then the discriminant $4a^3 + 27b^2$ is 0.

9. Show that $P + Q = Q + P$ for any two points on an elliptic curve.

10. The points $(12, 3)$ and $(1, 9)$ are on an elliptic curve over Z_{31}. Find the curve.

Computer-Assisted Problems

11. Find all points on the elliptic curve $y^2 = x^3 + 200x + 192$ over Z_{281}.

12. Find all points on the elliptic curve $y^2 = x^3 + 285x + 111$ over Z_{379} for which the y co-ordinate is 0.

5.2 ELLIPTIC CURVE CRYPTOGRAPHY

5.2.1 Elliptic Curve Groups and the Discrete Logarithm Problem

At the foundation of every cryptosystem is a hard mathematical problem that is computationally infeasible to solve. The discrete logarithm problem, which we discussed in Chapters 2 and 3, is the basis for the security of the elliptic curve cryptosystem.

As we saw in the previous section, selecting an point in a elliptic curve group, we can double it to obtain the point $2P$. Then we can add the point P to the point $2P$ to obtain the point $3P$. The determination of a point nP in this manner is referred to as Scalar Multiplication of a point. *The Elliptic Curve Discrete Logarithm Problem (ECDLP)* is based on the intractability of scalar multiplication products.

The discrete logarithm problem with a multiplicative notation is given elements r and q modulo a prime p, find a number k such that $r = q^k \pmod{p}$.

Definition 5.10 When the elliptic curve group is described using additive notation, *the elliptic curve discrete logarithm problem is given points P and Q in the group, find a number k such that $Pk = Q$.*

Example 5.9 In the elliptic curve group defined by $y^2 = x^3 + 9x + 17$ over Z_{23}, what is the discrete logarithm k of $Q = (4, 5)$ to the base $P = (16, 5)$? One way to find k is to compute multiples of P until Q is found. The first few multiples of P are $P = (16, 5)$, $2P = (20, 20), 3P = (14, 14), 4P = (19, 20), 5P = (13, 10), 6P = (7, 3), 7P = (8, 7)$, $8P = (12, 17), 9P = (4, 5)$. Since $9P = (4, 5) = Q$, the discrete logarithm of Q to the base P is $k = 9$.

In a secure application, k would be large enough such that it would be infeasible to determine k in this manner.

The group theory that we developed in Chapter 3 is still relevant here. In fact, the idea of order of an element from Definition 3.5 is critical in dealing with the ECDLP. In multiplicative notation, the order of a modulo n is the smallest positive integer e such that

$a^e \equiv 1 \pmod{n}$. In elliptic curve notation, the order of a point P becomes the smallest positive integer e such that $e * P \equiv O \pmod{n}$.

Although, given an elliptic curve, there is no simple formula for determining the number of points on it, there is a formula. As we noted in the last section, the number is approximately the size of the underlying field. But a theorem due to Hasse [23; p 82] states that the number of points on an elliptic curve over a field with p elements (including the point at infinity) differs from $p + 1$ by at most $2\sqrt{p}$. There are efficient algorithms that can be used to determine the precise number of points on a particular elliptic curve [20]. Although we will not worry too much about this issue, it has implications in terms of the existence of a primitive root for the group (see Theorem 3.2). Cryptosystems based on elliptic curves follow the ElGamal scheme protocol and, therefore, assume that we can choose a primitive root. However, as we pointed out in Section 3.1, a primitive root is not essential. What we need is a good choice for this element that will avoid giving away the secret key. There are algorithms and tests in the literature to ensure that a good choice is made in any implementation of elliptic curves, but these will not be our concern here.

5.2.2 An Elliptic Curve ElGamal System

Key Generation

Each user chooses an elliptic curve E modulo some large prime p, and a point P on E. These parameters form part of the user's public key. Each user chooses a (secret) random a in $[2, p - 2]$ and computes $aP = Q \pmod{p}$. The user's public key is (p, P, Q) and private key is a.

Suppose that two parties, Alice and Bob now want to use this scheme. Alice may have a message she wants to send to Bob. To be usable, this message has to be identified with a point on Bob's elliptic curve. This can be done using a scheme that identifies a certain fixed set of messages with points on the curve. We will consider this in some of the exercises and problems. In the following, we assume that Bob has generated a random b in $[2, p - 2]$ and $bP = Q \pmod{p}$.

Encryption

Alice generates a message as a point R on Bob's elliptic curve E.
She obtains Bob's public key (p, P, Q), where $Q = bP$, b is Bob's secret.
She chooses $a \in [2, p - 2]$ randomly.
She computes aP and $R + aQ \pmod{p}$.
She sends $c = (aP, R + aQ)$ to Bob.

Decryption

Bob receives $c = (aP, R + aQ)$. To recover R, he computes $(R + aQ) - baP = R + abP - baP = R \pmod{p}$, where b is his random secret.

Example 5.10   We must first generate an elliptic curve. Let us use the prime $p = 8831$ and take a random point $P = (4, 11)$ that we want to be on the curve $y^2 \equiv x^3 + ax +$

$b \pmod{p}$. If we choose any fixed value for a, then substituting the co-ordinates of P will determine b. We take $a = 3$ in which case, $b = 45$.

Bob chooses the above curve, prime and point P to generate his public key $(8831, P, a_B P) = (8831, (4, 11), (413, 1808))$, where his secret $a_B = 3$.

Alice has a message, represented as a point $P_m = (5, 1743)$ of Bob's elliptic curve, that she wishes to send to Bob. Alice downloads Bob's public key and chooses a random number $a_A = 8$. She sends to Bob $8P = (5415, 6321)$ and $P_m + 8(a_B P) = (6626, 3576)$. Bob first calculates $a_B(8P) = 3(5415, 6321) = (673, 146)$. He now subtracts this from $(6626, 3576) : (6626, 3576) - (673, 146) = (6626, 3576) + (673, -146) = (5, 1743)$, and he has recovered the message. (Note that we subtracted points using the rule $P - Q = P + (-Q)$.)

Example 5.11   Nicky wants to set up his cryptosystem using the elliptic curve $y^2 = x^3 + 2x + 14 \pmod{17}$ with point $P(1, 0)$. He chooses a large (relative to the prime chosen) secret 14. Since P has second co-ordinate 0, $Q = 14P$ will be the identity O (see Definition 5.8). When Maria sends the encrypted message $c = (aP, R + aQ)$ to Nicky, using her secret a, the pair will reveal the message R: she actually sends $c = (aP, R + O) = (aP, R)$ and any interceptor can see it.

Example 5.11 points out that it is unwise to use a point P in a public key (p, P, Q) that has y co-ordinate 0.

We pointed out after the corollary to Theorem 4.6, Euler's criterion, that half the elements modulo a prime will be squares and half non squares. We use this fact in the next example to establish a method of identifying a number in base 10 with a point on an elliptic curve.

Example 5.12   We want to represent the message 2 as a point (x, y) on the curve $y^2 = x^3 + 7x + 11 \pmod{31}$. We embed the message into the x-co-ordinate of a point on the curve, but we do not know if the point $x = 2$ gives a solution to the equation, so we use a two-digit number, the first of which is 2. By the Corollary to Euler's criterion, there is a high probability of finding a square for y^2 with only two or three attempts. So we try to solve for the y co-ordinate of each of $(20, y)$, $(21, y)$, $(22, y)$, and so on. The first three corresponding y^2 values are 29, 26, and 1. Disregarding for the moment that we have an obvious square root for the last value, we note that 31 is congruent to 1 modulo 4, and we try Theorem 4.4 to find a square root for the first two. Since $\gcd(2, 15) = 1$, we proceed to determine the inverse of 2 (mod 15), which is 7. For 29, $29^7 = 27 \pmod{31}$ and $26^7 = 26 \pmod{31}$. Checking, $27^2 = 16 \pmod{31}$ while $26^2 = 25$ and so neither 29 nor 26 is a square. However, 1 is a square, and we choose $+1$ as a square root and associate the message 2 with the point $(23, 1)$. The receiver has to know in advance that the message can be retrieved from this point by taking the x co-ordinate and deleting the last digit.

We can also perform a key exchange protocol based on elliptic curves.

5.2.3 Elliptic Curve Key Exchange (ECKE)

We assume that parties A and B (often called Alice and Bob) want to exchange information secretly but are only able to communicate over insecure channels such as the Internet or telephone lines. The protocol set out here permits them to use these insecure channels to exchange information in such a way that after several communications, they share a single value known only to them and then can use this value as a key to conceal further communications.

1. In this first step, A and B agree on common parameters, which do not have to be kept secret from anyone else. These are
   - an elliptic curve E over a large prime p,
   - a point P on the curve.

   Now each user, A and B generates their own public key independently by
   - choosing a secret integer: $x_A < p$ for A and $x_B < p$ for B,
   - and computing their public key: $(p, P, x_A P) \pmod p$ for A and $(p, P, x_B P) \pmod p$ for B.

   A and B now publish their respective public keys wherever they like. In particular, they need to know each other's public keys and can send them to each other directly over an insecure channel.

2. Users A and B now establish a common value as follows:
   B computes $x_B x_A P \pmod p$ using his private key.
   A computes $x_A x_B P \pmod p$ using her private key.
   But both are the same:
   $K_{AB} = x_A x_B P \pmod p$.

Example 5.13   Alice and Bob want to exchange a key using an elliptic curve scheme. To do so, they agree on a public fixed point P on an elliptic curve $E : y^2 \equiv x^3 + ax + b \pmod p$. They choose $p = 7211$ and $a = 1$ and $P = (3, 5)$. This gives $b = 7206$. Randomly, Alice chooses $x_A = 12$ and Bob chooses $x_B = 23$. They keep these private, but publish $x_A P$ and $x_B P$.

   These points are

$$x_A P = (1794, 6375) \quad \text{and} \quad x_B P = (3861, 1242).$$

Alice now takes $x_B P$ and multiplies by x_A to get the key:

$$x_A(x_B P) = 12(3861, 1242) = (1472, 2098).$$

Similarly, Bob takes $x_A P$ and multiplies by x_B to get the key:

$$x_B(x_A P) = 23(1794, 6375) = (1472, 2098).$$

And now they have the same key.

5.2.4 Computer Examples

1. We want to represent the message 12345 as a point (x, y) on the curve $y^2 = x^3 + 7x + 11$ (mod 593899). We embed the message into the x-co-ordinate of a point on the curve. If we use 12345 as an x-co-ordinate itself, it may not have an associated y value (from substituting into the equation and finding a square root of y^2). Instead, we will add an extra digit to the beginning of this number and see which gives us a square. The probability is high that we will find a solution after only two tries. Write $x = 12345-$ and find a value of the missing last digit of x such that there is a point on the curve with this x-co-ordinate.

   Solution. We need $z = x^3 + 7x + 11$ to be a square (mod 593899). Since 593899 is congruent to 3 modulo 4, we use Proposition 4.5: raise z to the $(p + 1)/4$ power to calculate a potential square root, then square it to see if it is actually a square root. Note that if z is a square, then if we raise it to the power $(p - 1)/2$, we would get 1 (mod p).

   We successively substitute the number 12345–into $x^3 + 7x + 11$ with the blank running through 0, 1, 2, ... until we get a square mod 593899:

   - $p := 593899$;
     $p := 593899$
   - $z := 123450^3 + 7 * 123450 + 11$;
     $z := 1881365964489161$
   - $> z\&^{((p-1)/2)} \mod p$;
     593898
   - $> z := 123451^3 + 7 * 123451 + 11 \mod p$;
     $z := 426106$
   - $z\&^{((p-1)/2)} \mod p$;
     1
   - Therefore, z is a square mod p. To find a square root, the same proposition gives
   - $z\&^{((p+1)/4)} \mod p$;
     423090

   And we find that $(123451, 423090)$ is a point on the curve.

2. Antonia and Jose agree to set up a key exchange protocol using the same elliptic curve, prime and discovered point P as in computer Example 1 of this section. Show how they set up a common key.

   Solution. Both parties choose secrets. To keep our computations to a minimum, we assume that Antonia chooses $x_A = 2$, and Jose chooses $x_B = 3$. Antonia computes $x_A P$ and Jose computes $x_B P$. Using Definition 5.7, $2P = (s^2 2 * 123451, -423090 + s(123451(s^2 2 * 123451))$, where $s = (3 * 123451^2 + 7)/2 * 423090$ (mod 593899). Thus, $s = 321493 * 252281^{-1}$ and $2P = (3214932 * 252281^{-2} - 246902, -423090 + 431610 * 252281^{-1} - 473126 * 252281^{-3}) = (371641, 440083)$.

For $3P$, we add $2P$ to P using Definition 5.5. Here, the slope is $(252281 - 431610 * 252281^{-1} + 473126 * 252281^{-3}) * (370353 - 3214932 * 252281^{-2})^{-1} = 165382$ and so the x-co-ordinate of $P+2P = 1653822 - 123451 - 3214932 * 252281^{-2} + 246902 = 474084$ and, therefore, the y-co-ordinate is $-423090 + 165382 * 474084 = 82363$.

Now Antonia computes $x_A x_B P \pmod{p}$ using her private key and Jose computes $x_B x_A P \pmod{p}$ using his private key. The common result (doubling $x_B P$ for instance) is $(572289, 124604)$.

The efficiency of a cryptographic algorithm depends on the key length and the calculation effort that is necessary to provide a prescribed level of security. Thus, even using the same key size, algorithms based on differing types of computation may perform quite differently. For instance, a 160-bit key used in an ECC scheme and a 1369-bit key used in RSA or in ElGamal based on the standard discrete logarithm problem are expected to be equally efficient [24]. Thus, elliptic curve systems can be run effectively on much smaller key sizes than the other systems that we have seen. However, many assumptions must be made about how the algorithms are implemented and what else the computations are used for (example to sign electronically, which we will see in Chapter 6). The article [25] gives a good analysis of the factors that must be taken into consideration. Paar and Pelzl [35] in their Table 6.1 compare bit lengths needed for several cryptosystems to achieve the same level of security.

Currently, Certicom (http://www.certicom.com), which produces elliptic curve cryptographic software, has an arrangement to install ECC on palm pilot (http://www.palm.com) and on blackberry (http://www.blackberry.com) products. The use of ECC in wireless devices is very popular and likely to continue.

Since elliptic curve cryptosystems are based on the discrete logarithm problem, their underlying security is directly related to it. If the elliptic curve is chosen with care [29; pp. 130 and 316], an elliptic curve cryptosystem resists most attacks to which other schemes based on the discrete logarithm will fall. For instance, an index-calculus attack (discussed in Section 2.4) can be avoided, while only Pollard's attack (Section 2.3) and the Baby Step Giant Step attack (Section 2.4) remain threats. In these last two attacks, we saw that the number of steps needed to guarantee success is approximately the square root of the size of the modulus used. Thus, if a modulus of size about 2^{180} is used (so the modulus is about 180 bits in size), then about 2^{90} steps are needed to provide reasonable security. In fact, a bit-length of 256 is common in elliptic curve implementations.

Nonetheless, implementation of ECC on small portable devices can lead to ad hoc attacks that target the platform rather than the cryptography itself.

Further Reading. Several introductory cryptography texts discuss elliptic curve cryptosystems. Some of those with good examples include [19, 28, 35]. All three of these books mention Hasse's theorem on the number of points of an elliptic curve. The theorem implies that if a curve with 2^n elements is needed, then a prime of about n bits should be used. Also, see [37].

Ellliptic curve cryptography (ECC) allows for efficient implementation due to shorter underlying bit lengths key sizes $(160\dots256$ bit) when compared to RSA or DLP in finite fields $(1024\dots4096$ bit) at an equivalent level of security [59]. This results in faster computations and lower power consumption, as well as memory and bandwidth savings [43], [15] and [34] also discuss performance.

Modern security protocols such as SSL and TLS are widely used in e-commerce applications. These are arithmetic-intensive public key primitives; the use of SSL increases computational cost of transactions by a factor of 5–7 [21] in comparison with various parameters such as throughput, utilization, cache sizes, file access sizes, and network load on the server. In addition, several weaknesses of these protocols exist and are well known including the possibility of session hijacking [9].

5.2.5 Problems

1. Choose an elliptic curve, a prime p, a point on E, and generate your own public key.

2. Use the elliptic curve $y^2 = x^3 + 7x + 15$ to encrypt the message 1 using Chiara's public key $(29, (3,11), (5, 28))$.

3. Show how Chiara decrypts the message in question 2 given that her secret is 3.

4. Check that half the elements modulo 31 are square.

5. Binh has chosen the elliptic curve $y^2 \equiv x^3 + 2x + 15$ and public key $(17, (1, 1), (8, 13))$. Maria notices that the prime is very small and she decides to attack the public key to recover Binh's secret. Show how she does this.

6. Jakob and Ronghua want to exchange a key using an elliptic curve scheme. To do so, they agree on a public fixed point $P = (2, 7)$ on an elliptic curve $E : y^2 \equiv x^3 + 4x + 7 \pmod{13}$. Randomly, Jakob chooses a secret $x_A = 2$ and Ronghua chooses $x_B = 3$. Find their public keys.

Computer-Assisted Problems

7. Represent the message 23 as a point (x, y) on the curve $y^2 = x^3 + 19x + 11 \pmod{311}$.

8. Jurgen generates the message $R = (216, 52)$ as a point on Sonu's elliptic curve $y^2 = x^3 + 363x + 252$ and obtains Sonu's public key $(499, (21, 121), (114, 27))$. He chooses the secret $a = 3$. What is Jurgen's encrypted message that he sends to Sonu?

9. Decrypt the above message given that Sonu's secret is 2.

10. Tricia and Egon use the same elliptic curve $y^2 = x^3 + 333x + 57$ over the prime 509 with point $P(1, 30)$ to set up a key exchange. They independently choose their secrets (2 and 3, respectively). Tricia receives $(14, 293)$ from Egon and uses it to generate the key $(400, 28)$. Egon receives $(9, 27)$ from Tricia. Show that he generates the same key.

5.3 THE ELLIPTIC CURVE FACTORING SCHEME

In this section, we describe how elliptic curves can be used to factor numbers suspected of being composite. We saw in Section 2.2 that Fermat's Little Theorem can be used to check if a number is prime or not. In fact, it cannot definitively prove that a number is prime, as some composite numbers pass the FLT test.

We can also use elliptic curve cryptography to test if a number is prime. This is because when adding points, we need to compute an inverse for the slope. If we add enough points together and the modulus is in fact composite, there is a high probability that along the way we will be unable to compute an inverse because we found a factor of the modulus. Again, if all point additions are correctly computed, this is no guarantee that the modulus is a prime.

This method of factoring was first described formally in [24], but we give a brief algorithm here for the method.

EC Algorithm for Factoring

1. Input a value n for testing.
2. Choose an elliptic curve E and a point P on it modulo n.
3. Choose a bound b and compute all multiples of P up to bP.
   If the computations in Step 3 fail, output a divisor of n;
   End.
4. Otherwise, choose a new curve and point.

We illustrate this with an example.

Example 5.14 We wish to test if the number 15 is prime or not by attempting to factor it. We choose an elliptic curve modulo 15: say $y^2 = x^3 + 3x + 4$. We need a point on the curve that we will then repeatedly add to itself for a while to see if we encounter a problem. It is easy to see that $P = (0, 2)$ is on the curve. Doubling, it using the formula $s = (3x_P^2 + a)/(2y_P) \pmod{p}$, $x_R \equiv s^2 - 2x_P \pmod{p}$, and $y_R = -y_P + s(x_P - x_R) \pmod{p}$, we get slope $\frac{3}{4} \equiv 3*4 \equiv 12 \pmod{15}$ and so $2P = (9, 10)$. Instead of computing $3P$ at this point using a different formula, we could just as well reuse the above formula to compute $4P$. In this case, the slope is $21/20$ and now we have an interesting situation where $20 \equiv 5 \pmod{15}$ is not relatively prime to the modulus 15. In this case, there is no need to apply the EA to find the common factor; it is 5. So we have factored 15.

For large values of the modulus, a large number of additions must be done, and this is time consuming. We use two special commands available for Maple. However, Matlab (www.mathworks.com.au) and Magma [8; p. 706] software also have elliptic curve over finite modulus commands available. In Matlab, $ECADP(x1, y1, x2, y2, A, p)$ adds the points $(x1, y1)$ and $(x2, y2)$ on the elliptic curve with x coefficient A over the modulus p. Note that the points may be the same; also, one point along with the coefficient A

determines the constant value on the curve. In Magma, the command is a basic $R :=$ $P + Q$, assuming that the curve and modulus have been prespecified. An alternate option, of course, is to write a piece of code separately and let it run for as long as needed.

Example 5.15 In Maple, the command
> $multell([0, 2], 3, 1, 4, 19)$
provides the point (0,2), the number of multiples (3) that we want to compute, the coefficients a and b of the elliptic curve, in this case 1 and 4, and finally the modulus to be used, 19. So we are working on the elliptic curve $y^2 = x^3 + x + 4$ modulo 19 here. Note that the point (0,2) is on this curve. The command produces $3P$: [5, 1].

In case we are testing to see if the modulus is a prime or composite number, we need to worry about the fact that the computations may not work at every stage. Thus, we use a command that lists each multiple of the starting point and lets us know when a common divisor with the modulus has been found. The following command does this for us with the same curve and point:
> $multsell([0, 2], 3, 1, 4, 19)$;
[[1, [0, 2]], [2, [6, 6]], [3, [5, 1]]].

Here, $P, 2P$, and $3P$ are all listed. Since the modulus is a prime, there is no problem computing these multiples.

The examples of Section 5.3.1 illustrate how these commands work when the modulus is not a prime. In some cases, both here and in the problems, a bound has to be chosen arbitrarily. Of course, the modulus itself is an approximate upper bound as we do not expect many more points on the curve than the modulus (see Section 5.2 where this was discussed); but where this is a large number, we need to choose a much smaller bound. In general, the square root of the modulus may be sufficient.

5.3.1 Computer Examples

1. Factor 323 using the elliptic curve $y^2 = x^3 + x + 4$ and point (0,2) on it.
   Solution. We use the multsell command in Maple and compute up to $30P$:
   > $multsell([0, 2], 30, 1, 4, 323)$;

[[1, [0, 2]],	[2, [101, 215]],	[3, [252, 39]],
[4, [106, 308]],	[5, [166, 49]],	[6, [294, 265]],
[7, [122, 102]],	[8, [39, 109]],	[9, [200, 87]],
[10, [276, 236]],	[11, [286, 233]],	[12, [84, 278]],
[13, [85, 134]],	[14, ["factor =," 17]]].	

   Maple has found a factor 17 of the modulus and so $323 = 17 * 19$.

2. Factor 3900353.
   Solution. We will test this using the Maple multell command for elliptic curves. Pick a random point, say (1,1), and a random value of the first coefficient a on the elliptic curve we will construct, say $a = 123$. Now choose b so that (1,1) lies on the curve $y^2 = x^3 + 123 * x + b$. We find $b = -123$. Now choose a bound, say $B = 30!$ and compute
   > $multell([1, 1], factorial(30), 123, -123, 3900353)$;

The output is [factor=, 1109].
The other factor is
> 3900353/1109; 3517.

5.3.2 Problems

1. Use the curve $y^2 = x^3 + 11x + 4$ modulo 20 with point $P(1, 16)$ doubling P each time to try to factor 20.

2. We want to factor a number and begin with the general form of an elliptic curve: $y^2 = x^3 + ax + b$, choose a, then a point which will then determine b. Say we choose $a = 0$ and point $P = (1, 1)$. Is it the case that each multiple of P will be on the curve?

3. Choose an elliptic curve and a point and use these to factor 18.

4. Use the curve $y^2 = x^3 + 4x + 9$ modulo 25 with point $P(0, 3)$ doubling P each time to reach $8P$, to try to factor 25. List the slopes you derive.

Computer-Assisted Problems

5. Find $700P$ where $P = (105, 1087)$ is on the elliptic curve $y^2 = x^3 + 29x + 56$ modulo 1097.

6. Use the point $(1,5)$ on the elliptic curve $y^2 = x^3 + 16x + 8$ to factor the number 13837.

6

DIGITAL SIGNATURES

When sending a letter, it is customary to sign it. A signature indicates the source of the message in the letter and is important to the receiver who can then better interpret the contents and understand the context. If the letter promises to deliver goods or transfer money, then the signature is especially important as the sender can be held responsible in a court of law if she does not follow through on the promise. However, the signature is also important for the sender. The receiver of an unsigned letter may attribute it to a specific person who did, in fact, not write it. Thus false allegations may be made, leading to an argument.

In the digital world, signatures are necessary for exactly the reasons cited above. The standard digital equivalent of a hand-written signature on paper is provided by a *hash function*, described in Section 6.1, along with some secret information that belongs to the sender. Since documents can be very long, extending from a single digit or word to a lengthy legal tome, we need a mechanism, which encompasses all of the data inside it, to ensure that nothing can be deleted or changed unobtrusively. A hash function is a function in the mathematical sense that can be applied to data of any size and produce a small (usually fixed size) output. It needs to satisfy the condition that any two distinct documents must have different hashes (hash outputs).

Public Key Cryptography: Applications and Attacks, First Edition. Lynn Margaret Batten.
© 2013 by The Institute of Electrical and Electronics Engineers, Inc. Published 2013 by John Wiley & Sons, Inc.

6.1 HASH FUNCTIONS

A hash function is a function that satisfies certain properties needed in digital applications. Since the primary use of hash functions is for signing messages and for differentiation of messages or documents, we require several conditions of any hash function h.

Definition 6.1   A *hash function* is a function that satisfies the following properties:

1. It can be applied to any sized message.
2. It produces a fixed-length output.
3. For any message m, it is easy to compute $h(m)$.
4. Given c it is computationally infeasible to find m such that $h(m) = c$. (This is known as the *one-way property*.)
5. Given x it is infeasible to find y such that $h(y) = h(x)$. (This is known as the *weak collision resistant property*.)

Definition 6.2   This last condition is sometimes strengthened to the following condition, in which case, we refer to the hash function as a *strong hash function*.

6. It is infeasible to find any x and y such that $h(y) = h(x)$. (This is known as the *strong collision resistant property*.)

Given a message m and a hash function h, we refer to $h(m)$ as the hash of m.

Properties 1 and 3 make hash functions convenient to use, whereas Property 2 makes the output easy to use in storage or for look up tables. Properties 4, 5, and 6 focus on the design of the hash function and the applications it is used for. Properties 5 and 6 help to ensure that, when a message is sent, the receiver actually obtains the correct message unchanged by an attacker. This is known as *message authentication*. Since these properties imply that an attacker cannot substitute a new message with the same hash as the old message, the sender just has to send the message along with the hash to the receiver. The receiver then hashes the message and compares it with the received hash. Of course, an attacker could capture both the message and the hash and replace them with a new message and its hash. One way to avoid this attack is for the sender to send the hash over a secure channel, which is practical since it is small. Another solution is for the sender to sign the message in some way. We will describe how this can be done later in the section.

Property 4 is useful in a different kind of way. For instance, storing hashes of passwords in a computer system, rather than the passwords themselves, is a safe way of managing passwords. When a password is entered, it is hashed and the hash compared with the stored list. There is no danger of password theft, either by an internal or external attacker, as passwords cannot be retrieved from their hashes. (Note that we generally assume that everyone knows which hash function was used—this is not secret information.) However, there are no known functions which are provably one-way. As we saw in the descriptions of RSA and ElGamal, the encryption functions used are simply assumed to be computationally difficult to reverse.

Properties 1 and 2 imply that a hash function is not a 1–1 function (as described in the proof of Theorem 2.3). In fact, in general, many different inputs to h must result in the same output if messages can be much bigger than the output size. This contradicts a desire to use hash functions to identify the messages they are applied to. This is also a problem for Properties 4, 5, and 6 since if many messages hash to the same output, this increases the chances of finding at least one for a given output. We return to these problems later in the section.

Example 6.1   The function f takes as input any positive integer x and outputs $x^3 + 1$. We ask if f is a hash function. Certainly, any length of positive integer can be input, so Property 1 is satisfied. However, the size of the output will vary depending on the input, so Property 2 is not satisfied. At this point, we can say that f is not a hash function. However, let us check more of the properties. It is relatively easy to compute a cube, even for very large integers, so Property 3 is alright. Properties 4, 5, and 6 all want us to try to retrieve x from $x^3 + 1$. Technically, this requires a cube root. Letting $y = x^3 + 1$, we write $x^3 = y - 1$ and then take the cube root of $y - 1$. Since we know that the value $x^3 + 1$ was computed starting from a value x, we know that a cube root exists. Also, a cube root will be unique (unlike a square root). There are algorithms available (for example, see `http://www.itl.nist.gov/div897/sqg/dads/HTML/cubeRoot.html`) to compute cube roots, and so, in theory, we would be able to retrieve the message.

Definition 6.3   A (hash) *collision* is the name we give to the situation where two different inputs have the same hash value. The concept is identical to that used for collisions in cycle-finding algorithms discussed in Section 2.4. An example of a collision in a function is with $g(x) = x^2 + 1$ since g sends both $+1$ and -1 to the same output. The function g would not be a good choice for a hash function (see Problem 3 of Section 6.1.2).

To analyze how frequently collisions can happen, we look at probabilities. Suppose we have 23 people in a room and want to determine the probability that two of them have the same birthday? We can turn this around and ask what is the probability that they all have different birthdays?

If there are 365 days in the year, the first person uses up one of them, so the second person has probability $(1-1/365)$ of having a different birthday. The next person has probability $(1-2/365)$, and so on. The probability of all 23 people having different birthdays is then the product:

$$\left(1 - \frac{1}{365}\right) * \left(1 - \frac{2}{365}\right) * \left(1 - \frac{3}{365}\right) * \ldots * \left(1 - \frac{22}{365}\right) = 0.493.$$

So the probability of two of the group having the same birthday is $1 - 0.493 = 0.507$, which is more than half.

This seems a little astonishing when the number 23 is much smaller than 365. If we try this for 40 people, there is an 89% probability of a match.

The next proposition gives the general result.

Proposition 6.1   *A basket contains N balls, numbered 1 to N. One at a time, m balls
are randomly taken from the basket, the number checked, and the ball replaced. The
probability that at least two of the tested balls had the same number is* $1 - \prod_{i=1}^{m}(1 - \frac{i}{N})$
which is larger than $1 - e^{-m(m-1)/2N}$, *where e is the exponential function.*

Proof. As in the argument preceding the proposition, we count the chances of no match
and then subtract this from 1. This is

$$Pr(\text{match}) = 1 - \prod_{i=1}^{m-1}\left(1 - \frac{i}{N}\right).$$

We now use the fact that for all real numbers x, it is the case that $1 - x \leq e^{-x}$ [36]. It
follows that

$$\prod_{i=1}^{m}\left(1 - \frac{i}{N}\right) \leq \prod_{i=1}^{m}e^{-i/N} = e^{-\sum_{i=1}^{m}\frac{i}{N}} = e^{-m(m-1)/2N}.$$

Hence $1 - \prod_{i=1}^{m}\left(1 - \frac{i}{N}\right) \geq 1 - e^{-m(m-1)/2N}$ as claimed.   □

This is known as the Birthday Paradox, since the probability is over 0.5 of a match
when r is far less than 50% of N. In fact, if there are N objects and we have about $\sqrt{N}$
people, the probability of a match is about 50%. There are clear implications for hash
collisions. If we have a given message out of a set of N and want to know the probability
of a collision with it, this is just the chance of the remaining messages colliding with it,
which is $1/(N - 1)$. But if we are simply looking for any pair out of N to collide, the
chances are much greater.

Since we want a hash function to be able to take a very large input, it is common for
it to use data blocks—plaintext broken into segments of equal size that we saw in Section
3.2. The most common hash functions use a method called *cipher-block-chaining*, which
works on blocks.

Let M be a message of any size and break it into equal size parts as, for instance, in
Computer Example 2 of Section 3.2.1. (A common block size is 64 bits.) Now take any
encryption algorithm that can be applied to data of this block length. (RSA, ElGamal, and
elliptic curve encryption are all possible, as are many standard nonpublic key algorithms.)
If either the original message or the last block has too few bits, then we can pad it with
0s to complete to the required size.

Label the blocks B_i, where i begins at 1 and ends at some fixed n. Then we apply
the encryption algorithm recursively to the blocks, each time adding in the result of the
previous encryption. This is shown in Figure 6.1 where we input B_1, apply the encryption
algorithm E with a fixed key k, output H_1, then XOR H_1 with B_2 to produce the input

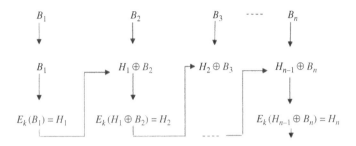

Figure 6.1. Cipher-block-chaining of an iterative hash function.

to E_k in round 2. (Note that the XOR operation is only possible if H_1 and B_2 have the same length, so E must output blocks of the same length as the input.) This continues until each block has been used; the output is a single block. The output of E_k at each round is either in a fixed size or in some fixed range and so can be standardized to meet requirement 2 of Definition 6.1. Requirement 3 follows if the encryption algorithm is easy to compute; requirements 4 and 5 follow if the encryption algorithm is difficult to invert.

Example 6.2 Consider the message 100001011110001001110101011. In order to hash it to a 6-bit output using the cipher-chaining method, we need an encryption algorithm that takes as input blocks of fixed size and that outputs a 6-bit string. Suppose we have such an encryption algorithm E and that E takes as input 6-bit strings. We then break the message into equal 6-bit lengths, deciding on whether this is done from the left or from the right. In this case, we choose to break up the message starting from the left. Thus, the input blocks after padding the last one, are $B_1 = 100001$, $B_2 = 011110$, $B_3 = 001001$, $B_4 = 110101$, $B_5 = 010000$.

Now we choose a key k and apply E. Suppose that $E_k(B_1) = H_1 = 101010$. Then, as input to the next round, we XOR H_1 with B_2 to obtain 110100. Suppose that $E_k(110100) = H_2 = 100111$. We XOR H_2 with B_3 to obtain 101110. Suppose that $E_k(101110) = H_3 = 001011$. We XOR H_3 with B_4 to obtain 111110. Suppose that $E_k(111110) = H_4 = 011111$. We XOR H_4 with B_5 to obtain 001111. Suppose that $E_k(001111) = H_5 = 110100$. This is the final output of the hash function.

In general, a major part of a hash function is a compression function which reduces a large amount of data to the predetermined fixed output length. A good compression function makes use of as many input bits as possible in producing the output. The example in Section 6.1.2 uses every bit of the input as long as the encryption algorithm does. However, the following example is not a good compression function.

Example 6.3   Let 1010101010110000000000101010111 be the input to a hash function H that compresses a binary string of any length to a 5-bit string by taking the first 3 bits and concatenating them with the last 2 bits. Thus,

$H(1010101010110000000000101010111) = 10111$. This is not a good compression function as most of the bits are not used in producing the output. It is clearly not a good hash function as we can easily find many strings which hash to 10111—just replace the digits between the first 101 and the last 11 with any set of digits at all!

We now look at two of the most well known and used cryptographic hash functions. Both the SHA family and the MD family are authorized for use by many government organizations [56, 61].

6.1.1 SHA-1

This hash function was the second in line as a standard invented by the U.S. National Security Agency (NSA). The first version, now known as SHA-0, was published in 1993 and subsequently dropped because weaknesses were found. The NSA replaced it with SHA-1 as a standard in 1995.

Most of the operations in the SHA-1 system are elementary swaps and row or column exchanges, implementing Shannon's ideas of confusion and diffusion (see Chapter 1). In the current standard implementation [63, 67], each message input block of 512 bits is broken down into blocks of size 160 and then further into 32-bit blocks and is processed in the same way. The output from each message block is used as input to the next one. There is a complex function applied to each message block which is designed to avoid two different messages having the same hash. There is also a compression function to reduce the whole message to 160 bits.

Figure 6.2 shows one iteration of the compression function.

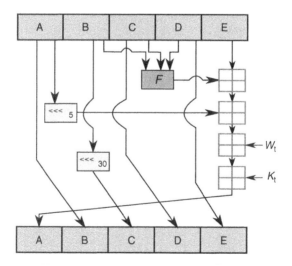

Figure 6.2. The SHA-1 operations (see [43]).

Notation

- A, B, C, D, and E are 32-bit words.
- F is a nonlinear function mapping a 96-bit string to a 32-bit string.
- $<<<n$ denotes a circular left bit rotation by n places; n varies for each operation.
- The symbol $\boxplus$ denotes addition modulo 2^{32}. (Note that this is just XORing the bits in the bit representation of the input.)
- W_t is the result of combining A, B, C, D, and E after a left bit rotation has been applied to A, and F has been applied to B, C, and D and the result combined with E.
- K_t is a 32-bit constant.

The output is again labelled as a concatenation of A, B, C, D, and E and processed as input through a second round.

Example 6.4   We perform a toy example with one round of SHA-1 using Figure 6.2 on a 20-bit input 11010100001010101001, where $A = 1101$, $B = 0100$, $C = 0010$, $D = 1010$, and $E = 1001$. Let F map a 12-bit string to a 4-bit string by $F(abcdefghjkmn) = ahkn$ XOR $dcfe$ XOR $gbmj$. K_1 is the 4-bit constant 1010.

We compute the input to W_1 first: from A it is 1011. (On a 4-bit string, a left rotation by 5 bits is the same as a left rotation by 1 bit.) From B, C, and D, it is $F(010000101010) = 0000$ XOR 0000 XOR 1111 = 1111. These are then added modulo 2^{32} (XORing) with E. So W_1 is 1011 XOR 1111 XOR 1001 = 1101. We now produce the output that we will refer to as A', B', C', D', and E'. $A' = W_1$ XOR $K_1 = 1101$ XOR 1010 = 0111; $B' = A = 1101$; C' is produced by shifting B left by 30 bits, or equivalently in our case, by 2 bits to get 0001; $D' = C = 0010$ and $E' = D = 1010$.

Note that in SHA-1, the original blocks A, C, and D, without change, become blocks in the output (B', D', and E'). All of the original blocks are used in determining A' while C is just a shift of B.

6.1.2 MD5

MD5 stands for "Message Digest 5" because it is the fifth revision of a message digest algorithm devised by Ron Rivest of RSA Laboratories. Like SHA-1, MD5 is a target for those trying to find weaknesses in cryptographic hash functions. Although both have been adopted as standards in many government organizations around the world, they are now both suspect and an open call for a hash function to replace them has been made. We give more details about this later in this section.

A 128-bit input state is divided into four 32-bit words, denoted A, B, C, and D. There are four rounds; each round is composed of similar operations based on a different nonlinear function F.

The four functions used are

$$F(X, Y, Z) = (X \wedge Y) \vee (\neg X \wedge Z)$$
$$G(X, Y, Z) = (X \wedge Z) \vee (Y \wedge \neg Z)$$
$$H(X, Y, Z) = X \oplus Y \oplus Z$$
$$I(X, Y, Z) = Y \oplus (X \vee \neg Z),$$

where $\oplus$, $\wedge$, $\vee$, and $\neg$ denote the XOR, AND, OR, and NOT operations, respectively.

Notation

- A, B, C, and D are 32-bit words.
- F is one of the above nonlinear functions mapping a 96-bit string to a 32-bit string.
- $<<< s$ denotes a left bit circular rotation by s places; s varies for each round.
- The symbol $\boxplus$ denotes addition modulo 2^{32}. (Note that this is just XORing the bits in the bit representation of the input.)
- M_i is the result of combining A, B, C, and D after B, C, and D have been put through F.
- K_i is a 32-bit constant, different for each round.

The output is again labeled A, B, C, and D to be put through the next round.

Example 6.5   We perform a toy example with one round of MD5 using Figure 6.3 on a 16-bit input 1110100101001001, where $A = 1110$, $B = 1001$, $C = 0100$, and $D = 1001$. We use F is $I(X, Y, Z) = Y \oplus (X \vee \neg Z)$, K_1 is the 4-bit constant 1011 and $s = 3$.

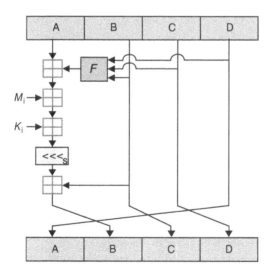

Figure 6.3.   The MD5 operations (see [38]).

We compute the input to M_1 first: from A it is 1110. From B, C, and D, it is C XOR $(B$ OR $(NOTD)) = 0100$ XOR $(1001$ OR $0110) = 0100$ XOR $1111 = 1011$. So M_1 is the sum of 1110 and 1011 modulo 2^{32} which is 1110 XOR $1011 = 0101$.

We now produce the output that we will refer to as A', B', C', and D'. $A' = D = 1001$; $C' = B = 1001$; $D' = C = 0100$; B' needs additional computation. We XOR M_1 with K_1 which gives 0101 XOR $1011 = 1110$; then we do a left rotation of this result by three bits, resulting in 0111. This is added modulo 2^{32} to B giving 0111 XOR $1001 = 1110 = B'$.

Note that input blocks B, C, and D are used directly as output blocks C', D', and A'. Only the input block A is used, in conjunction with the other input blocks, to produce an entirely new section of the output.

In the next section, we will consider digital signatures on data. Hash functions can be used to perform this job. In using a hash function as a signature, a receiver wants to check that a message received actually came from the person who sent it. We describe two scenarios that manage this situation. In both scenarios, we avoid encrypting the message, as, in general, it may be a very large message and public key schemes are not efficient for encrypting large messages.

Scenario 1

Atul wants to send a document D to Antonio and wants to make sure that Antonio knows it came from Atul and that it was not altered. Atul uses a hash function h to compute $h(D)$ and then applies his own private key from a private key encryption scheme to $h(D)$ to get $E(h(D))$. He sends D along with $E(h(D))$ to Antonio. Antonio verifies that $E(h(D))$ came from Atul by decrypting it with Atul's public key. He then verifies the hash by hashing D independently. The steps are shown in Figure 6.4.

See Section 6.1.1, Computer Example 1, for an example of Scenario 1.

Scenario 2

Feena wants to send a document D to Miriam and wants to make sure that Miriam knows it came from Feena and that it was not altered. Feena and Miriam agree beforehand on a secret value s. Feena concatenates s with D to obtain D'. (The notation is $D' = D||s$.)

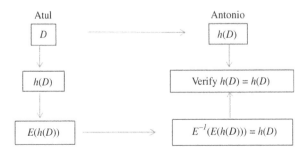

Figure 6.4. Atul sends data to Antonio.

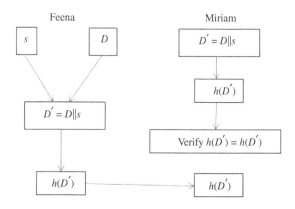

Figure 6.5.   Feena sends a document to Miriam.

She then uses a hash function h to compute $h(D')$ and sends this along with D to Miriam. When Miriam receives D and $h(D')$, she concatenates s with D to obtain D' and checks that the hash of this is the same as the hash she received. The details are shown in Figure 6.5.

This second scenario is also known as a *message authentication code* or *MAC*. In a MAC, the hash is applied to both the message and to a shared secret. In our scenario, we concatenated the two, but the hash could also be a function which applies to a paired input (for example, $f(x, y) = xy$ which maps the pair (5,11) to the single value 55).

Definition 6.4   A *message authentication code (MAC)* is a hash function used together with a shared key specifically to provide authentication.

Thus, MACs provide

- message authentication, provided by the hash and
- sender authentication, provided by the shared secret.

See Section 6.1.1, Computer Example 2, for an example of a MAC.

If a shared secret is available, it can be used to encrypt D before it is hashed. Then D can be transmitted in encrypted form on an insecure channel without fear that it can be read.

Note that Property 5 of Definition 6.1 is a critical property in applications such as signing as it prevents forgeries from taking place; if Atul signs document D using the hash function h to obtain $h(D)$, Feena cannot obtain $h(D)$ using a different document D' and so cannot pretend to be Atul.

6.1.3   The Search for New Hash Functions

Many attacks on hash functions have appeared in recent years, the best of which is [11]. Even those established in standards have been shown to have significant weaknesses. Thus, a competition to select a new hash function or hash functions is being run by NIST with a target of 2012 for winners to be selected. See `http://csrc.nist.gov/groups/ST/hash/index.html` for more details about this competition and its timeline.

The European Centre of Excellence in Cryptography, ECRYPT, is assisting the competition by storing and testing new candidates. See [62] for the SHA-3 Zoo of proposals and for details on attacks on them to date. The eHash main page at `http://ehash.iaik.tugraz.at/wiki/The_eHash_Main_Page`, which is maintained by the Technical University of Graz in Austria, has the most recent information about the proposals and can assist you if you are interested in analysing any of them.

6.1.4 Computer Examples

1. Atul wants to send the message
   $m = 08220811111200171019070818220404100041303$ to Antonio.
   Apply the block method to find a hash. Use blocks as in Computer Example 2 of Section 3.2.1 and apply the hashing method of Example 6.2 using the encryption function on bits $E(xyzw) = wzyx$ and normal addition instead of XOR, deleting the leftmost digit if the sum has five digits.
   Solution. We choose message blocks of size 4 and so take 10 messages $B1 = 0822$, $B2 = 0811$, $B3 = 1112$, $B4 = 0017$, $B5 = 1019$, $B6 = 0708$, $B7 = 1822$, $B8 = 0404$, $B9 = 1004$, $B10 = 1303$. (Note that if we had had only two digits in the last message, we would have added 00 to pad it out). Then $H1 = E(B1) = 2280$; $H2 = E(2280 + 0811) = E(3091) = 1903$; $H3 = E(1903 + 1112) = E(3015) = 5103$; $H4 = E(5103 + 0017) = E(5120) = 0215$; $H5 = E(0215 + 1019) = E(1234) = 4321$; $H6 = E(4321 + 0708) = E(5029) = 9205$; $H7 = E(9205 + 1822) = E(1027) = 7201$; $H8 = E(7201 + 0404) = E(7605) = 5067$; $H9 = E(5067 + 1004) = E(6071) = 1706$; $H10 = E(1706 + 1303) = E(3009) = 9003$.
   This is the final output of the hash function. (This problem could have been done by writing an algorithm.)

2. Feena wants to send Miriam the text string
   $D = xo45mn20ssthij69n0b81az375gheifkln39bid0m0spr0w$ and wants to make sure that Miriam knows it came from Feena and that it was not altered. Feena and Miriam have agreed beforehand on a secret value $s = mno$. Feena concatenates s with D to obtain D' and uses the MD5 hash function h to compute $h(D') = 1173b404b3d04efad863c28c6465d7da$ and sends this along with D to Miriam. Explain how Miriam checks that the message came from Feena and has not been altered. (Note: to calculate an MD5 hash, you can locate several websites which do this for you, or alternatively, see question 5 in Section 6.1.5.)
   Solution. When Miriam receives D and $h(D')$, she concatenates $s = mno$ with D to obtain D' and checks that the hash of this is the same as the hash she received. She obtains

$D' = xo45mn20ssthij69n0b81az375gheifkln39bid0m0spr0wmno$ and the
MD5 hash of this is $1173b404b3d04efad863c28c6465d7da$ that confirms that
Feena did indeed send this message and it has not been changed.

Further Reading. Chapter 11, Section 11.4 of [35] explains how messages are
preprocessed before the SHA-1 hash function is applied. Also, the compression function
is described in detail.

6.1.5 Problems

1. List four reasons for using a hash function.
2. Show that the function f of Example 6.1 has no collisions.
3. Explain why the function $g(x) = x^2 + 1$ is a poor choice for a hash function.
4. If the hash function h has 10,000 possible inputs and all outputs are 8-bits long, on average, how many inputs will have the same hash?
5. Try to find a collision with SHA-1 and MD4 by downloading HashCalc (for free) to your computer from http://www.slavasoft.com/hashcalc/ (Figure 6.6).
6. Find two text strings that differ in one place and whose hashes have no common places at all.
7. What is the minimum number of people in a classroom to ensure with 100% probability that two people have the same birthday?
8. On Tuesday, John receives a digital cheque from Mirna along with an encrypted hash function. He prints the cheque and takes it to the bank and the bank authenticates the fact that it came from Mirna, using Mirna's public key and checking the hash function, and debits her account. John puts the amount in his account. On Wednesday, John prints and takes the same cheque to the bank, and again it is authenticated and John deposits the money in his account. If Mirna only wanted John to cash the cheque once, how could she have prevented its reuse?
9. Veelasha and Saran share the same secret 001. Veelasha wants to send the message $m = 110100011$ to Saran using a MAC based on the encryption algorithm of Example 6.2. What does Saran receive and how does he confirm that it came from Veelasha?

Computer-Assisted Problems

10. Jodi wants to send Terry the message $m = ux571mnopffhi89s0dBA234$ and wants to make sure that Terry knows it came from Jodi and that it was not altered. They have agreed beforehand on a secret value $s = uU4$.
    Jodi concatenates s with m to obtain m' and uses the SHA-1 hash function h to compute $h(m') = 0f451dffc40384faabbb216fc4f2488e23b349ef$ and sends this along with m to Terry. Explain how Terry checks that the message came from Jodi and has not been altered.

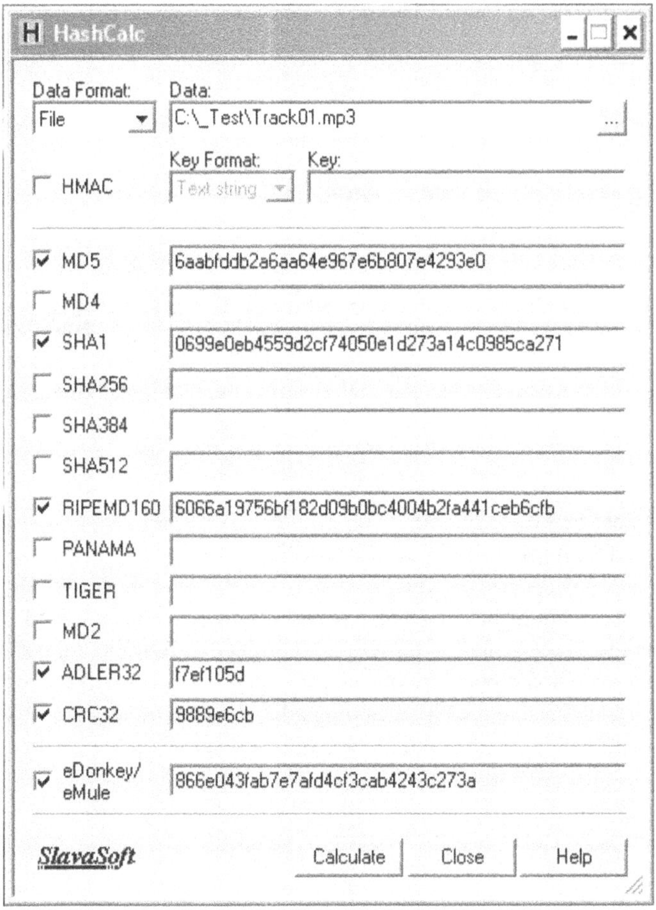

Figure 6.6. HashCalc.

11. Erik wants to send the message $m = 7am$ to Jessica and wants to make sure that she knows it came from Erik and that it was not altered. He also does not trust the channel that he is using and wants to keep the message secret using his RSA encryption scheme with private key $d = 48305$. He plans to send Jessica $d(m)$ and $h(m)$, where h is the hash function CRC32 (see question 5). To apply his RSA scheme with $n = 823091$, Erik first converts his message into a number using the standard alphabetic conversion modulo 26. He leaves 7 as a number and obtains 070012. Erik then computes $d(m) = 70012^{48305} \pmod{823091} \equiv 425992$ (we used Maple). He also computes $h(70012) = 0fe9d888$. (Note that he could also have computed the hash of m in its original format.) Jessica now receives $d(m)$ and $h(m)$ from Erik. She knows that he used his RSA scheme and she looks up his public parameters: ($n = 823091$, $e = 17$). Show how she

determines the message, she knows that it came from Erik and has not been changed.

12. Use the toy one-round version of MD5 as described in Example 6.5 to calculate the hash of 01011100000110000.

6.2 DIGITAL SIGNATURE SCHEMES

As we saw in the last section, Bob can check that the message he received is the one intended using a hash function. But if Alice sends him a message, how can he be sure it is Alice and not someone posing as Alice who sent it? A MAC using a common secret is one way to verify this; but it may not always be feasible to establish such a common secret. In this section, we look more closely at digital signatures. Digital signatures provide the ability to

- verify author, date, and time of signature,
- authenticate message content,
- be verified by third parties to resolve disputes.

A digital signature should be attached somehow to the message signed. It must use information unique to the sender to prevent both forgery and denial. It must be relatively easy to produce and should be relatively easy to recognize and verify.

A forgery could be achieved by attaching a legal signature to a new message or by attaching a fraudulent digital signature to a given message. Digital signatures should be computationally infeasible to forge.

Generally, there are two categories of digital signature schemes: those involving only the sender and receiver and those involving a third party.

- The first type is called a "direct" scheme.
- The second type is called an "arbitrated" scheme.

6.2.1 Direct Digital Signature Schemes

Direct signature schemes are useful in environments where the receiver is trusted by the sender. To bind the signature to the message, a sender first signs the message and then encrypts the signed message. The message itself need not be encrypted. The signature can be some digital information that identifies the sender, including a name. It is a good idea to add time and date information to the signature so that a receiver cannot argue that it was sent too late and has now become invalid. This may also prevent reuse of a document as in a digital cheque—see Problem 8 of Section 6.1.5.

However, in this type of scheme, the receiver could tamper with the message or signature after it was received and could claim that it was not properly signed. Direct digital signature schemes cannot manage this situation.

Let us suppose that Bob has a document that he sends in plaintext to Alice and asks her to sign. We show how this can be done with a direct signature scheme based on RSA.

6.2.2 Using RSA for Signing

Bob has a document m that Alice agrees to sign.

1. Alice generates two large primes p and q and computes $n = pq$. She chooses e_A such that $1 < e_A < \phi(n)$ with $\gcd(e_A, \phi(n)) = 1$ and calculates d_A such that $e_A d_A \equiv 1 \pmod{\phi(n)}$. She publishes (e_A, n) and keeps (d_A, p, q) secret.
2. Alice's signature is $y \equiv m^{d_A} \pmod{n}$.

She makes (m, y) public, and in particular, sends it to Bob. So Alice has "signed" the document m by raising it to her secret key d_A.

If m is bigger than n, she will have to break m into blocks and use a block-chaining approach as we saw in the previous section.

How Does Bob Verify that It was Alice Who Signed the Message?

1. He downloads Alice's public key (e_A, n).
2. He calculates $z \equiv y^{e_A} \pmod{n}$.

Of course, $y^{e_A} \equiv m^{d_A e_A} \equiv m \pmod{n}$.

So Bob has checked that only the private key known to Alice was used.

RSA Signature Variation—Blind Signature. In a variation of the above scheme, it is possible to get Alice to sign a document without knowing its contents. (This might be necessary in a legal situation where Alice simply "witnesses" the document, but does not need to know its contents.)

1. Alice chooses p, q, n, e_A, and d_A as above.
2. Bob has the message m that he wants Alice to sign without letting her see it. He chooses a random integer $k \pmod{n}$ with $\gcd(k, n) = 1$. He computes $t \equiv k^{e_A} m \pmod{n}$ and sends t to Alice.
3. Alice signs t by computing $s = t^{d_A} \pmod{n}$ and sends this back to Bob.
4. Bob computes $sk^{-1} \pmod{n}$:

$$sk^{-1} \equiv t^{d_A} k^{-1} \equiv k^{e_A d_A} m^{d_A} k^{-1} \equiv km^{d_A} k^{-1} \equiv m^{d_A} \pmod{n}.$$

So Bob has received the same signed message Alice would have sent if she had m.

The idea of using a random variable, as above, to "hide" things and then divide it out later is a common one.

Example 6.6 Alice chooses $p = 7919$ and $q = 101$. So $n = 799819$. She chooses $e = 9007$. So $d = 715143$ is the inverse. Now Bob sees e and n. He has a message $m = 57131$ that he wants Alice to sign, but not see. Bob now chooses a random $k = 5 \pmod{n}$ and computes $t \equiv k^e m \equiv 5^{9007} * 57131 \pmod{n}$. So $t = 465204$. He sends this to Alice and she signs it with d: $s = t^d \equiv 536325$. Alice sends s back to Bob. Bob confirms by checking $sk^{-1} \equiv 536325 * 5^{-1} \equiv 107265$ that should be m^d (mod n). He can check that $107265^e \equiv 57131$.

6.2.3 Using ElGamal for Signing

The ElGamal scheme can also be used for signing a document. In this scenario, we assume that Alice sees the document m.

1. As usual, she chooses a prime p and a primitive root α. She chooses a secret integer a, $1 < a \le p - 2$, and calculates $\beta \equiv \alpha^a$ (mod p). She publishes p, α, and β. The value of a is kept secret.
2. Alice selects a secret random k such that $\gcd(k, p - 1) = 1$. She computes $r \equiv \alpha^k$ (mod p), $0 < r < p$. She computes $s \equiv k^{-1}(m - ar)$ (mod $p - 1$). The signed message is the triple (m, r, s), that she sends to Bob.
3. Bob verifies the signature:
   he downloads (p, α, β) and computes $v_1 \equiv \beta^r r^s$ and $v_2 \equiv \alpha^m$ (mod p).

CLAIM: The signature is valid if and only if $v_1 \equiv v_2$ (mod p). We explain why: since $s \equiv k^{-1}(m - ar)$ (mod $p - 1$), we have $sk \equiv m - ar$, so $m \equiv sk + ar$ (mod $p - 1$). Thus, $v_2 \equiv \alpha^m \equiv \alpha^{sk+ar} \equiv (\alpha^k)^s(\alpha^a)^r \equiv r^s \beta^r$ (mod p). Note that for Eve to sign as Alice, she needs to know a. So this must be kept secret by Alice.

Example 6.7   Alice wants to sign $m = 151405$. She chooses $p = 225119$ and $\alpha = 11$. She chooses a secret a and computes $\beta \equiv \alpha^a \equiv 18191$ (mod p). To sign, she chooses a random k and computes $r \equiv \alpha^k \equiv 164130$ (mod p). Then $s = k^{-1}(m - ar) \equiv 130777$ (mod $p - 1$). Alice sends the triple $(m, r, s) = (151405, 164130, 130777)$ to Bob who can verify that it was really Alice who signed by comparing $\beta^r r^s$ and α^m (mod p).

6.2.4 Arbitrated Digital Signature Schemes

Definition 6.5 An *arbitrated digital signature scheme* is a digital signature scheme that requires a trusted third party as part of the signature generation and verification. Such a scheme is used to deal with situations where the receiver may not be trusted.

Note that a trusted third party in this situation both helps to generate a signature and then to determine (independently of the sender) that the signature is valid. This requires a suitable level of trust in the arbiter. It can be implemented with either private key algorithms or public key algorithms and the arbiter may or may not see the message.

For those wishing to read further about the use of arbitration in digital signatures, we refer to the *Handbook of Applied Cryptography* [29].

6.2.5 The Digital Signature Standard

The NIST is a U.S. Federal Technology Agency that develops and promotes measurement, standards, and technology to improve security and quality of life (see http://www.nist.gov). NIST has developed a number of cryptographic standards including one for a digital signature, which they call the *Digital Signature Algorithm* or **DSA**. The DSA was designed by NIST in conjunction with the U.S. National Security Agency in the early 90s, revised in 1993, 1996 and then again in 2000. It is based on the discrete logarithm problem and is a variant of the ElGamal digital signature scheme. SHA-1 is the recommended hash function to be used with it.

The distinctive difference between this scheme and the ElGamal scheme is that DSA works in a proper subgroup of the full group modulo p in order to make the computations faster. There is an underlying assumption that it is no easier to attack the subgroup than the full group.

Definition 6.6 A *subgroup* of a group G under an operation "." is a subset of G which itself forms a group under "." . (See Definition 3.2.)

As a consequence of Theorem 3.1, we know that the set of all nonzero elements modulo a prime forms a group under multiplication. We base the next example on this fact.

Example 6.8 The set of integers modulo the prime $p = 48731$ forms a group G under multiplication if we ignore 0. This group has 48730 elements. We now look for a subgroup of G. Note that Euler's Theorem implies that $g^{48730} \equiv 1 \pmod{48731}$ for any element g of G. It follows by Proposition 3.3, that the order of any element in G must divide 48730. We, therefore, take a look at the factors of 48730: $2 * 5 * 11 * 443$. Thus any element of G has order 1 (the identity itself), or some product of the factors of 48730. Is it possible for all elements of G to have order 48730? Theorem 3.1 and Proposition 3.3 say no: because each such element would be a primitive root, there are only $\phi(\phi(48730)) = 6144$ of them. So all other elements of G must have smaller order. We try $g = 1234$ in G. The Maple command produces order$(1234, 48731) = 24365 = 5 * 11 * 443$. Thus, the set of all elements which are powers of 1234 in G produce a subgroup of G with 24365 elements. For instance, $1234^{62} \equiv 15980$ is in this subgroup. We leave it as an exercise to show that the definition of subgroup is satisfied (see the problem set).

The DSA has three components: key generation, signature generation, and signature verification. We show each of them here.

DSA Key Generation

Alice picks and publishes (p, q, g, y):

- she chooses p, a 160 bit prime;
- she chooses a large prime q, which divides $p - 1$;

- she chooses a primitive root h (mod p) and computes $g = h^{(p-1)/q}$ (mod p)
  - so $g^q = 1$ (mod p);
- she chooses a secret a between 1 and $q - 1$ and calculates $y = g^a$ (mod p).

In both signature generation and verification below, Alice and Bob work in the subgroup modulo q of the group modulo p.

Signature Generation

To sign the message M Alice:

- generates a random signature key $k, k < q$.

Then she computes a signature pair:

- $r = (g^k \pmod{p}) \pmod{q}$.

(In determining r, an initial computation is done (mod p) and then this is reduced (mod q).)

- $s = k^{-1}(H(M) + ar) \pmod{q}$, where H is a hash of M.

Note that k^{-1} is computed modulo q. Also H needs to be a function that maps to an integer computable modulo q.

Alice sends Bob the signature (r, s) with the message M.

Signature Verification

Bob receives M and the signature (r, s). To *verify* Alice's signature, he computes

- $w = s^{-1} \pmod{q}$,
- $u_1 = (H(M)w) \pmod{q}$,
- $u_2 = (rw) \pmod{q}$,
- $v = (g^{u_1} y^{u_2} \pmod{p}) \pmod{q}$.

(Here again, an initial computation is done (mod p) and then this is reduced (mod q).)

If $v = r$ then the signature is verified.

Verification works because we have $H(M) = -ar + ks \pmod{q}$. So $wH(M) = -arw + k \pmod{q}$. Therefore,

- $k = wH(M) + arw \pmod{q} = u_1 + au_2$ and so
- $g^k = g^{u_1 + au_2} = (g^{u_1} y^{u_2} \pmod{p}) \pmod{q}$.

Thus, $v = r$.

See Computer Example 3 of Section 6.2.1 for an example of how someone would set up a digital signature based on the DSA, and in particular, how she would deal with the hash function.

Example 6.9   We work through the three stages of the DSA with small primes. Also, to simplify the computation, we do not hash the message. Let $p = 23$ and $q = 11$ (so $11|(23 - 1)$ is satisfied). We choose a primitive root 5 modulo 23 and use it to produce $g = h^{(p-1)/q} \equiv 2 \pmod{23}$. From the secret $a = 3$, we get $y = g^a \equiv 8 \pmod{23}$. Now Alice posts ($p = 23$, $q = 11$, $g = 2$, $y = 8$).

Alice now uses her DSA setup to sign the message $M = 7$; M is chosen in the smaller group F_{11}^* (the nonzero elements modulo 11). She chooses a random value k, also in F_{11}^*, say $k = 5$, and computes

$$r = (g^k \pmod{p})(\bmod\ q) \equiv (32 \pmod{p})(\bmod\ q) \equiv 9$$

and

$$s = k^{-1}(M + ar)(\bmod\ q) \equiv 9 * 34 \equiv 9 \pmod{11}.$$

Alice now sends ($r = 9$, $s = 9$, $M = 7$) to Bob who confirms that Alice has signed M by computing g^k in two ways. First of all, $r = g^k$, by definition, was received by Bob. Second, Bob uses s, which contains Alice's secret a:

$$v = g^{u_1} y^{u_2}, \quad \text{where,} \quad u_1 = M * s^{-1} \pmod{11} = 7 * 9^{-1} \equiv 2$$

$$\text{and} \quad u_2 = r * s^{-1} \pmod{11} = 9 * 9^{-1} \equiv 1.$$

So $v = (2^2 * 8^1 \pmod{p})(\bmod\ q) \equiv 9$.

Since $v = r$, Bob knows that Alice did sign the message.

6.2.6 Computer Examples

1. Bob has a document $m = 103$ that Alice agrees to sign. The document must be signed within 1 week, that is, by March 11, 2012. He appends this date as 1103 to m to get 1031103 and sends this to Alice. Show how Alice signs using her RSA scheme and how Bob confirms that she signed.

   Solution.   Alice uses an RSA scheme based on primes 1223 and 1987, so $n = 2430101$. Her public key is $e_A = 948047$. Her decryption key is $d_A = 1051235$.

   Alice's signature on the dated message is $y = 1031103^{1051235} \pmod{2430101} = 1160264$. She sends this to Bob.

   We show how Bob verifies that it was Alice who signed the message:

   He first downloads Alice's public key (948047, 2430101), and then he calculates $z = 1160264^{948047} \pmod{2430101} = 1031103$. So Bob has checked that only the private key known to Alice was used.

2. Alice's public ElGamal parameters are $p = 641$, $\alpha = 3$ and $y = 3^a = 88$ where a is her secret key. Zoe wants to send the message $m = 121$ to Bob pretending to be Alice. She does not know Alice's secret key a, so she uses her own, z. She generates $\beta = 3^k \equiv 480 \pmod{p}$ and $\gamma = (121 - 480z)k^{-1} \pmod{p-1} \equiv 532$, where k is a random number relatively prime to $p - 1$. Bob receives (480, 532) along with $m = 121$ (the order in the pair is important!). Show how he knows that the message did not come from Alice.

   Solution. To verify Alice's signature has been used, he computes 3^{121} $\pmod{641} \equiv 300$ and $88^{480} * 480^{532} \pmod{641} \equiv 191$. Since they do not match; he knows Alice did not sign.

3. Carol uses the DSA with public parameters $(22531, 751, 4488, 1467 = 4488^{321} \pmod{22531})$. We determine her signature on the document $M = 816$. (Note that we do not know the primitive root she used. Her secret a is the exponent 321.)

   Solution. Carol must choose $k < 751$ to compute r and s as above. Suppose that she chooses $k = 700$. Then $r = (4488^{700} \pmod{22531})$ $\pmod{751}$. We use Maple to obtain $r = 13929 \pmod{751} = 411$.

   Now $s = 700^{-1}(H(816) + 321 * 411) \pmod{751}$, where H is chosen to be SHA-1. First of all, $700^{-1} \pmod{751} = 589$. Also, SHA-1 applied to 816 as a text string yields

   $$f022da4e40566305c0c8f39fd8f4b83dd5368834.$$

To obtain a numerical value from this, we do a simple translation of ASCII (the American Standard Code for Information Interchange) that takes characters $0 - 9$ to $48 - 57$, lower case a – z to $97 - 122$, and upper case A – Z to $65 - 90$. The result is $H(M) = 10248505010097521015248535454514853994899561025157102100561025298383310010035333638383334$, which is 657 modulo 751. Therefore, $s = 589(657 + 321 * 411) \pmod{751} = 95$. Thus, Carol's signature on 816 is (411, 95).

Further Reading. *The Handbook of Applied Cryptography* [29] provides an introduction to digital signatures on pages 22 and 23 and specifically deals with arbitrated digital signatures on pages 472 and 473. This last page describes ESIGN, a digital signature scheme with security based on the difficulty of integer factoring. The DSA is presented on page 452 of [29] and an example given on page 453. On page 446 of [19], an example of the DSA is provided. In [28], an example is presented and examined on pages 158 and 159, and is then written in the open-source language Sage on pages 160 and 161.

6.2.7 Problems

1. Let G be the group Z/p^* under multiplication, where p is a prime and zero has been removed from the set Z/p. Let g be any element of G. Show that the set of all positive integer powers of g forms a subgroup of G.

2. Jo has a message $m = 57131$ that he wants Eddie to sign but not see. Eddie uses an RSA scheme with $n = 2430101$. His encryption key is $e = 948047$; his decryption key is $d = 1051235$. Jo chooses a random number $k = 7 \pmod{n}$ and computes $t = k^e m = 7^{948047} 57131 \equiv 2173015 \pmod{2430101}$. Jo sends $t = 2173015$ to Eddie. Show how Eddie signs m without seeing it and how Jo confirms the signature.

3. Alice derives an ElGamal signature scheme using $p = 5023, \alpha = 5$ and $y = 5^a = 3796$. Her computations yield $\beta = 5^r \equiv 2294$ and $\gamma = (444 - 2294a)r^{-1} \equiv 3740$, where $m = 444$ is the message. Determine if Bob should accept the signed message as valid.

4. Go to http://www.nist.gov/index.html and describe NIST from this website. Locate NIST's cryptographic algorithm testing page. Locate the DSS document written by NIST in 2000. Which hash function is recommended? Give the page number where this is written.

Computer-Assisted Problems

5. Jeremy does not trust Mattia, to whom he must send a signed message. To allow for arbitration in case of a dispute, he uses an ElGamal scheme in which he publishes his public keys $p = 225119, \alpha = 11$, and $\beta = \alpha^a \equiv 18191 \pmod{p}$, where a is his secret key. However, to sign $m = 35991$, he engages a trusted third party, Felicia, to provide him with a random value k, relatively prime to $p - 1$, and to compute $r = \alpha^k$. Jeremy now sends Felicia $m - ar$ and she computes $s \equiv k^{-1} (m - ar) \pmod{p - 1}$ and sends this to Jeremy. Jeremy now sends (m, r, s) to Mattia. Explain (i) why Mattia cannot claim that Jeremy did not sign correctly and (ii) why Felicia cannot determine Jeremy's secret a.

6. Using Carol's signature $(411, 95)$ on $M = 816$ in Example 3 of Section 6.2.1, show how Jackie, who receives both of these, would verify that Carol's signature was indeed used.

6.3 ATTACKS ON DIGITAL SIGNATURES

In this section, we look at some of the attacks possible on digital signatures. The first one is based on the very simple concept of the Birthday Paradox, essentially described in Section 6.1.

6.3.1 The Birthday Attack

Since, in general, hash functions map long strings to much shorter strings, collisions are expected. The Birthday Paradox can be used to estimate the probability of collisions. The next proposition and its corollary show us how to use such collisions in an attack. Compare them with Proposition 6.1.

Proposition 6.2   *A basket contains N balls, n of which are red and $N - n$ of which are green. One at a time, m balls are randomly taken from the basket, checked for colour, and then replaced. The probability that at least one red ball was taken out is $1 - (1 - n/N)^m$.*

Proof. We count the probability that none of the m balls pulled from the basket is red. (This is one minus the probability that every one of them is green.) Now Pr(a green ball being taken) $= (N - n)/N$ and so the probability that all m balls taken are green, since they are replaced and can be taken again, is $((N - n)/N)^m$. Therefore, the probability of pulling a red ball in m tries is $1 - ((N - n)/N)^m$, which is the same as the stated formula.   □

Corollary 6.1   *Two tables each contain M items labeled 1 to M. A selection of m items is taken from each table. The probability of taking two entries with the same label is $1 - ((M - m)/M)^m$.*

Proof. Name the tables Table 1 and Table 2. First we select the m items from Table 2, note their labels, take the items in Table 1 with those same labels and paint them red. From here on, we ignore Table 2. Now we consider Table 1 to be the "basket" of Proposition 6.2 and consider the $M - m$ items not painted red to be painted green. By the proposition, the probability of choosing a red item from Table 1 is $1 - ((M - m)/M)^m$. This is the desired probability.   □

Example 6.10   Suppose a hash function h with hash output of length 64 bits is used by Jo to sign messages. Cleo wants to get Jo to sign a fraudulent message. She generates 2^{32} variations of a valid message, all with essentially the same meaning, and produces their hashes. She also produces 2^{32} variations of a fraudulent message along with their hashes. We determine the probability that one of the fraudulent messages has the same hash as one of the valid messages. To match our example with Corollary 6.1, first note that there are 2^{64} possible hash values in all. We consider two tables, named 1 and 2, that contain all of the hash values (the hash values are the labels of items in the table). Now we select the 2^{32} items from each table that were labeled with hash values of the messages generated by Cleo. By the Corollary, the probability of a collision is $1 - ((2^{64} - 2^{32})/2^{64})^{2^{32}} = 0.34916$. So Cleo has a good chance of convincing Jo to sign a fraudulent message. She can increase the probability by producing more hashes, say 2^{40}.

If the hash output in Example 6.10 were 128 bits, the above attack is much harder to implement as the attacker must generate a very large number of hashes and store them. (See the computer examples and problems.) Current attacks on hash functions typically focus on collisions on the rounds used in compression [11].

6.3.2 Intruder-in-the-Middle Attack

Oscar has recently learned to play chess and claims that he can play against two grandmasters simultaneously and either win one game or draw both games. He lets one grandmaster $G1$ move first and moves first himself with the other one $G2$. When $G1$ moves, Oscar makes the identical move with $G2$. He then waits for $G2$ to move before making that same move with $G1$. So Oscar actually has $G1$ and $G2$ playing against each other. If $G1$ plays a final winning move, Oscar can play that same move against $G2$ to win. If Oscar and $G1$ draw, then so will Oscar and $G2$. (Oscar does not expect to win against $G1$!)

Oscar has been using the "intruder-in-the-middle" attack (also known as the "man-in-the-middle" attack) against two chess grandmasters. We define this ploy more formally:

Definition 6.7   An *Intruder-in-the-Middle (IITM) attack* is an attack whereby two people (or computers) believe that they are communicating directly with each other, whereas all communication between the two is intercepted by a third party, the Intruder, who receives and forwards messages between the two parties.

An intruder-in-the-middle can, therefore, read all messages from both parties. Even if these messages are encrypted, we assume that Oscar was involved in setting up the key agreement and so knows all necessary keys.

If you get an e-mail telling you to go to a website and update account information, how can you be sure that the website is legitimate? It is very easy to use an intruder-in-the-middle attack and set up a false website that records your details and sends them to Eve. A similar attack can be played against many cryptographic systems. Here, we look at how this can be done with Diffie–Hellman key exchange, which we saw in Chapter 2.

6.3.3 Intruder-in-the-Middle and Diffie–Hellman

Alice and Bob agree on a prime p and a primitive root g (which can both be public). Each selects a random number, say Alice chooses x and Bob chooses y, where $0 < x, y < p - 1$. They compute g^x and g^y and send them to each other. Each then generates a (symmetric) session key $K = g^{xy}$, which is used both for encryption and decryption.

Now put Eve in the middle. She intercepts g^x and g^y that are not received by Bob and Alice. Instead, she sends each of them the same g^z for some z. So Alice actually computes g^{xz} and Bob computes g^{yz} while Eve can compute both of these too. Now Eve can sit quietly and un-noticed read all messages between Alice and Bob as follows: Alice sends a message encrypted with g^{xz} to Bob but Eve intercepts it, decrypts it with g^{xz}, reads it, encrypts it with g^{yz} and sends it to Bob.

The standard way to stop this attack by Eve is to use an arbitrated digital signature scheme. This involves a trusted third party (whom we will call Trent) who will authenticate the other parties. So we get an "authenticated key agreement scheme." Each user now has a digital signature, which they will use to sign. For each signature, Trent has a verification algorithm that he applies to confirm (or not) the signature.

Alice and Bob set up everything as before and send each other g^x and g^y. So Eve could still intercept. However, before they proceed to use the resulting key K, each of them verifies the signatures on the exchanged keys as follows:

- Bob sends $K(sig B(g^x, g^y))$ to Alice.
- Alice applies K again to obtain $sig B(g^x, g^y)$. (Eve could still be in the middle to this point!)

Now Alice asks Trent to verify that this is Bob's signature.

If Eve has intercepted, she has both g^x and g^y but does not know $sig B$. If she applies some other signature to g^x and g^y then the verification $ver B$ would not verify it.

It is important that Trent be trusted. He could actually be an "Eve" in disguise!

Example 6.11 Nam and Paulo hire Trent, a trusted third party, to assist them in setting up a common symmetric key. Oscar does not know that they have hired a trusted third party, and he proceeds to use the intruder-in-the-middle attack to capture their key.

Nam and Paulo agree on a prime $p = 2663$ and a primitive root $g = 2$ and each selects a random number; Nam chooses $x = 1085$ and Paulo chooses $y = 1701$. They compute $g^x \equiv 252$ and $g^y \equiv 1524$ (mod 2663) and send them to each other. Oscar intercepts and sends each his value $g^z \equiv 2^{101} \equiv 1352$ (mod 2663). Thus, Oscar generates the key $K_1 = g^{xz} \equiv 121$ with Nam and the key $K_2 = g^{yz} \equiv 41$ with Paulo.

Trent has provided both Nam and Paulo with digital signatures sigN and sigP, respectively. Nam and Paulo proceed to verify that their keys are correct

- Nam sends $K_1(sigN(g^x, g^z))$ to Paulo, but this is intercepted by Oscar, who has K_1 and applies it to get $sigN(g^x, g^z)$. Since Oscar does not know sigN or its inverse, all he can do is apply K_2 and hope for the best. He forwards $K_2(sigN(g^x, g^z))$ to Paulo.
- Paulo receives $K_2(sigN(g^x, g^z))$ and applies K_2 again to obtain $sigN(g^x, g^z)$. He asks Trent to verify that the message has been sent with Nam's signature and also asks Trent for the message. Trent applies the inverse of Nam's signature, revealing the pair (g^x, g^z). This confirms that Nam's signature was used, but Paulo does not recognize g^x. So he suspects that someone has interfered and contacts Nam to re-establish a new common key.

6.3.4 An Attack on RSA Signatures: What if Eve Uses Alice's Signature?

Note that in the RSA signature scheme, Alice's signature, $y = m^{d_A}$, was made public. Since y uses both the message m and d_A, if an attacker Eve wants to reuse y with another message, it will not work.

However, Eve can do the following:

Eve chooses y_1 first and then takes Alice's public key e_A. She computes $m_1 = y_1^{e_A}$ (mod n). She then sends m_1 and y_1 to Bob, pretending that she is Alice. Bob receives these, computes $y_1^{e_A}$ and, of course, gets m_1. So he believes the message came from Alice.

While there is nothing to stop Eve from doing this, if she first chooses y_1 as above and applies e_A, her resulting message m_1, will likely be garbage. Her real challenge is to start with a sensible message m_1, use Alice's e_A and find a y_1 that fits the modulus equation. But this is difficult.

Example 6.12 Eve knows about the birthday paradox and decides to use it to trick Jimmie into believing that he has received a message from Sven.

She generates 2^{16} variations of a valid message, all with essentially the same meaning, and computes them modulo $n = 3398909$, which is the RSA modulus that Jimmie uses in his digital signature scheme.

She also randomly takes 2^{16} values y modulo n and, for each of them, computes y^{e_J} (mod n), where e_J is Jimmie's public RSA key.

We determine the probability that a valid message will be a match for some y to Jimmie's public key using the corollary to Proposition 6.2. Each table contains the $n = 3398909$ numbers modulo n. Note that $2^{16} < 2^{21} < n < 2^{22}$. By the corollary, the probability of a collision is $1 - ((2^n - 2^{16})/2^n)^{2^{16}}$, which is very close to 1.0. Eve can, therefore, choose a valid message as a power of some y to Jimmie's public key and send it to Sven, who will believe that it came from Jimmie.

6.3.5 Protecting ElGamal with Signatures

We first review the ElGamal encryption scheme.

Alice's public key is $(p, \alpha, y = \alpha^a)$, where p is a prime, α is a primitive root, and her secret is a.

She chooses a random $r \in [1, p - 2]$.

She computes $\beta \equiv \alpha^r$ (mod p) and, given a message m modulo $p - 1$ to sign, she computes $\gamma \equiv (m - a\beta)r^{-1}$ (mod $p - 1$).

She sends (β, γ, m) to Bob. (Notice that at this stage, if Bob had r, he could get a and conversely.)

The pair (β, γ) represents the signed message; Bob will check that this matches m.

Bob needs to check also that only Alice could have provided the pair (β, γ) for the message m. So her private key must have been used.

To confirm this, he needs to use her public key to check to see if two values match:

- He computes α^m (mod p) directly (recall that m is modulo $p - 1$).
- He then computes $y^\beta \beta^\gamma$ (mod p) $\equiv \alpha^{a\beta}\alpha^{r(m-a\beta)r^{-1}} \equiv \alpha^{a\beta}\alpha^{m-a\beta} = \alpha^m$.

So the two values match.

The first computation just used m, but the second relied on using Alice's secret key a. Notice that computations in the exponent are done modulo $\phi(p)$.

6.3.6 Oscar Tries to Trick Bob

Oscar has shown up again and wants to harass Bob by sending strange messages that seem to come from Bob's colleagues. Here is how he sends Bob something from Alice.

Oscar uses Alice's ElGamal setup with her public key $(p, \alpha, y = \alpha^a)$.

He picks random values $r_1, r_2 \in [1, p - 2]$.

He computes $\beta_1 \equiv \alpha^{r_1}y^{r_2}$ (mod p) and $\gamma_1 \equiv -\beta_1 r_2^{-1}$ (mod $p - 1$).

Oscar then sends (β_1, γ_1) with message $m_1 = \gamma_1 r_1$ (mod $p - 1$) to Bob.

Bob receives the message and verifies in the usual way: $y^{\beta_1}\beta_1^{\gamma_1}$ (mod p) $\equiv \alpha^{m_1}$.

These give the same value. Hence, Bob is sure the message came from Alice.

If Oscar chooses his message m_1 first, then in order to execute this attack, he must choose his r_1 and r_2 such that $m_1 = -\alpha^{r_1} y^{r_2} r_2^{-1} r_1$, where α and y are specified by Alice's public key. This is very difficult to do, and so his messages to Bob will not make sense. Bob will, of course, then check directly with Alice and discover that Oscar has been playing tricks.

6.3.7 Oscar Captures a Message with a Signed Version

Suppose Oscar has captured a message m from Alice (intended for Bob), along with the signed version (β, γ) (even if a hash has been used). Oscar checks if m^{-1} exists (modulo $p - 1$). If yes, he proceeds to pick his own message m_1.

Oscar then computes $t = m_1 m^{-1} \pmod{p-1}$ and $\gamma_1 = t\gamma \pmod{p-1}$.

Since $\gcd(p-1, p) = 1$, Oscar can use the CRT to compute a solution to the system

$x \equiv \beta t \pmod{p-1}$
$x \equiv \beta \pmod{p}$.

He calls this solution β_1.

Oscar now sends (β_1, γ_1) and m_1 to Bob knowing that he will use Alice's parameter setup to verify. Bob in fact computes $\alpha^{m_1} \pmod{p}$ and

$$y^{\beta_1} \beta_1^{\gamma_1} \equiv \alpha^{a\beta_1} \beta^{t\gamma} \equiv \alpha^{a\beta t} \alpha^{rt\gamma} \equiv \alpha^{t(a\beta + r\gamma)}$$

$$\equiv \alpha^{tm} \equiv \alpha^{m_1 m^{-1} m} \equiv \alpha^{m_1} \pmod{p}.$$

So the verification is confirmed.

However, Oscar needs to be lucky on two counts to pull this off: first, he needs $m^{-1} \pmod{p-1}$; second, his CRT solution β_1 will be (mod $p(p-1)$) and so in general will be outside Z_p. Bob always should reject the message if the parameters of the message received are not in the correct range.

Example 6.13 Oscar has captured the message $m = 487$ along with the signed pair $\beta = 1723$ and $\gamma = 7045$ in Alice's scheme with $p = 7481$, $\alpha = 6$ and $y = 5979$. He checks that m^{-1} exists mod $(p-1)$ and since it does, proceeds to choose his own message $m_1 = 2222$. We show how Oscar can now fraudulently attach Alice's signature to this message and how Bob might suspect that Oscar has used this attack.

Oscar computes $m^{-1} = 983 \pmod{7480}$ and $t = m_1 m^{-1} \pmod{p-1} = 66$ and $\gamma_1 = t\gamma \pmod{p-1} = 1210$.

Oscar now uses the CRT to compute a solution β_1 to the system

$$x = \beta t \pmod{p-1} = 1518$$

$$x = \beta \pmod{p} = 1723.$$

We can use Maple to do this for us:
> *chrem*([1518, 1723], [7480, 7481]); 54425998.
Oscar now sends (54425998, 1210) and 2222 to Bob.

Bob may notice that one of the values that he receives is larger than the prime p used and so be suspicious that Oscar has been meddling with his messages. On the other hand, if he fails to check this, he will simply compute $y^{\beta} \beta^{\gamma} \pmod{p} = \alpha^m$ and verify Alice's signature.

6.3.8 Alice Reuses a Random Number

As in the ElGamal encryption scheme, it is important that Alice not reuse a random number.

If she does, here is what Oscar can do.

If r is used for two message m_1 and m_2, then the signed messages are (β, γ_1) and (β, γ_2). $\beta = \alpha^r$ and $\gamma_1 = (m_1 - a\beta)r^{-1}$, $\gamma_2 = (m_2 - a\beta)r^{-1}$ (mod $p-1$).

Oscar knows (we can assume) m_1, m_2, β, γ_1, and γ_2.

Oscar computes $\gcd(p-1, \gamma_2 - \gamma_1) = g$, say. He then looks for an equation involving $\gamma_2 - \gamma_1$.

Now $\alpha^{m_2 - m_1} \equiv \beta^{\gamma_2 - \gamma_1} \equiv \alpha^{r(\gamma_2 - \gamma_1)}$ (mod p).

So the exponents on the generator α must be equal (mod $p-1$): $m_2 - m_1 \equiv r(\gamma_2 - \gamma_1)$ (mod $p-1$).

Since $g|(p-1)$ and $g|(\gamma_2 - \gamma_1)$, g must divide $m_2 - m_1$ and we can write

$$(m_2 - m_1)/g \equiv r(\gamma_2 - \gamma_1)/g \ (\text{mod} \ (p-1)/g).$$

Recall: This is in integers; we do not compute g^{-1}!

Now Oscar has r since in the modulus, $r = [(m_2 - m_1)/g][(\gamma_2 - \gamma_1)/g]^{-1}$ (mod $(p-1)/g$). And recall that once Oscar has r, he has Alice's secret a and can now impersonate her.

Example 6.14   For the same El Gamal setup with $\alpha = 2$ and $p = 103$, Zoe reuses her random number r to sign two messages : $m_1 = 45$ and $m_2 = 91$ that she sends to Alan. The signed messages are $(32, \gamma_1 = 43, 45)$ and $(32, \gamma_2 = 93, 91)$.

Alan sees that the first entries of each triple are the same and so knows that Zoe has reused her random number. He computes $\gcd(p-1, \gamma_2 - \gamma_1) = \gcd(102, 93 - 43) = 2$.

He sets $m_2 - m_1 \equiv r(\gamma_2 - \gamma_1)$ (mod $p-1$), or $46 \equiv r * (93 - 43)$ (mod 102) and is able to divide through by 2 to obtain $23 = r * 25$ (mod 51).

Alan can now solve for Zoe's random number r : $23 * 25^{-1}$ (mod 51) $= 5$. Since we reduced $p-1$ by 2, either $r \equiv 5$ (mod 102) or $r \equiv 51 + 5$ (mod 102). Alan only needs to check $\beta = 2^r$ (mod 103) to see that $r = 5$ is correct. Alan can now compute Zoe's secret a from $\gamma_1 = (m_1 - a\beta)r^{-1}$, or $43 \equiv (45 - a * 32) * 41$ (mod 102) which gives $a \equiv (45 - 43 * 41^{-1}) * 32^{-1}$ (mod 102). However, we cannot take the inverse of 32 modulo 102, and so we step back to obtain: $32a \equiv (45 - 43 * 41^{-1}) \equiv 34$ (mod 102) and then divide through by 2s to obtain $16a \equiv 17$ (mod 51) giving $a = 17$. Again, we need to check the two values of a: 17 and $17 + 51 = 68$ modulo 102. The first is correct.

6.3.9 Computer Examples

1. This example is a slight variation of Example 6.10. Suppose a hash function h with hash output of length 64 bits is used by Jo to sign messages. Cleo wants to get Jo to sign a fraudulent message. She generates 2^{33} variations of a valid message, all with essentially the same meaning, and also produces their hashes.

She also generates 2^{33} variations of a fraudulent message along with their hashes. What is the probability that a legitimate message will have the same hash as some fraudulent message?

Solution. Cleo has chosen 2^{33} hashes from each of the message sets. By the Corollary, the probability of a collision is $1 - (1 - 2^{33}/2^{64})^{2^{33}}$, which is approximately 0.9864. (Use decimal values 1.0, and so on if your software will not compute.)

2. Oscar, the attacker, uses Alice's scheme setup parameters $p = 5023$, $\alpha = 5$, and $y = 5^a = 3796$. Oscar picks random $r_1, r_2 \in [1, p - 2]$, $r_1 = 205$, and $r_2 = 1021$. He computes $\beta_1 = 5^{205}3796^{1021} \pmod{p} = 1287$ and $\gamma_1 = -\beta_1 r_2^{-1} = -1287 * 4417 \pmod{p - 1} = 225$. Oscar then sends (β_1, γ_1) with message $m_1 = \gamma_1 r_1 = 927 \pmod{p - 1}$ to Bob. Show why Bob thinks this message has been signed by Alice.

Solution. Bob checks by computing $5^{927} \pmod{5023} \equiv 600$ and also $y^\beta \beta^\gamma$ $\pmod{p} = 3796^{1287}1287^{225} \equiv 600$. Since the two computations match, Bob will assume that Alice signed this message.

3. For the same ElGamal setup with $\alpha = 2$ and $p = 2357$, Ari reuses his random number r on two messages: $m_1 = 132$ and $m_2 = 678$ that he sends to Jennie. Show how Jennie obtains Ari's random number from the signed versions $(1779, \gamma_1 = 643, 132)$ and $(1779, \gamma_2 = 669, 678)$.

Solution. Jennie notices that the triples have the same first values and so she knows that Ari has reused his random value. She has Ari's public information $(2357, 2, 799)$. She computes $\gcd(p - 1, \gamma_2 - \gamma_1) = \gcd(2356, 26) = 2$.
She sets $m_2 - m_1 \equiv r(\gamma_2 - \gamma_1) \pmod{p - 1}$, or $546 \equiv 26r \pmod{2356}$ and is able to divide through by 2 to obtain $273 \equiv 13r \pmod{1178}$.

Alan can now solve for Zoe's random number r: $273 * 13^{-1} \pmod{1178} \equiv 21$. Since he reduced $p - 1$ by 2, either $r \equiv 21$ or $r \equiv 1178 + 21 \pmod{2356}$. Alan only needs to check $\beta = 2^r \pmod{2357}$ to see that $r = 21$ is correct.

Further Reading. Paar and Pelzl [35] give a clear analysis in Section 10.4.3 of their book of the computational effort needed to attack the DSA. An attacker might try to sove the discrete logarithm in the larger group modulo p, or in the smaller group, modulo q. However, the attacks available do not apply equally to both situations and, as explained in [35], the attack complexities are comparable when the sizes of p and q are appropriately chosen.

Mao [27], Section 10.4.9, discusses the need for a better formatlisation of provable security for digital signatures. Menezes et al. [29] discuss more esoteric digital signature schemes such as "short signatures," "blind signatures," and "group signatures."

To summarize the problems that can be encountered in using digital signatures with the ElGamal scheme:

- *do not reuse random numbers;*
- *check that values are in the correct range;*
- *hash the message.*

6.3.10 Problems

1. In Example 6.10, suppose the hash function h has hash output of length 128 bits. Write the formula for the probability of a collision if Cleo produces 2^{32} hashes of both types of message.

2. Morshed uses an RSA scheme with modulus $n = 2430101$ and public key 948047. For added security when signing documents, he will only sign documents that, when converted in a number modulo n, are even and that are also even when signed with his private key. You know this arrangement, but nevertheless, want to send Malcolm a signed document and pretend that it came from Morshed. Explain how you do it.

3. This problem is based on Example 2 of Section 6.3.9. In this case, Oscar, the attacker, uses Alice's scheme setup parameters $p = 5023$, $\alpha = 5$ and $y = 5^a = 3796$. Oscar picks random $r_1, r_2 \in [1, p-2]$, $r_1 = 205$, and $r_2 = 1021$. He computes $\beta_1 = 5^{205}3796^{1021} \pmod{p} = 1287$ and $\gamma_1 = -\beta_1 r_2^{-1} = -1287 * 4417 \pmod{p-1} = 225$. Oscar then sends (β_1, γ_1) with message $m_1 = \gamma_1 r_1 = 927 \pmod{p-1}$ to Bob. Show why Bob thinks this message has been signed by Alice.

Computer-Assisted Problems

4. Oscar has captured the message $m = 487$ along with the signed pair $\beta = 1723$ and $\gamma = 7045$ in Alice's scheme with $p = 7481, \alpha = 6$, and $y = 5979$. He checks that m^{-1} exists mod $(p-1)$ and since it does, proceeds to choose his own message $m_1 = 1011$. Show how Oscar can now fraudulently attach Alice's signature to this message.

5. For the ElGamal setup with $\alpha = 11$ and $p = 3359$, Amanda reuses her random number r on two messages: $m_1 = 1321$ and $m_2 = 1678$ that she sends to Lisbeth. Show how Lisbeth obtains Amanda's random number from the signed versions $(646, \gamma_1 = 551, 1321)$ and $(646, \gamma_2 = 930, 1678)$.

6. In Example 1 of Section 6.3.9, suppose the hash function h has hash output of length 128 bits. Find a bound for the number of hashes that Cleo should compute for each set of messages to get the probability of a match near 0.5.

7. Eve combines the birthday attack with an RSA digital signature attack on Oscar. She generates 2^4 valid messages modulo $437(= 19 * 23)$, which is Oscar's RSA modulus. Oscar's encryption key is 31. Determine the probability of a match as in Example 6.12, and find a match.

7

PRIMALITY TESTING

As we saw in earlier chapters, prime numbers are essential to the construction of the cryptographic algorithms upon which much of the security available in computer and Internet systems used in everyday life is based. We do not know very much about prime numbers in fact. For example, given a random large number, there is no fast and easy test which tells you that it is definitely prime or definitely composite. If there were a fast method of factoring numbers into their prime components, this problem would be solved, but we look at this aspect in Chapter 8 and will see that this is not a way out of the problem!

To be sure that a number chosen as a prime for use in a cryptographic system is really a prime, several tests have been developed that can determine, with various levels of probability, the chances that the number is prime or not. In this chapter, we examine some of these tests.

The simplest approach to testing for "primeness" is the same as that for testing for factors: try division by each prime up to the square root of the number. Given that we need primes with more than 100 digits for our cryptosystems, this can be computationally prohibitive. (See Problem 1 in Section 7.1.2.) In general, we argue that if our resources cannot check primality in a reasonable period of time, then it is likely that the resources of an attacker cannot do so either. Thus, we are willing to give up certainty for speed, and

Public Key Cryptography: Applications and Attacks, First Edition. Lynn Margaret Batten.
© 2013 by The Institute of Electrical and Electronics Engineers, Inc. Published 2013 by John Wiley & Sons, Inc.

as long as a number is not shown, in a reasonable amount of time and with a reasonable set of tests, to be not prime, we assume that it is prime or at least prime-like. The tests we present in this chapter are based on this approach.

7.1 FERMAT'S APPROACH AND WILSON'S THEOREM

We saw in Section 2.3 that Fermat's theorem can be used to test if a number is prime. More precisely, if a modulus p is used with a value a in the statement of the FLT and the result is not 1, then p must be composite. The more values for a tested and returning 1, the more certain we become about the primality of p. Thus, we can associate a level of confidence with a conclusion that p is "probably prime." However, we saw in Chapter 2 that there are composite numbers which always pass the Fermat test. These are the *Carmichael numbers* defined in Computer Example 3 of Section 2.3.1.

Computer Example 2 of Section 2.3.1 defined a pseudoprime. We give a formal definition again here.

Definition 7.1   If some specific value for a satisfies Theorem 2.3 (the FLT) modulo n where n is composite, then we say that n is a (Fermat) *pseudoprime base a.*

Example 7.1   Since $2^{340} \equiv 1 \pmod{341}$, the number 341 is a pseudoprime base 2. (Note that 11 divides 341.)

The next result we consider in this section gives a definitive test for primality. It has two parts: the first part states that if p is prime, then a certain congruence modulo p must hold. The second part is the converse and states that if this same congruence holds modulo a number p, then p must be prime. However, instead of a congruence equation involving exponents, as used by Fermat and Euler, this result deals with factorials.

Recall that $n!$ means $n * (n-1) * (n-2) * \ldots * 2 * 1$. For instance, $6! = 6 * 5 * 4 * 3 * 2 * 1 = 720$.

Theorem 7.1 Wilson's Theorem
If p is a prime, then $(p - 1)! \equiv -1 \pmod{p}$.

Proof. The proof is based on the fact that any number in the range 1 to $p - 1$ has an inverse in this range (by the EA). We pair up each number in the factorial on the left of the modulus equation with its inverse. If a number and its inverse are different, their product is 1. The only problem is when a number is its own inverse, which is the case for both 1 and $p - 1$, for instance. We leave as an exercise to show that these are the only cases in which a number is its own inverse. (See the problem set.) So we can pair these two numbers up, which gives a product of -1. Thus, the product of all numbers between 1 and $p - 1$ is -1, as claimed.   □

Example 7.2   If $p = 19$, then $(p - 1)! = 6402373705728000$.
Using Maple, this is 18 modulo 19, which is -1.

It is actually the converse of Wilson's theorem that gives a nice way of checking if a number is a prime number:

Theorem 7.2   The Converse of Wilson's Theorem
For any positive integer n, if $(n-1)! \equiv -1$ (mod n), then n is a prime number.

Proof. Suppose n has a smaller prime divisor p. Then p appears in the list $(n-1)! = (n-1) * (n-2) \ldots 2 * 1$. So p divides $(n-1)!$.

But if $(n-1)! \equiv -1$ (mod n), we can write $(n-1)! + 1 = kn$, for some integer k. Now p also divides n, and so p must divide 1, which is a contradiction.   □

Theorem 7.2 is a true test of a prime. At first glance, this looks like a real break-through, until we realize that given a large n, computing $n!$ is very time consuming and needs a lot of storage space. Thus, in practice, Wilson's theorem is hardly used.

Example 7.3   We use the converse of Wilson's theorem to prove that 113 is a prime number. We need to evaluate 112! This can be done by hand, or with a calculator or with packaged software such as Maple. The result is
1974506857221074023536820372759924883412778680349753377966562950949
0285896977181144089422435502777936659795733823785363827233491968
63856218118507804642770944000000000000000000000000000000
which, taken modulo 113, is -1. Therefore, 113 is a prime.

7.1.1 Computer Examples

1. Check that 561 is a Carmichael number.
   Solution.   First we need to find a factor of it to show that it is not prime. It is easy to see that it is divisible by 3. We now run a test of Fermat's theorem. We need to test x^{560} (mod 561) for every x between 1 and 560. Writing code to do this shows that the result is always 1.
2. Use the site http://www.math.fau.edu/Richman/carm.htm to determine all pseudoprimes less than 1000 to base 5.
   Solution.   The output is 4, 124, 217, 561, 781.
3. Use the converse of Wilson's theorem to test $n = 1713$ for primeness.
   Solution.   Using Maple $1712! \equiv 0$ (mod 1713), which tells us that n is composite.

7.1.2 Problems

1. Given the number 111111111111111111111111111111 (30 1s), determine the number of trial divisions needed to divide by each prime up to its square root. If each division took an average of 1 ms, determine the time needed to try all prime divisors.
2. Show that modulo a prime p, the only numbers which are their own inverses are 1 and $p-1$.

3. Use Wilson's theorem to verify that $n = 13$ is prime.

4. Use Wilson's theorem to verify that 14 is composite.

5. Show that if n is a Fermat pseudoprime base 2 and base 3, then it is a Fermat pseudoprime base 6.

Computer-Assisted Problems

6. Show that 65 is a Fermat pseudoprime base 14.

7. Explain how to find a prime number between 9999999 and 8888888.

8. We want to test the number $n = 1234567$ using the converse of Wilson's theorem. Using any software, determine how long it takes to compute $(n - 1)!$ If your program stalls, note the time lapsed until it stalled.

7.2 THE MILLER–SELFRIDGE–RABIN PRIMALITY TEST

The Miller–Selfridge–Rabin test is an adaptation of Fermat's test, but cuts down the computation. Like the Fermat test, it is really a test for compositeness. It was developed by the three people mentioned in its name [29, 30, 32].

In the Fermat test, each value of a between 1 and $n - 1$ is raised to the power $n - 1$. In the Miller–Selfridge–Rabin test, we still try all values of a in this same range, but we raise them to a lower power, using just the odd part of n, and so reducing the computation.

The idea is based on two facts around the equation $a^{n-1} \equiv 1 \pmod{n}$. First, if n is indeed a prime, then $a^{(n-1)/2} \equiv 1$ or $-1 \pmod{n}$ are the only solutions of the corresponding quadratic equation $(a^{(n-1)/2})^2 \equiv 1 \pmod{n}$. (This follows from the Primitive Root Theorem and Proposition 3.4.) And if the solution is 1 and if $(n - 1)/2$ is even, then we can apply this again to obtain $a^{(n-1)/4} \equiv -1 \pmod{n}$ but not $\equiv 1$; this argument continues as long as the exponent is even.

Write $n - 1$ as $2^s d$, d odd, by factoring powers of 2 from $n - 1$. If n is prime, then the above discussion tells us that $a^{2^{s-1}d} = 1$ and -1 are the only solutions for the quadratic equation $a^{n-1} = (a^{(n-1)/2})^2 \equiv 1 \pmod{n}$. So, if $a^{2^r d} = 1$ for some r in the range 0 to $s - 2$, then we have found an additional root of $a^{n-1} \equiv 1 \pmod{n}$ and so, as we saw in Section 2.3, n must be composite.

Second, if n is in fact composite, the equation $(a^{(n-1)/2})^2 \equiv 1 \pmod{n}$ generally has more than two roots when $n - 1$ is even. Thus, we expect to find exponents t which properly divide $(n - 1)/2$ and for which $a^t \equiv 1$ or $-1 \pmod{n}$.

We formalize these points in the following results which are more general than needed here, but which we shall need in full generality in Chapter 8.

Proposition 7.1 *Let n be an odd positive integer at least 3 and a a positive integer modulo n such that $\gcd(a, n) = 1$. The equation $x^2 \equiv a^2 \pmod{n}$ has exactly two solutions (a and $-a$) precisely when n is prime.*

Proof. Clearly, $x \equiv a$ and $x \equiv -a$ are distinct solutions when n is prime. If n is composite and $a \equiv -a \pmod{n}$ then n divides $2a$ and this contradicts the fact that $\gcd(a, n) = 1$, so again, a and $-a$ are distinct solutions in this case. We refer to these as the *trivial solutions*. Suppose that $x \equiv b$ is a nontrivial solution. Thus $(b - a) * (b + a) \equiv 0 \pmod{n}$. If n is prime, we know from Section 5.1 that we are working in a field. Thus, every nonzero element has a multiplicative inverse. Since neither $b - a$ nor $b + a$ is zero, each has an inverse. Multiplying by the product of these inverses results in $1 \equiv 0$, which is a contradiction. So, if n is prime, there are precisely two solutions.

Now consider the case where n is composite. Write $n = r * s$, where $0 < r, s < n$ and $\gcd(r, s) = 1$. By the Chinese Remainder Theorem, Theorem 2.1, we can solve each equation $x^2 \equiv a^2 \pmod{r}$ and $x^2 \equiv a^2 \pmod{s}$ separately, giving us (at least) the solutions $x \equiv a, -a \pmod{r}$ and $x \equiv a, -a \pmod{s}$. If $a \equiv -a \pmod{r}$ or $\pmod{s}$, noting that both r and s are odd, we use the same argument as above to contradict the fact that $\gcd(a, n) = 1$. We then use the CRT method to combine these into four solutions modulo n. Thus if n is not prime, the quadratic equation has more than two solutions. $\square$

Corollary 7.1 *Let n be a positive integer at least 2. If $b^2 \equiv a^2 \pmod{n}$, $0 < a, b < n$ where b is not a or $-a$, then n is composite and $\gcd(b - a, n)$ and $\gcd(b + a, n)$ are nontrivial factors of n.*

Proof. If n is at least 3, the fact that n is composite follows from the proposition. Since $(b - a) * (b + a) \equiv 0 \pmod{n}$, each term $b + a$ and $b - a$ must divide n and each is nonzero, and not 1. If $n = 2$, the conditions of the Corollary cannot be satisfied. $\square$

The Miller–Selfridge–Rabin algorithm first reduces $n - 1$ by all of its even component and then picks random values for a in the appropriate range and checks for values of a to the exponent which are 1 or -1. It relies on Proposition 7.1 and its corollary in the special case that $a = 1$.

To ensure that the algorithm does not continue for too long, a bound k on the number of tries is established. The larger this bound, the more confidence that we have in the result of the algorithm. We provide two versions of the algorithm. The first version, the long one, explains why each step works. The second version, the short one, is more useful in practice. We refer to the second one as the MSR algorithm to distinguish the two.

7.2.1 The Miller–Selfridge–Rabin Algorithm (Long Version)

Input: $n > 1$, an odd integer to test for primality; k, a parameter that determines the accuracy of the test.

Write $n - 1$ as $2^s d$, d odd, by factoring powers of 2 from $n - 1$.

- Repeat k times:
  - pick a randomly in the range $[2, n - 1]$
  - if $a^{n-1} \neq 1 \pmod{n}$ or $\gcd(a, n) \neq 1$ return composite (using the FLT).STOP
  - otherwise, suppose $a^{n-1} = 1 \pmod{n}$ and continue.

0th step

- if $a^d = 1$ or -1 (mod n), then n may be prime (using Proposition 7.1, since the square is 1 and we did not find nontrivial solutions) and we continue.
- otherwise, continue.

1st step

- if $a^{2d} = 1$, and $a^d \neq 1$ or -1, then we have a nontrivial solution a^d to the equation. We conclude (by the corollary to Proposition 7.1) that n is composite. STOP
- if $a^{2d} = -1$, the fact that $a^{4d} = 1$ and we have not found a nontrivial solution to this, indicates (using Proposition 7.1) that n may be prime and we continue.
- otherwise, continue.

rth step, $1 \leq r \leq s - 1$

- if $a^{2^r d} = 1$ and $a^{2^{r-1}d} \neq -1$ or 1, then we have a nontrivial solution $a^{2^{r-1}d}$ to the equation. We conclude (by the Corollary) that n is composite.   STOP
- if $a^{2^r d} = -1$, the fact that $a^{2^{r+1}d} = 1$ and we have not found a nontrivial solution to this, indicates (using Proposition 7.1) that n may be prime and we continue.
- otherwise, continue.

sth step

- then $a^{n-1} = a^{2^s d} = 1$ (recalling an early assumption). If $a^{2^{s-1}d} \neq -1$ or 1, then this equation has a nontrivial solution $a^{2^{s-1}d}$. We conclude (by the Corollary) that n is composite.   STOP
- Otherwise, n is probably prime. We return and test another value for a.
- When k values of a have been tried and the algorithm has never returned composite and stopped, then return probably prime and stop.

In general, if we come across values that are not 1 or -1 in this algorithm, we have found nontrivial solutions to an equation in the next stage and conclude that n is composite. Otherwise, we continue through the fixed set of k rounds until the end and conclude that n is probably prime. If the output is *composite*, we are certain that n is composite. If the output is *probably prime*, the related probability is a function of the k chosen.

In practice, k should run over a reasonably large number of values of a, but will be limited by the time available. Since $a^2 \equiv (n - a)^2 \equiv (-a)^2$ (mod n), raising to an even power hides the difference between a and $-a$, so that once a particular value for a has been tested, the value $-a$ can be eliminated from the test. (This is also true of Fermat's test of course.)

Next we give the abbreviated version of the Miller–Selfridge–Rabin algorithm. Go through it carefully to see that it is really the same as the longer version.

7.2.2 The MSR Algorithm (Short Version)

Input: $n > 1$, an odd integer to test for primality; k, a parameter that determines the accuracy of the test.

Write $n - 1$ as $2^s d$, d odd, by factoring powers of 2 from $n - 1$.

- Repeat k times:
  - pick a randomly in the range $[2, n - 1]$
  - if $a^{n-1} \neq 1 \pmod{n}$ or $\gcd(a, n) \neq 1$ return *composite*.   STOP
  - otherwise, continue.

  1st step
  - if $a^{2d} = 1$, and $a^d \neq 1$ or -1, conclude that n is *composite*.   STOP
  - otherwise, continue.

  rth step, $1 \leq r \leq s - 1$
  - if $a^{2^r d} = 1$ and $a^{2^{r-1} d} \neq -1$ or 1, conclude that n is *composite*.   STOP
  - otherwise, continue.

  sth step
  - if $a^{2^{s-1} d} \neq -1$ or 1, then conclude that n is *composite*.   STOP
  - return and test another value for a.

- When k values of a have been tried and the algorithm has never returned composite and stopped, then return *probably prime* and stop.

Example 7.4 Suppose we wish to determine if $n = 21$ is (probably) prime using the short version of the algorithm test. We first write $n - 1 = 20$ as $2^2 \cdot 5$, so that we have $s = 2$ and $d = 5$. We randomly select $a = 2 < n$ and check the value of 2^{20} which is 4. Thus, we can stop immediately and declare that 21 is definitely composite. Note that $3^{20} = 9$ and $\gcd(3, 21) = 3$, and $5^{20} = 4$, so we would have quickly discovered the result with a small value for k.

Definition 7.2 Let n be odd and $n - 1 = 2^s d$, d odd. Let a be a number satisfying $\gcd(a, n) = 1$, $a^d \neq 1$ and $a^{2^r d} \neq -1 \pmod{n}$ for all r in the range $[0, s - 1]$. Then we say that a is an *MSR witness* for the compositeness of n.

What are the chances of finding an MSR witness to confirm that a number is indeed composite? The next proposition, which we state without proof, says that the chances are good. A proof can be found in [56, Theorem 10.6].

Proposition 7.2 *Let n be an odd composite number. Then at least 75% of the numbers in the range 2 to $n - 1$ are MSR witnesses for the compositeness of n.*

Recall that we pointed out that since the algorithm continually squares, once a value for a has been checked, its negative is taken care of. Thus, if we have tested just over one-eighth of the values in the range 2 to $n - 1$ (none of which is the negative of another) and the MSR test has not returned composite, then by Proposition 7.2, it is certain that n is prime.

7.2.3 Computer Examples

1. Test $n = 1729$ for primality using the Miller–Selfridge–Rabin test.
   Solution.   Write $n - 1 = 2^6 * 27$, so $s = 6$. Select $a = 2$. Check $2^{1728} \equiv 1$,
   which is true.

   Then $x_0 \equiv 2^{27} \equiv 645 \pmod{1729}$ is not ± 1 and $s \neq 1$.
   We set $r = 1$ and compute $x_1 \equiv 2^{2*27} \equiv 1065 \pmod{1729}$, that is not 1 or -1.
   We set $r = 2 \neq s - 1$. So repeat the previous step increasing r.
   $x_2 \equiv 2^{4*27} \equiv 1 \pmod{1729}$. This means that we have found a nontrivial solution
   to $x^2 \equiv 1 \pmod{n}$, which is 2^{2*27}.
   The MSR algorithm now tells us that n is composite.

2. Test 38200901 for primality using the Miller–Selfridge–Rabin test.
   Solution.   We first try the base $a = 2$ and check $a^{n-1} \equiv 1$, which is 1.
   Thus, Fermat's theorem tells us nothing.
   Write $n - 1 = 2^2 * 9550225$.
   Now, using Maple, we check various powers of 2, starting with 9550225, then
   square it, each time checking for $+1$ or -1:
   $>$ 2&^$((n - 1)/4)$ mod n; 12629190 and
   2&^$((n - 1)/2)$ mod n; -1. At this point, it looks as if n is prime.
   Let's try base 3. First, $3^{n-1} \equiv 1$ and 3 does not divide n. Then
   $>$ 3&^$((n - 1)/4)$ mod n; 25571711
   and 3&^$((n - 1)/2)$ mod n; -1.
   Again, n is acting like a prime. We will try one more value for a, $a = 5$.
   First, $5^{n-1} \equiv 1$ and 5 does not divide n. Then
   $>$ 5&^$((n - 1)/4)$ mod n; -1 and
   5&^$((n - 1)/2)$ mod n; 1. We conclude at this point that n is probably
   prime.

7.2.4 Problems

1. Test $n = 13$ for primality using the Miller–Selfridge–Rabin test with the values
   of a being 7 and 9.

2. Use Theorem 3.1 and Proposition 3.4 to give an alternate proof of the half of
   Proposition 7.1 that reads "Let n be a positive integer at least 3. The equation
   $x^2 \equiv 1 \pmod{n}$ has exactly two solutions (1 and -1) if n is prime."

3. The Primitive Root Theorem tells us that composite numbers of the form $n = p^r$,
   p an odd prime, have primitive roots and so Proposition 3.4 applies. Then an
   equation of the form $a^{48} \equiv 1 \pmod{49}$ will have exactly two solutions for a^{24},
   1 and -1. Thus, each of the steps 0 through $s = 4$ of the Miller–Selfridge–Rabin
   test would return "probably prime."

   (a) Test this for the values $a = 2$ and $a = 5$.

   (b) Since 49 is in fact composite, indicate how, in the Miller–Selfridge–Rabin
       test, that this might be discovered.

Computer-Assisted Problems

4. Determine if $n = 221$ is (probably) prime or composite using the MSR test choosing $a = 137$ as the base.
5. Determine if $n = 38200901201$ is (probably) prime or composite using the MSR test.

7.3 TRUE PRIMALITY TESTS

In this section, we state two deterministic primality tests and give examples. Each test is related to a theorem.

7.3.1 Pocklington's Theorem

We give a proof below. A reader interested in examining an alternate proof can look at [17; Section 24.3].

Theorem 7.3 Pocklington's Theorem
Let $n = ab + 1$ with $b > \sqrt{n} - 1$, $n > 2$. Suppose that for every prime divisor q of b there exists an integer m such that $m^{n-1} \equiv 1$ (mod n) and $\gcd(m^{(n-1)/q} - 1, n) = 1$. Then n is prime. (Otherwise, we know nothing.)

Proof. Let $n = ab + 1$ and suppose that for each prime divisor q of n, there is an m_q such that

$$m_q^{n-1} \equiv 1 \pmod{n} \tag{7.1}$$

and

$$\gcd(m_q^{(n-1)/q} - 1, n) = 1 \tag{7.2}$$

STAGE 1. Let p be any prime divisor of n. Under conditions (7.1) and (7.2) on b, we shall first show that b divides $p - 1$. (This part will be true even if n is composite.)

We do this by writing $b = q_1^{e_1} * q_2^{e_2} * \ldots * q_r^{e_r}$ where the q_i are the distinct prime divisors of b and each exponent e_i is at least 1. The plan is to show that each $q_i^{e_i}$ divides $p - 1$. It follows then that the product, b, of all the $q_i^{e_i}$ divides $p - 1$.

The argument is the same for each $q_i^{e_i}$, so we work with a general prime divisor q of b and assume it appears exactly e times.

So, for the prime divisor q of b, let m_q satisfy (7.1) and (7.2). Define $c = m_q^{(n-1)/q^e} \pmod{p}$. The number $(n - 1)/q^e$ is an integer since $n - 1 = a * b$ and q^e divides b. We now determine the order of c modulo p.

Consider $c^{q^e} = m_q^{n-1}$; since n divides $m_q^{n-1} - 1$ by assumption (7.1), it is also true that p divides it. And so, $c^{q^e} \equiv 1 \pmod{p}$.

By Proposition 3.2, the order of c modulo p divides q^e. Thus, it is a power of q. Suppose $c^{q^s} \equiv 1 \pmod{p}$ where $s < e$. Then $1 \equiv (c^{q^s})^{q^{(e-1-s)}} = c^{q^{(e-1)}}$. This means that

p divides $c^{q^{(e-1)}} - 1 = m_q^{(n-1)/q} - 1$, and since p also divides n, we have contradicted assumption (7.2). So c^{q^s} cannot be $1 \pmod{p}$ where $s < e$, and we have proved that the order of c is q^e modulo p.

However, Proposition 3.2 also tells us that q^e divides $\phi(p) = p - 1$. Since this is true for every prime divisor of b, we conclude that b divides $p - 1$.

STAGE 2. Now suppose that $b > \sqrt{n} - 1$.

If n is not a prime, it has a smallest prime divisor p which must satisfy $\sqrt{n} > p$. Also, we know that b divides $p - 1$ and so $p - 1 \geq b$, in which case, $p > b$. Putting these three inequalities together, we get the contradiction $\sqrt{n} > p > b > \sqrt{n} - 1$. So n cannot have a proper prime divisor and must be prime itself.

This completes the proof. □

A basic assumption of Theorem 7.3 is that we need to be able to factor $n - 1$. But this is always even in practice, and so can be done trivially using 2 as one of the factors. However, any factorization of $n - 1$ can be used.

In addition, the values a and b play a symmetric role; there is no importance in the order. If b is not bigger than $\sqrt{n} - 1$, then a must be (why?) and then a test of prime divisors of a can be made instead of those of b. Thus, this apparent condition of the theorem is actually simply satisfied.

When applying the theorem, the difficult part is finding a value for m satisfying the conditions required. However, when testing an m, if the gcd condition fails, and if the gcd is not itself a multiple of n, we can conclude that n is composite. Also, if $m^{n-1} \not\equiv 1 \pmod{m}$ then n is not prime by the FLT.

Example 7.5 We test $n = 54419$ using Pocklington's theorem. First, write $n - 1 = 54418 = 2 * 27209$ and let $b = 27209$. Now $b > \sqrt{n} - 1$. (If it had not been, we would have turned to a.) We need to be able to compute all prime divisors of b. In fact, b is prime, so there is just one.

Now we look for an m such that $\gcd(m^2 - 1, n) = 1$ and $m^{n-1} \equiv 1 \pmod{n}$. We start with $m = 2$ and claim that $2^{n-1} \equiv 1 \pmod{n}$ and $\gcd(3, n) = 1$. (See Problem 1 of Section 7.3.4.) By the theorem, n is prime.

7.3.2 Proth's Theorem

We give a proof of this theorem here, but before doing so, we need to introduce the concept of quadratic residue.

Definition 7.3 If c is a square modulo n, then c is called a *quadratic residue* (mod n). Otherwise, it is called a *quadratic nonresidue*.

Example 7.6 The number 2 is a quadratic residue (mod 7) as $2 \equiv 3^2 \pmod{7} \equiv (-3)^2$. However, 3 is a quadratic nonresidue (mod 7).

For the proof of Proth's theorem, we also need the result on quadratic residues which is the Corollary to Euler's criterion, Theorem 3.3.3.

Theorem 7.4 Proth's Theorem [13]
Let n be odd and write $n = 2^k t + 1$ where t is odd. Suppose $2^k > t$. Then n is prime if and only if, for some quadratic nonresidue c, $c^{(n-1)/2} \equiv -1$ (mod n).

Proof.

(a) Suppose n is prime. Then for any quadratic nonresidue c, we have $c^{(n-1)/2} \equiv -1$ (mod n) by Euler's criterion.

(b) Suppose $c^{(n-1)/2} \equiv -1$ (mod n) for some quadratic nonresidue c. We use Pocklington's theorem, using $b = 2^k$ and so $q = 2$ is the only prime divisor. The conditions $c^{n-1} = [c^{(n-1)/2}]^2 \equiv 1$ (mod n) and $\gcd(c^{(n-1)/2} - 1, n) = \gcd(-2, n) = 1$ are met. Since $2^k > \sqrt{n} - 1$, n is prime. □

Compare Proth's Theorem with the Corollary to Euler's criterion, Theorem 4.6. The corollary tells us that if n is prime, it is the case that $c^{(n-1)/2} \equiv -1$ (mod n) for every quadratic nonresidue c. But Proth's theorem tells us that if n has a certain form, it is prime if $c^{(n-1)/2} \equiv -1$ (mod n) holds for at least one quadratic nonresidue c. This assists with applying the theorems to specific values of n in Proth's form, since, if n is indeed prime, any quadratic nonresidue that we take should satisfy the equation. If every quadratic nonresidue fails to satisfy the equation, then we can conclude that n is composite. This raises the question of how to find quadratic nonresidues. There are some good methods for doing this efficiently, but we will not cover them in this book.

Example 7.7   We use Proth's theorem to test 113. We write $113 = 112 + 1 = 2^4 * 7 + 1$. Since $2^4 > 7$, we can proceed. We need a quadratic nonresidue c for which $c^{56} \equiv -1$ (mod 113). We can list all the quadratic residues by taking squares, the remaining values are the nonresidues. Since $x^2 = (113 - x)^2$ for any x modulo 113, we only need to compute squares for a up to 56. If the number -1 is a square, then $-x^2$ is a square for any square x^2, and so we can automatically add it. In the list of quadratic residues, we compute squares beginning at 1. If -1 appears in this list, we will begin to add negatives of numbers not already appearing, and stop when we reach 56 values. $QR = \{1, 4, 9, 16, 25, 36, 49, 64, 81, 100, 8, 31, 56, 83, 112$ (this is -1, so we include any negatives not already appearing, as well as new squares from here on), 109 (-4), 104 (-9), 97 (-16), 88 (-25), 32 (-81), 13 (-100), 105 (-8), 82 (-31), 57 (-56), 30, 63, 50, 98, 15, 91, 22, 52, 61, 102, 77 (also -36), 11, 60, 53, 111, 2, 51, 62, 106, 7, 72 (33^2), 41, 26, 87, 95, 18, 99, 14, 69, 44, 28, 85$\}$. We try $c = 3$ which is not in the above set. Since $3^{56} \equiv -1$ (mod 113), we can conclude by Proth's theorem that 113 is prime.

If the value tested in Example 7.7 had been composite, we would have needed to test all quadratic nonresidues before concluding this. So the full procedure can be quite lengthy and automating it becomes necessary. Notice that once a quadratic nonresidue is found, multiplying it by a quadratic residue will produce another nonresidue.

7.3.3 Computer Examples

1. Test $n = 104759 = 2 * 52379 + 1$, where 52379 is a prime, using Pocklington's theorem.
   Solution. We need to look for an integer m such that $\gcd(m^2 - 1, n) = 1$ and $m^{n-1} \equiv 1 \pmod{n}$. We start with $m = 2$ and check that $2^{104758} \equiv 1 \pmod{104759}$ and $\gcd(2^2 - 1, 104759) = 1$. Since both conditions are true, and 52379 is the single prime we need to find m for, we conclude by Pocklington's theorem, that n is prime.

2. Use Proth's theorem to test $n = 40961$ for primality given that 3 is a quadratic nonresidue modulo 40961.
   Solution. Write $n - 1 = 40960 = 2^{13} * 5$. Since $2^{13} > 5$, we can proceed. Checking, $3^{20480} \pmod{40961} \equiv -1$ and so n is prime.

7.3.4 Problems

1. Verify using fast exponentiation that, in Example 7.5 with $n = 54419$, $2^{n-1} \equiv 1 \pmod{n}$ and $\gcd(3, n) = 1$.

2. Test $n = 89$ for primality using Pocklington's theorem.

3. Pepin discovered [6] that Proth's theorem can be applied to an infinite set of numbers of a certain form because they all have 5 as a quadratic nonresidue. Pepin's numbers are of the form $F_n = 2^{2^n} + 1$ and are called *Fermat numbers*.

   (a) List F_1, F_2, F_3, and F_4.

   (b) Verify that Proth's theorem applies to F_3.

Computer-Assisted Problems

4. Check the Distributed Search for Fermat Number Divisors at `http://www.fermatsearch.org/` and determine the latest known Fermat factors of Fermat numbers. Why is this an important issue?

5. Test $n = 7369$ for primality using Pocklington's theorem.

6. Use Proth's theorem to test if 209 is prime.

7.4 MERSENNE PRIMES AND THE LUCAS–LEHMER TEST

Marin Mersenne (1588–1648) was a Frenchman who lived about the same time as Fermat, and who also loved numbers. One of his major contributions, which is useful these days in cryptography, is the idea of a *Mersenne number*: $M_n = 2^n - 1, n \geq 2$. (Compare with Fermat numbers, Problem 3 of Section 7.3.2.)

Examples are $M_2 = 3$, $M_3 = 7$, and $M_4 = 15$. As of 2011, the longest known primes are Mersenne primes. This is partly because computations in Z_n for n of this form are efficient. See [66] for more information.

It was originally thought that all Mersenne numbers were prime numbers if the exponent n was prime. This is false, since $M_{11} = 2^{11} - 1 = 2047 = 23 * 89$.

Let us look at why M_n *cannot* be prime if n is not.

Suppose $n = ab$. Then

$$2^{ab} - 1 = (2^a)^b - 1 = (2^a - 1)[(2^a)^{b-1} + (2^a)^{b-2} + \ldots + 2^a + 1]$$

And in general, the factors on the right are nontrivial.

Notice that we also get from this the result that $2^a - 1 | 2^{ab} - 1$ and can state this even more generally for any positive integer c:

Proposition 7.3   *Let a and n be positive integers. If a divides n, then $c^a - 1$ divides $c^n - 1$.*

Example 7.8   We factor $M_{12} = 2^{12} - 1 = 4095$.
The exponent, 12, is composite, so 4095 is definitely composite (which is easy to see since it ends in 5). Factoring:
$2^{12} - 1 = (2^3)^4 - 1 = (2^3 - 1)((2^3)^3 + (2^3)^2 + (2^3) + 1) = 7 * 585$.
Alternatively, $2^{12} - 1 = (2^4)^3 - 1 = (2^4 - 1)((2^4)^2 + 2^4 + 1) = 15 * 273$.
And again, $2^{12} - 1 = (2^6)^2 - 1 = (2^6 - 1)(2^6 + 1) = 63 * 65$.
We can now pick out the prime factors: 32, 5, 7, 13.

We are now ready to see a new test for primality, that applies specifically to Mersenne numbers. By the above discussion we may assume that n is prime.

7.4.1 The Lucas–Lehmer Test

1. Input $M_n = 2^n - 1$, $n \geq 3$.
2. Set $s_1 = 4$ and compute $s_j \equiv s_{j-1}^2 - 2 \pmod{M_n}$ recursively for $j = 2, 3, \ldots n - 1$.
3. If $s_{n-1} \equiv 0 \pmod{M_n}$ output prime and STOP.
   Otherwise, output composite and STOP.

Notice that the first few terms computed are always 4, 14, 194, 37634 if the modulus is at least six digits. Once we hit M_n, they will change.

This test is unusual in that it always gives a definite answer.

Example 7.9   We test $M_{11} = 2^{11} - 1 = 2047$ for primeness.
Computing the values $s_1, s_2, \ldots, s_{10}$, we get the list 4, 14, 194, 788, 701, 119, 1877, 240, 282, 1736 (mod 2047). The last value is not zero, so $2^{11} - 1$ is not prime.

7.4.2 Computer Examples

1. Use the Lucas–Lehmer test on $M_{13} = 2^{13} - 1 = 8191$.
   Solution.   Computing the values $s_1, s_2, \ldots, s_{12}$, we get the list 4, 14, 194, 4870,

$3953, 5970, 1857, 36, 1294, 3470, 128, s_{12} \equiv 0 \pmod{8191}$. Therefore, 8191 is prime.

7.4.3 Problems

1. Proposition 7.3 indicates that Mersenne numbers with even exponent n have smaller Mersenne numbers as divisors. Find proper Mersenne number divisors for each of the first five Mersenne numbers with even exponent.
2. Completely factor M_8 into primes using the material of this section.
3. Completely factor M_{10} into primes using the material of this section.

Computer-Assisted Problems

4. Check the "Great Internet Mersenne Prime Search" website at `http://www.mersenne.org/prime.htm` and determine the largest Mersenne prime currently known.
5. Use the Lucas–Lehmer test on $M_{17} = 2^{17} - 1 = 131071$.

7.5 PRIMES IS IN *P*

The expression "primes is in P" actually means that there is a polynomial-time deterministic algorithm for testing whether a number is prime or not. The result came as a complete surprise in 2004 when Manindra Agrawal, Neeraj Kayal, and Nitin Saxena at the Indian Institute of Technology in Kanpur discovered a proof based on a polynomial version of the Euclidean Algorithm. Until their paper appeared, no one knew if it was possible to test deterministically for primality in real time.

7.5.1 Polynomial Rings

To understand the algorithm, we need first to introduce some notation.

Notation

Let $p(x)$, $q(x)$, and $g(x)$ be polynomials in the variable x with coefficients from a set R. Then $p(x) \equiv q(x) \ (\textbf{mod} \ g(x))$ means that $g(x)|[p(x) - q(x)]$. (That is, $g(x)$ divides into $p(x) - q(x)$ or, equivalently, $p(x) - q(x)$ is a multiple of $g(x)$.)

Alternatively, we can write $p(x) - q(x) = g(x) * f(x)$ for some polynomial $f(x)$. We need to have consistency of the coefficients used. If we assume that the coefficients of p, q, and g are all from the same fixed set R, then those of f must also be from R.

Notation

The set of polynomials in the variable x with coefficients from the set R is denoted by $R[x]$.

Definition 7.4 We say a polynomial $p(x)$ in $R[x]$ *divides* a polynomial $q(x)$ in $R[x]$ if there is a polynomial $r(x)$ in $R[x]$ such that $p(x)r(x) = q(x)$.

Example 7.10 Over the real numbers, $x^3 - 1 = (x - 1)(x^2 + x + 1)$. So, by Definition 7.4, both $x - 1$ and $x^2 + x + 1$ divide $x^3 - 1$. Note that $x - 1$ does not divide $x^3 - 2 = (x^3 - 1) - 1$.

Example 7.11 We check if $x^2 + 1$ divides $x^4 + 1$ over Z_3. We need to write $x^4 + 1 \equiv (x^2 + 1)(ax^2 + bx + c)$ for some $a, b, c \in Z_3$ for this to be true.

If $a = 0$, we will not get the x^4 term: in fact by multiplying out and comparing exponents we need $1 = a, 0 = b, 0 = a + c, 0 = b$, and $c = 1$. But $0 = a + c = 1 + 1$ is not true in Z_3. So the answer is no.

An improvement on this trial and error approach would be good! Hence, we have the next subsection that tells us how we can divide polynomials.

7.5.2 A Division Algorithm for Polynomials

Just as for integers, we can divide "smaller" polynomials into "larger" ones. In fact, we can divide a degree m polynomial into a degree n polynomial if $m \leq n$. The remainder will usually be nonzero.

We assume our coefficient set forms a field (as defined in Section 5.1).

Example 7.12 Let R be the integers modulo 7. Divide $3x^2 + 1$ into $4x^3 + 5x + 2$.

$$3x^2 + 1 \overline{)\ \begin{array}{l} \frac{4}{3}x \\ 4x^3 + 5x + 2 \\ \underline{-4x^3 - \frac{4}{3}x} \\ \frac{11}{3}x \end{array}}$$

We need to solve $3x \equiv 4 \pmod 7$. Since $\gcd(3, 7) = 1$, we can use the EA to find the inverse of 3 modulo 7 and thus find x. The answer is 6. Multiplying $6x$ by $3x^2 + 1$ and subtracting the result from $4x^3 + 5x + 2$ results in a remainder of $4x^3 + 5x + 2 - (4x^3 + 6x) = 6x + 2$.

In general, we will need inverses of the coefficients to divide polynomials and so requiring that the coefficients be from a field provides these.

7.5.3 A Euclidean Algorithm for Polynomials

Let F be a field and consider the set of polynomials $F[x]$. This set itself will not necessarily be a field! [See Problem 1 of Section 7.5.2.]

To copy the EA for integers, not only do we need to be able, given $p(x)$ and $q(x)$, to write $p(x) = q(x)h(x) + r(x)$, we need an extra condition on the "remainder" $r(x)$. It has to be "less than" $q(x)$ in some sense.

We manage this by looking at the degrees.

Notation

Given a polynomial $p(x)$, deg $p(x)$ denotes its *degree*, that is, the highest power of x which appears in it.

Given $p(x)$ and $q(x)$, with $\deg(p) \geq \deg(q)$, we can write

$$p(x) = q(x) * h(x) + r(x), \quad \text{where} \quad r(x) = 0 \quad \text{or} \quad \deg r < \deg q.$$

We can continue dividing with $q(x)$ and $r(x)$, decreasing the degrees of the remainders each time until we finally obtain a 0 remainder. (This is the same idea as in the EA for integers.)

We can then use the same method as for the integer EA to pick out the gcd of $p(x)$ and $q(x)$ and write it as a polynomial combination of the two polynomials.

Example 7.13   We apply the EA for polynomials to find the gcd of $p(x) = x^6 + x^3 + 2$ and $q(x) = x^2 + x + 1$ over Z_3:

$$
\begin{array}{r}
x^4 - x^3 + 2x - 2 \\
x^2 + x + 1 \overline{) x^6 + x^3 + 2} \\
\underline{x^6 + x^5 + x^4} \\
-x^5 - x^4 + x^3 + 2 \quad \text{The degree is} > 2 \\
\underline{-x^5 - x^4 - x^3} \\
2x^3 + 2 \quad \text{The degree is} > 2 \\
\underline{2x^3 + 2x^2 + 2x} \\
-2x^2 - 2x + 2 \\
\underline{-2x^2 - 2x - 2} \\
1 \, (in \, Z/3) \quad \text{The degree is} < 2, \text{ so stop.}
\end{array}
$$

So we can write

$$x^6 + x^3 + 2 = (x^2 + x + 1)(x^4 + 2x^3 + 2x + 1) + 1.$$

So the gcd of the two polynomials is 1. Now take the remainder 1 and write

$$1 = x^6 + x^3 + 2 - (x^2 + x + 1)(x^4 + 2x^3 + 2x + 1).$$

By Definition 3.1, every nonzero element of a field Z_p is a unit (an invertible element).

Notation

If the only common divisor of two polynomials $p(x)$ and $q(x)$ is a unit, we write $\gcd(p(x), q(x)) = 1$.

Note that 2 is a unit in $Z/3$, so if we had obtained a greatest common divisor of 2, we would still write $\gcd(p(x), q(x)) = 1$.

Notation

We write $f(x) \equiv g(x)$ (mod $h(x), n$) to mean that all of f, g, and h are considered to have coefficients in Z_n and that $h | (f - g)$.

We are now ready to state the general primality test discovered by Manindra Agrawal, Neeraj Kayal, and Nitin Saxena [1]. It applies to any positive integer, gives a necessary and sufficient condition (and so always determines if a number is prime or composite) and they were able to give a polynomial time deterministic algorithm for this result.

Theorem 7.5 A Polynomial Primality Test

If a and n are integers with $n > 1$ and $\gcd(a, n) = 1$, then n is prime if and only if $(x + a)^n \equiv x^n + a$ (mod n) for every such a.

We do not prove this, but add some comments. The theoretical time complexity of their algorithm is $O(\log_2^{12}(n))$, but in practice, it is much faster.

Example 7.14 Let us apply the polynomial test for $n = 11$. We need to determine if the equation $(x + a)^{11} \equiv x^{11} + a$ (mod 11) holds for all a from 1 to 10.

Computing the left-hand side for a general a, we get

$$x^{11} + 11x^{10}a +_{11} C_2 x^9 a^2 + \cdots +_{11} C_{10} x a^{10} + a^{11}.$$

Where $_n C_m$ is the combinatorial notation for the number of ways that m objects can be chosen from n objects. For instance, $_3 C_2 = 3$.

All the middle terms are a multiple of 11 and so are 0 (mod 11) and disappear. Since $a^{11} \equiv a$, this equals the right-hand side.

NOTE: If n is not a prime, the middle terms are not expected to disappear.

Example 7.15 We apply the polynomial test to $n = 6$.

Computing the left-hand side for a general a, we get $x^6 + 6x^5 a +_6 C_2 x^4 a^2 + \cdots + _6 C_5 x a^5 + a^6 = x^6 + 6x^5 a + 15 x^4 a^2 + 20 x^3 a^3 + 15 x^2 a^4 + 6 x a^5 + a^6$. Now modulo 6, not all of these coefficients disappear. We are left with $x^6 + 3x^4 a^2 + 2x^3 a^3 + 3x^2 a^4 + a^6$, which is not the same as the right-hand side: $x^6 + a$ when a is not 0.

7.5.4 Computer Examples

1. Apply the polynomial test to $n = 97$.
   Solution. The polynomial we need to check is $x^{97} + 97 x^{96} a +_{97} C_2 x^{95} a^2 + \cdots + 97 x a^{96} + a^{97}$ (mod 97). All the coefficients need to be evaluated modulo 97. We do two of them manually and the rest by computer: $_{97} C_2 = 97 * 96/2$ which is divisible by 97 and so is 0. And $_{97} C_3 = 97 * 96 * 95/6$ which is divisible

by 97 and so is 0. Continuing by computer, we see that all coefficients except the first and last are 0 modulo 97. Therefore, by the polynomial test, 97 is prime.

2. Apply the polynomial test to $n = 91$.

Solution. The polynomial we need to check is $x^{91} + 91x^{91}a +_{91} C_2 x^{91} a^2 + \cdots + 91xa^{91} + a^{91}$ (mod 91). All the coefficients need to be evaluated modulo 91. We do several manually and the rest by computer: $_{91}C_2 = 91 * 90/2$ which is divisible by 91 and so is 0. And $_{91}C_3 = 91 * 90 * 89/6$ which is divisible by 91 and so is 0. Also, $_{91}C_4 = 91 * 90 * 89 * 88/24$ which is divisible by 91 and so is 0; and $_{91}C_5 = 91 * 90 * 89 * 88 * 87/120$ which is divisible by 91 and so is 0. Then $_{91}C_6 = 91 * 90 * 89 * 88 * 87 * 86/720$ is divisible by 91 and so 0. But $_{91}C_7 = 91 * 90 * 89 * 88 * 87 * 86 * 85/5040$ is not divisible by 91. Continuing, we will see that several other coefficients are not 0. Thus, by the polynomial test, 91 is composite.

Further Reading. Section 6.3 of [52] is devoted to primality testing and the Miller–Selfridge–Rabin test is presented there as the Miller–Rabin test. Primes and primality testing are also the subject of Section 3.4 of [19].

We made the observation earlier that to maintain security it is not always necessary to have an actual prime: a pseudo-prime will suffice as long as it acts sufficiently like a prime and is resistant to factoring. As we saw in Section 7.2, it is possible to identify an integer which has a "high probability" of being a prime. Garrett considers such numbers in Section 24.5 of [17] where the concept of a "certificate of primality" is proposed. For instance, in the MSR test, the collection of data supporting the "probable primeness" of an integer would become part of its certificate of primality.

7.5.5 Problems

1. Show that the set of polynomials over Z_7 does not form a field.
2. Show in general that if a and p are integers with p prime and $\gcd(a, p) = 1$, $(x + a)^p \equiv x^p + a$ (mod p).
3. Find all solutions of $x^5 + 2x^3 + 1 = 0$ in $Z/5$.
4. Apply the polynomial test to $n = 4$.
5. Find the gcd of the polynomials $x^3 - 1$ and $x^3 - 6x^2 - 9x + 14$ over the real numbers.

Computer-Assisted Problems

6. Apply the polynomial test to $n = 101$.
7. Apply the polynomial test to $n = 119$.

8

FACTORING METHODS

As many of the cryptographic systems in common use today are based on the difficulty of factoring, we need to understand just how difficult this is. To ensure the security of the system, knowing the resources needed by an attacker will determine parameters we choose such as the key size, length and type of prime or composite modulus, and so on. Recall that a mathematical attack on the RSA scheme takes one of three forms:

- factor $n = p * q$, hence compute $\phi(n)$ and then d;
- determine $\phi(n)$ directly (without factoring) and compute d;
- find d directly by some means other than the above.

Currently, it is believed that all these approaches are equivalent to factoring n; in other words, any one of the three approaches, from a mathematical perspective, is just as difficult as actually factoring. However, there is no known proof of this.

Our focus in this chapter is on several of the most efficient (under current computing conditions) factoring algorithms available today. Factoring numbers has been a subject of interest for hundreds of years and a popular part of the subject of Number Theory [10]. There have seen slow improvements to factoring algorithms over the years with, in 2011, numbers of just over 200 digits being factored in "reasonable" time.

Public Key Cryptography: Applications and Attacks, First Edition. Lynn Margaret Batten.
© 2013 by The Institute of Electrical and Electronics Engineers, Inc. Published 2013 by John Wiley & Sons, Inc.

Recall that Theorem 4.1, the Unique Factorization Theorem, stated that any integer greater than 1 can be factored into a product of primes in a unique way, up to order of the primes. The ultimate goal of factoring a number n is to find this unique representation as a product of primes. However, finding a single factor, prime or not, of n allows us to reduce the factoring problem to n divided by its factor and so is a smaller and easier problem. Hence, the approach of factoring algorithms is to find a single proper factor (not 1 or n).

The algorithms that we have chosen include several based on Fermat's work (including an adaptation of the Miller–Selfridge–Rabin method that we saw in Chapter 7 used for primality testing), two methods due to Pollard, called $p - 1$ and rho, respectively, a quadratic sieve method (the oldest factoring concept of them all), and a relatively recent method based on continued fractions. And do not forget that we saw how to use elliptic curves in a factoring method in Section 5.3.

8.1 FERMAT AGAIN

8.1.1 Fermat's Difference of Squares Method

Fermat's factoring methods based on a difference of squares go back to the year 1643. They are still used almost 400 years later.

Suppose $x, y \in Z_n$, $x \not\equiv \pm y \pmod{n}$. Suppose, however, that $x^2 \equiv y^2 \pmod{n}$. Proposition 7.1 tells us that in this case, n must be composite. We obtain $(x - y) * (x + y) \equiv 0 \pmod{n}$ and so $\gcd(x \pm y, n)$ cannot be 1. In particular, if $x > y$, then $0 < x - y < n$ and so n and $x - y$ must have a nontrivial positive common factor that can easily be found by the EA.

There is a similar, but slightly more complicated argument for $x + y : 0 < x + y < 2n$ and if $x + y \neq n$, then n and $x + y$ must have a nontrivial positive common factor. But $x + y = n$ is also possible in this case, which would imply $x \equiv n - y \equiv -y$ and we are assuming this is not true. So in fact $\gcd(n, x + y)$ is also nontrivial and yields a proper factor of n.

If n is an RSA modulus (a product of two odd primes), then $x - y$ and $x + y$ will be the two primes.

The methods, that we examine in this section deal with various ways that two squares can be congruent modulo n, or equivalently, that n divides a difference of squares.

Suppose now that n is composite and write $n = rs$, where $1 < r < \sqrt{n}$ so that $s > r$. Then we can always write

$$n = \left[\frac{s + r}{2}\right]^2 - \left[\frac{s - r}{2}\right]^2.$$

That is, we know that any composite n is equal to a difference of squares! However, these squares will not be integers if r and s have different parity (one odd and one even). We need both $s - r$ and $s + r$ to be even in order to obtain integers. In our case, we are not interested in n even as we are trying to factor it. So without any loss in generality, we can assume that all of n, r, and s are odd.

Based on this observation, Fermat looked for values of the form $y^2 - n$ until one of them is a perfect square. His list starts at $y = \lfloor\sqrt{n}\rfloor + 1, \lfloor\sqrt{n}\rfloor + 2$, and goes to $(n-1)/2$. The algorithm is described in the following example. The argument above indicates that this algorithm will eventually succeed; the maximum number of steps needed to find a perfect square is $(n-3)/2 - \lfloor\sqrt{n}\rfloor$. (Recall the notation $\lfloor m \rfloor$ for any real number m, means the largest integer less than or equal to m. For example, $\lfloor -2.395 \rfloor = -3$.)

Example 8.1   We use the Fermat approach to factor $n = 899$. We need to be able to calculate square root of n, but this is computationally much easier than factoring. Construct the sequence $x_1 = (\lfloor\sqrt{n}\rfloor + 1)^2 - 899 = (29+1)^2 - 899 = 1$, $x_2 = (\lfloor\sqrt{n}\rfloor + 2)^2 - 899 = (30+1)^2 - 899 = 62$, and so on. In fact, we can stop at the first line since this already gives us a square:
$899 = 30^2 - 1^2 = 29 * 31$.
Knowing a factorization, we can also verify the formula above based on the factors:

$$899 = \left(\frac{29+31}{2}\right)^2 - \left(\frac{31-29}{2}\right)^2 = 900 - 1.$$

The Miller–Selfridge–Rabin primality test that we discussed in Chapter 7 also tries to generate a difference of squares where one of the squares is 1. We can easily adapt the method to be a factoring method.

8.1.2 Using the Miller–Selfridge–Rabin Algorithm to Factor

Using the $x^2 \equiv y^2$ modulo n principle, the Miller–Selfridge–Rabin algorithm for primality testing can be adapted to find a divisor of n. Recall that we generated squares in this method: $a^d, a^{2d} = (a^d)^2, a^{2^2d} = (a^d)^{2^2}$, and so on. If we get to the point where $(a^d)^{2^r} \equiv 1 \equiv (a^{d2^{r-1}})^2 \pmod{n}$ for some r, then $\gcd(a^{d2^{r-1}} - 1, n)$ may be a nontrivial factor of n.

Example 8.2   We factor $n = 1729$ using the Miller–Selfridge–Rabin test. This refers to Computer Example 1 in Section 7.2.1. In this example, we obtained $x_2 \equiv 2^{4*27} = 2^{54*2} \equiv 1 \pmod{1729}$. Therefore, we can check the greatest common divisors of $2^{54} - 1$ and $2^{54} + 1$ with 1729. These are 133 and 13, respectively. We have thus found proper factors of 1729 and can write it as $13 * 133$.

8.1.3 Euler's Factoring Method

As we have seen at several points in the text, Euler was ingenious in extending Fermat's ideas. Almost 100 years after Fermat discovered his difference of squares method, Euler spotted an extension of it, which we now describe.

Euler noticed that if n had two different particular representations in a similar form, then, modulo n, two squares could be obtained which were equivalent modulo n and Fermat's basic method could be applied to $x^2 \equiv y^2 \pmod{n}$.

He decided to look for $n = x^2 + ay^2 = z^2 + aw^2$ for integers x, y, z, w, and a. Then he rewrote this as follows:

$$(xw)^2 \equiv (n - ay^2)w^2 \equiv -ay^2w^2 \equiv y^2(z^2 - n) \equiv (zy)^2 \pmod{n}.$$

But are these multiple representations possible? And if so, how do we find them? We consider these issues in the next examples.

Example 8.3   The number $59 = 3^2 + 2 * 5^2$ cannot be written any other way as $x^2 + 2y^2$. However, $28 = 1^2 + 3 * 3^2 = 5^2 + 3 * 1^2$. This last equality can be used to derive, as in Euler's formula, $1 \equiv 15^2 \pmod{28}$. Hence, checking the $\gcd(15 - 1, 28)$, we find that 14 divides 28.

To find such representations of n, Fermat's list method can be adapted. Instead of simply looking for squares as in $x_1 = (\lfloor \sqrt{n} \rfloor + 1)^2 - 899 = (29 + 1)^2 - 899 = 1$, we now look for the right-hand side that contains a square. (Note that $x_1 = 17$ can be written as $x_1 = 17 * 1^2$, and in this case, we could choose $a = 17$.) However, we are now after two "matching" equations in the sense that the same value "a" used by Euler must be present. Also, we will only use positive x and y.

A simple observation of the equation $n = x^2 + ay^2$ tells us that n must be a quadratic residue modulo a. Thus, if $a = 2$, then n must be odd; if $a = 15$, n must be congruent to 1, 4, 6, 9, or 10 (mod 15).

Example 8.4   We show that the number $n = 301$ can be written in two ways as $x^2 + 5y^2$ and use this to factor n. The possible values for y^2 run from 0 to about $301/5$, or 60. So we need only test $y^2 = 0, 1, 4, 9, 16, 25, 36, 49$. We obtain exactly two results: $301 = 11^2 + 5 * 6^2$ and $16^2 + 5 * 3^2$. Using Euler's method, we obtain the difference of squares: $(11 * 3)^2 \equiv (6 * 16)^2 \pmod{301}$. We now check $\gcd(33 - 96, 301) = 7$, and $\gcd(33 + 96, 301) = 43$. It is now easy to verify that $301 = 7 * 43$.

8.1.4 Kraitchik's Method

Many years later, in 1945 in fact, Maurice Kraitchik [56] went back to Fermat's basic method of finding x and y such that $x^2 \equiv y^2 \pmod{n}$ to factor n. He observed that $x^2 - y^2$ is a multiple of n. So to factor n, Kraitchik looked for equations of the form $kn = x^2 - y^2$ for k a positive integer. (Without loss of generality, we can assume that $x > y$.)

For instance, if $3n = x^2 - y^2$, then $3n = (x - y)(x + y)$. Since 3 is a prime number, it must divide at least one of the terms $x + y$, $x - y$. If it divides $x - y$, we can factor n into integers as $n = (x + y) * (x - y)/3$. In general, if k is chosen to be prime, then it must divide one of the terms $x - y$ or $x + y$.

Example 8.5   We use Kraitchik's method to factor 24. Note that $5 * 24 = 13^2 - 7^2 = (13 - 7)(13 + 7)$. So $24 = 6 * (20/5) = 6 * 4$.

It is easy to adapt Fermat's algorithm to find a Kraitchik-type representation. It will be faster than the Fermat algorithm as there are more possibilities generating a factorization. Usually, we test only for k prime. We avoid $k = 2$ as this implies that n is even and we would never find a solution if n is odd. See Section 8.1.5 for an example.

Kraitchik's method is the basis of the quadratic sieve, one of the most efficient methods still in use today. We describe the quadratic sieve method in the next section.

8.1.5 Computer Examples

1. Use Fermat's algorithm to factor 426749.
   Solution.   The square root of 426749 is approximately $653.26\ldots$ Starting at $y_i = 654$, we compute the sequence x_i as described in Example 8.1.

y_i	$y_i^2 - 426749$
654	967
655	2276
656	3587
657	4900

   We observe that $4900 = 70^2$ is a square. So write $426749 = (657 + 70)(657 - 70) = 727 * 587$. Since 727 and 587 are prime, we have obtained the prime factorization of 426749.

2. Use Euler's method to factor 10817.
   Solution.   We can write a routine to test if 10817 is a quadratic residue modulo primes 3,5,7,11,13, and so on. This can be done by computing the squares modulo each number, or using Euler's criterion. It is not a quadratic residue modulo 3 or 5, but is a quadratic residue modulo 7, 11, and 13. We choose to use $a = 13$ and write a new routine to find solutions to $10817 = x^2 + 13y^2$. We obtain $25^2 + 13 * 28^2 = 103^2 + 13 * 4^2$. Euler's formula now gives us $(25 * 4)^2 \equiv (28 * 103)^2 \pmod{10817}$, or $100^2 \equiv 2884^2$. Testing $\gcd(2784, 10817) = 29$ and $\gcd(2984, 10817) = 373$, we see that we have factored 10817 as $373 * 29$.

3. Factor 899 using Kraitchik's method with k an odd prime.
   Solution.   We first set $k = 3$ and try to find $3 * 899$ as a difference of squares: $(29 + 1)^2 - 3 * 899 = -1797$.
   This is negative and so no good. In fact, we can move up to a value that gives positive results immediately:
   $(29 + 23)^2 - 3 * 899 = 7$
   $(29 + 24)^2 - 3 * 899 = 112$
   $(29 + 25)^2 - 3 * 899 = 219$
   $(29 + 26)^2 - 3 * 899 = 328$
   $(29 + 27)^2 - 3 * 899 = 439$
   $(29 + 28)^2 - 3 * 899 = 552$
   $(29 + 29)^2 - 3 * 899 = 667$
   $(29 + 30)^2 - 3 * 899 = 784 = 28^2$.

So $\quad 3*899 = (59-28)*(59+28) = 31*87.\quad$ Thus $\quad n = 31*(87/3) = 31*29$.

Further Reading. If the primality testing methods of Chapter 7 fail to verify that an integer is a prime, then the next step is to try to factor it. Chapter 8 examines some of the most useful integer factoring methods in use today. These methods are extremely important as they gauge for us the level of security of cryptographic systems whose integrity relies on the inability of an attacker to factor a composite integer. The reader is referred to [56] for a very nice history of factoring integers before computers came on the scene.

8.1.6 Problems

1. Confirm that if $n = rs$ with $1 < r < \sqrt{n}$ and $s > r$ then the equation representing n as a difference of squares given in this section is valid.
2. Confirm that the number $59 = 3^2 + 2*5^2$ cannot be written any other way as $x^2 + 2*y^2$.
3. Use the Fermat method to factor $n = 2079$.
4. Use Euler's method to factor 667 using $a = 7$.
5. (a) Find an example of an odd integer n that can be written as $pn = x^2 - y^2$ for some odd prime p and integers x and y.
   (b) Use this to factor n.
6. Write out the Kraitchik algorithm that generalizes Fermat's factorization.

Computer-Assisted Problems

7. Factor 221 using the MSR test. (See Problem 4 of Section 7.2.4.)
8. Try Euler's method to factor 10817 choosing $a = 7$ and 11. (See Computer Example 2 in Section 8.1.5.)
9. Use Kraitchik's method to factor $n = 1226987$ using $k = 3$.

8.2 THE QUADRATIC SIEVE

Kraitchik's algorithm to write a difference of squares as a multiple of n is the basis of the idea of the quadratic sieve discovered in the 1980s [41, 42]. In subsequent years, with improvements contributed by many people, sieving methods have turned out to be the most efficient known methods for factoring.

The idea is somewhat of a trial and error method and similar to some of the other methods that we have seen in this book, targets small prime factors. While the idea is simple, for very large n, a lot of data may need to be stored and compared, so it is best to use tables. We illustrate the concept in the next example.

Example 8.6 We want to factor the number 91. At a first glance, we do not see how to choose values for x and y such that $x^2 \equiv y^2$ (mod 91). We decide to play a little with some squares on the left and see what happens to the right-hand side. $14^2 \equiv 2 * 7$ (mod 91) and $21^2 \equiv 7 * 11$ (mod 91). Note the common number 7 in both the right-hand sides. If we combine the two equations, we get $(14 * 21)^2 \equiv 2 * 7^2 * 11$ (mod 91). We seem to be on our way to constructing a square on the right. We randomly choose another square: $29^2 \equiv 2 * 11$ (mod 91). We were very lucky with this choice, as now, patching the three equations together, we obtain $(14 * 21 * 29)^2 \equiv 2^2 * 7^2 * 11^2$ (mod 91) $\equiv (2 * 7 * 11)^2$.

Let us see if this now gives us a factor of 91: check the gcd$(14 * 21 * 29 - 2 * 7 * 11, \ 91) =$ gcd$(8526 - 154, \ 91) =$ gcd$(8372, \ 91) = 91$. So we are unlucky as the gcd is the number that we are trying to factor. We try now gcd$(14 * 21 * 29 + 2 * 7 * 11, \ 91) =$ gcd$(8680, \ 91) = 7$. This time we have factored 91 as $7 * 13$. We could also have reduced 8372 modulo 91 before testing. This would have given 336 and gcd$(336 - 154, \ 91) = 91$ while gcd$(336 + 154, \ 91) = 7$, and we obtain the same result.

With a very large number to be factored, it is easy to see that the number of combinations of partial squares can be very large. In order to try to limit the computations necessary, we decide on some basic approaches. In particular, we would like the right-hand sides that we will patch together to have only "small" primes in them. This limits the number of combinations. What do we mean by "small"? Its definition often depends on the person who has to do the work, and how much time and patience they have, as well as on the computer being used, and its capacity. *So in the first stage, begin by choosing a base $\mathcal{B}$ of primes from 2 up to some reasonable number, depending on the number to be factored.*

In the next stage, we need to choose numbers to use as squares on the left-hand side of our equations. We take numbers about the square root of n (just a touch bigger is good), square them modulo n and factor them. Because of the way they are chosen, modulo n the squares should not be too large, and this increases the chances of them having factors in our list. *If their factors include small primes in $\mathcal{B}$, we keep these numbers in a list.* If not, we discard them. This technique is called the *quadratic sieve* method. (The word "quadratic" refers to the fact that we are using squares; the word "sieve" refers to the fact that we are excluding all but a few primes and only choosing numbers which contain these small primes.) Note that, in testing the factors, we do not try to directly factor the number, but simply test for divisibility by the primes in the base.

Example 8.7 We use the quadratic sieve to factor 437. First we choose a base of primes. Let $\mathcal{B} = \{2, 3, 5, 7\}$. Then we calculate the square root of 437, which is just below 21, and begin to square values from 21 on. In each case, we divide the square by the numbers in $\mathcal{B}$ to see if we get a factorization. So $21^2 = 441 \equiv 4 = 2^2$ (mod 437).

We have found a square in the very first step. So next we check to see if this will factor 437 for us. The difference of squares $(21 - 2) * (21 + 2) = 19 * 23$. The gcd$(19, 437) = 19$. The gcd$(23, 437) = 23$. Thus, $437 = 19 * 23$.

If we had been unsuccessful in this first attempt, we would have tried $22^2 = 484 \equiv 47 \equiv 22 * 11^2 \pmod{437}$. The prime 11 is not in our base, but we can enlarge $\mathcal{B}$ to include it as it is the next prime in the list. Nonetheless, adding 11 does not help as we see that the number 47 is not a square.

Trying $23^2 = 529$, we see that no primes in $\mathcal{B}$ divide into it, so we cannot factor it. Trying $24^2 = 576 \equiv 139 \equiv 26 * 32 \pmod{437}$, we see that 139 is not a square, and so on.

Definition 8.1   Let $\mathcal{B}$ be a set of prime numbers. We say that a number n is $\mathcal{B}$-smooth if all the prime factors of n are in $\mathcal{B}$. We call the largest element of $\mathcal{B}$ a *smoothness bound* for n, and also sometimes use the same symbol $\mathcal{B}$ for it. The context distinguishes between its use as a set or as a number.

In the quadratic sieve method, we choose a base of primes $\mathcal{B}$ and look for squares which are $\mathcal{B}$-smooth.

8.2.1 Computer Examples

For both of the examples in this section, a program should be written to find the needed differences of squares. In Maple, the commands might look like

```
quadrsieve := proc(x) local i, j, b, c, k, p;
p := {2, 3, 5, 7, 11, 13, 17, 19, 23, 29, 31, 37};
b[0] := 1;
c[0] := 1;
for i from 2000 to x do c[i] := i&^2 mod n : b[i] := c[i] :
    for j from 1 to 25 do
        for k from 1 to 12 do
if b[i] mod p[k] = 0 then b[i] := b[i]/p[k]
        end if: end do: end do:
    if b[i] = 1 then print (i, c[i], ifactor(c[i])) fi :
end do;
end proc;
```

In the above, x is used to mark the upper bound of the search. Since i begins at 2000, x will be something larger than this. The prime set has been chosen to contain 12 primes, which is the range of k. The variable n will be the specific number to be factored. We chose j to range up to 25; this marks the number of times the prime $p[k]$ occurs in the squares generated. It is highly unlikely that any prime will be contained more than 25 times. However, for extremely large numbers n, this bound can be raised. When $b[i] = 1$, we have divided out all primes in the base and no other primes remain. Thus, we have a square which factors using only our base primes.

In classic versions of Maple, the ampersand, &, used with $\wedge$ induces a fast exponentiation method of computing the result. In later versions, this has changed.

1. Use the quadratic sieve method to factor $n = 2043221$.

   Solution. We try a factor base $\mathcal{B} = \{2, 3, 5, 7, 11\}$. The integer 1430 is the smallest number larger than square root n. Using the algorithm above, we find $1439^2 \equiv 27500 = 2^2 * 5^4 * 11$ and $2878^2 \equiv 2^4 * 5^4 * 11$. Combining these two, we obtain $(1439 * 2878)^2 \equiv (2^3 * 5^4 * 11)^2$. But each side is 55000 squared and this will not produce a divisor of n. However, $3197^2 \equiv 4704 = 2^5 * 3 * 7^2$ and $3199^2 \equiv 2^3 * 3^7$. So $(3197 * 3199)^2 \equiv (11098)^2 \equiv (2^4 * 3^4 * 7)^2 = 9072^2$. Using a difference of squares gives $(11098 - 9072) * (11098 + 9072) \equiv 0 \pmod{n} \equiv (2026) * (20170)$. Using the EA to check gcds (or some software), we see that 1013 divides both 2026 and 2043221. Also 2017 divides both 20170 and n. Thus, we have factored n as $2017 * 1013$.

2. Use the quadratic sieve to factor $n = 3837523$.

   Solution. We first choose a base $\mathcal{B} = \{2, 3, 5, 7, 11, 13, 17, 19, 21\}$ of small prime numbers. The square root of n is just over 1958. Using the algorithm above beginning with 1958, we obtain

   $$1964^2 \equiv 3^2 * 13^3 \pmod{3837523},$$
   $$9398^2 \equiv 59375 = 5^5 * 19 \pmod{3837523},$$

   and

   $$19095^2 \equiv 2^2 * 5 * 11 * 13 * 19 \pmod{3837523}.$$

   This is good; we now have 2, 5, 13, and 19 squared. But we have 11 appearing only once. But we can use $17078^2 \equiv 2^6 * 3^2 * 11 \pmod{3837523}$.

   Now we multiply all four equations together modulo n.
   $(1964 * 9398 * 19095 * 17078)^2 \equiv (2^4 * 3^2 * 5^3 * 11 * 13^2 * 19)^2 \pmod{n}$.
   This is $2230387^2 \equiv 2586705^2$ and so $2230387 \equiv \pm 2586705 \pmod{n}$. So let us try the gcds:

   $$\gcd(2230387 - 2586705, 3837523) = 1093.$$

   We have found a divisor of n. In fact, $3837523 = 1093 * 3511$.

Further Reading. See [41] and [42] for some of the original work on the Quadratic Sieve. Appendix B of [28] describes the method and gives examples, including in Sage. Sections 5.4 and 5.5 of [31] describe variations on the basic quadratic sieve method; these sections contain further references.

8.2.2 Problems

1. Find a five-digit prime p where $p - 1$ can be factored into prime factors using only the prime 2.

2. Let $\mathcal{B} = \{2, 3\}$. List all $\mathcal{B}$-smooth numbers up to 100.

Computer-Assisted Problems

    3. Use the quadratic sieve method to factor $n = 12358397$.

8.3 POLLARD'S $P - 1$ AND RHO METHODS

While the quadratic sieve method works well, there are several methods, based on other ideas, which are also worth trying. John Pollard developed two quite different methods, which we consider in this section. The "$p - 1$" method, developed in 1974 [38] is useful for RSA moduli, normally the product of two large primes. It is based on an assumption that for one of the primes p in an RSA number n, the number $p - 1$ has only small prime factors. Of course, an RSA designer would want to avoid a $p - 1$ attack and so make sure that the modulus she chose did not have this property. However, in practice, primes are taken randomly from a table and often not checked.

8.3.1 Pollard's $p - 1$ Method

Consider the prime $p = 281$. The number $p - 1 = 2^3 * 5 * 7$ has a factorization into small primes. As we saw in the previous section, there is some lack of clarity about what is meant by "small." This will remain unclarified. But, as in the quadratic sieve method, we can be flexible enough to increase the size of the base set if necessary.

    The idea of the algorithm is that if p is a prime such that $p - 1$ is $\mathcal{B}$-smooth for some set $\mathcal{B}$, and if B is the largest prime number in $\mathcal{B}$ (the smoothness bound for $p - 1$), then the small factors in $p - 1$ would each appear in B factorial.

    For example, if $B = 7$, then $7! = 7 * 6 * 5 * 4 * 3 * 2 * 1$ is divisible by each of 2, 3, 5, and 7. If this happens, then we can write $B! = k(p - 1)$ for some integer k and use the FLT to get $a^{B!} \equiv (a^{(p-1)})^k \equiv 1 \pmod{p}$ for any $0 < a < p$.

    We can conclude that $p | a^{B!} - 1$.

    Now let us return to the general factoring situation where we are trying to factor a number n for which the above p is a prime divisor. We know that p divides n as well as the above difference. Hence, p must divide their greatest common divisor. That is, $p | \gcd(a^{B!} - 1, n) = d$.

    And of course, we can compute d using the Euclidean algorithm. If $1 < d < n$, we have found a nontrivial factor, d, of n. If $d = 1$, then perhaps our $\mathcal{B}$-smooth $p - 1$ does not exist; however, we can try a new base. If $d = n$, we have learnt nothing, and again could try a new base.

8.3.2 The Pollard $p - 1$ Algorithm

Input an odd integer n to be factored.
Choose a smoothness bound $\mathcal{B}$.
Let $a = 2$

- Compute $\gcd(a, n)$; if larger than 1, output a divisor of n and STOP.
- Compute $b \equiv a^{B!} \pmod{n}$ (in some efficient way)

- Compute $d = \gcd(b - 1, n)$
- If $1 < d < n$, output a divisor d of n and STOP.
  Otherwise try $a \to a + 1$ and repeat until $(n - 1)/2$ is reached.

Choose a new smoothness bound.

There are two variables in the algorithm, a and $\mathcal{B}$. Normally, values of a from 2 on will be tried. Note that since $\mathcal{B}!$ is always even, the same value for b will be obtained for both a and $-a$; so we only need to use values for a up to $(n - 1)/2$. Choosing $\mathcal{B}$ can be difficult. A simple approach is to begin with what seems to be a reasonable choice and then if it is not large enough, change it to the next prime in line. However, the running time of the algorithm is about $O(\mathcal{B} * \ln(n)/\ln(\mathcal{B}))$ so choosing a small $\mathcal{B}$ aids the computation.

Example 8.8 We use the Pollard $p - 1$ method to factor $n = 973$. Choose a smoothness bound $\mathcal{B} = 7$ and apply the algorithm. Choosing $a = 2$, the gcd with n is 1 and so we now compute $b \equiv 2^{7!} = 2^{3840} \pmod{973}$. This can be done using the fast exponentiation method used in Example 2.8 and later examples in the text. We obtain 925. The $\gcd(925 - 1, 973) = 7$ and so we have factored $n = 7 * 139$.

8.3.3 Pollard's rho Method

Pollard's rho method was published 1 year after his $p - 1$ method, in 1975, and extended in 1978 [38, 39, 41]. This algorithm is most useful in factoring numbers, which have some relatively small factor; it is not particularly effective for RSA moduli, which are the product of very large primes. The method is based on the Floyd cycling algorithm, which we discussed in Section 2.4, along with an adaptation of the Pollard attack on the Discrete Logarithm focusing on the use of the Euclidean Algorithm to find greatest common denominators.

8.3.4 The Pollard rho Algorithm

Input an odd integer n to be factored.

1. Choose a polynomial of degree at least 2 with coefficients modulo n (usually $f(x) = x^2 + 1$ is used).
2. Choose a random seed value x_0 and set $x_i = x_0$, $y_i = x_0$ with $i = 0$.
3. Repeat $i = i + 1$, $x_i = f(x_{i-1})$, $y_i = f(f(y_{i-1}))$ and check if $\gcd(x_i - x_j, n) > 1$ until $x_i = y_i$.

Output a proper factor of n OR return to Step 1 and use a different polynomial.

As discussed in Section 2.4, we know that a collision will eventually be found as the set of numbers available is finite. However, in practice, with very large values for n, we often do not want to compute n pairs in Step 3. In this case, we can trade off by adding a bound on i in that step. If no collision or nontrivial factor is found, we return to Step 1 and change the polynomial. It is also possible to begin with a list of polynomials for use.

The expected running time for the Pollard rho algorithm is $O(n^{1/4})$.

Example 8.9   We use Pollard's rho method to factor 221. First set $f(x) = x^2 + 1$ and $x_0 = 2$ and then compute:

$$x_1 = 5, x_2 = 26, x_3 = 14, x_4 = 197, x_5 = 135, x_6 = 104,$$
$$x_7 = 209, x_8 = 145, x_9 = 31, x_{10} = 78, x_{11} = 118, x_{12} = 2,$$

and we have a cycle with no tail.

We can write $x_0 = f(x_{11})$ and so $1 + 1 \equiv 118^2 + 1 \pmod{221}$, and $1^2 \equiv 118^2 \pmod{221}$. Now test the $\gcd(117, 221) = 13$ and $\gcd(119, 221) = 17$. Thus, $221 = 13 * 17$.

It may happen that two values of f are equal modulo a proper factor of n, but not modulo n itself. In general, we cannot see this in the computations, but it is a good reason for checking greatest common divisors regularly as in Step 3 of the algorithm. This is illustrated in the next example where the cycle is not apparent modulo n, but in fact $x_0 = x_6 \pmod{41}$, where 41 is a proper divisor of n.

Example 8.10   Let $n = 37351$ with seed $x_0 = 2$ and function $f(x) = x^2 + 1$. Then $x_1 = f(x_0) = 5, x_2 = 26, x_3 = 677, x_4 = 3146$, $x_5 = 36653$, and $x_6 = 1642 \pmod{n}$. Although we have not yet reached a collision, we start to check some greatest common denominators at this point. We check all $\gcd(x_i - x_j, n)$ for $i \neq j$ and see that these values are all 1 until we reach $\gcd(x_6 - x_0, n) = \gcd(1640, 37351) = 41$. We can now factor n into $41 * 911$.

We can see how the cycles would have occurred modulo 41: $x_0 = 2, x_1 = 5, x_2 = 26,$ $x_3 = 21, x_4 = 32$, $x_5 = 0$, $x_6 = 1, x_7 = 2$, so we have a collision here.

8.3.5 Computer Examples

1. We are given the RSA product of two primes to be $n = 3837523$. Factor it using the Pollard $p - 1$ algorithm.

    Solution.   Any prime factor of n would have about four digits. So choose $\mathcal{B}$ such that $\mathcal{B}!$ has four or five digits. Example $6! = 720$ and $7! = 5040$.

    We try $\mathcal{B} = 7$ with $a = 2$:

    $\mathcal{B} := 7; a := 2;$

    $b := a\&^{\wedge}(\mathcal{B}!) \mod n$; and so $b = 2494436$.

    However, $\gcd(b - 1, n) = 1$. So we try $\mathcal{B} = 8$:

    $\mathcal{B} := 8;$

    $b := a\&^{\wedge}(\mathcal{B}!) \mod n$; and so $b = 2468068$.

    However, again $\gcd(b - 1, n) = 1$.

    We switch to a new value for a, trying $a = 3$, with $\mathcal{B} = 7$.

    $\mathcal{B} := 7;$

$b := a\&^{\wedge}(\mathcal{B}!) \mod n$; yields $b = 3748991$.
This time $\gcd(b-1, n) = 1093$ and we have found a nontrivial factor of n. Thus, $n = 1093 * 3511$.

2. Use Pollard's rho method to factor $n = 2431$.

Solution. We write an algorithm to follow the steps of the rho method using 40 as the bound on the number of iterations:

```
rho:=proc(n) local i, x, y;
x[0] := 2;
y[0] := 2;
for i from 1 to 40 do
        x[i] := x[i − 1]^2 + 1  mod  n;
        y[i] := (y[i − 1]² + 1)^2 + 1  mod  n;
COMMENT: If we obtain a match, we will need to
compute gcds using x[i − 1]. So we print all values
of [i].
print(x[i]);
if  x[i] = y[i] then  print (i, x[i], x[i − 1]) end if
end do;
end proc;
```

With $n = 2431$, this procedure produces a cycle at step $i = 12$. The preliminary output is 2, 5, 26, 677, 1302, 798, 2314, 1535, 587, 1799, 741, 2107, 444, 226, 26, 677, and so on. The tail is $\{2, 5\}$ and the first cycle then starts. So we can set $5^2 + 1 \equiv 226^2 + 1 \equiv 26 \pmod{2431}$. Now we can look at the greatest common divisors: $\gcd(226 - 5, 2431) = 221$ and $\gcd(226 + 5, 2431) = 11$. We have factored 2431 as $221 * 11$.

Further Reading. For additional theoretical details of the Pollard $p - 1$ method, see [38], and for additional details on Pollard's rho method, see [39] and [41]. Descriptions of both methods, along with examples, can be found in [29] on pages 91, 92, and 93; page 125 of [29] lists references to some practical improvements of both the $p - 1$ and rho methods. See also [40] and [45].

Descriptions of both algorithms can be found in many texts on factoring relevant to cryptography. Over the years, variations of the algorithms and of the notation have developed. Mollin [31] discusses the $p - 1$ method in Section 6.2; McAndrew [28] presents the Pollard's rho method in Section 6.8 and implements it in Sage. Hoffstein et al. consider both methods in Ref. [19] but give a particularly nice description of the rho algorithm and its connection to the Floyd cycle-finding algorithm (Section 2.4 of this book) in Section 5.5.

8.3.6 Problems

1. Use Pollard's rho method to factor 35.
2. Use Pollard's $p - 1$ method to factor 221.

Computer-Assisted Problems

3. Use Pollard's rho algorithm to factor 1387.
4. Use Pollard's $p - 1$ method to factor 11663 using a factor base of $\{2, 3, 5\}$.

8.4 CONTINUED FRACTIONS AND FACTORING

The material in this section provides the background for an attack on the RSA scheme. It deals with special ways of writing numbers. It is the final factoring method that we discuss. Before the sieving methods were discovered to be so efficient, the continued fraction method was the best known.

Recall that a rational number has the form a/b, where a and b are integers; this set includes the case $b = 1$ and so all integers are considered to be rational. However, most real numbers are not rational. An example of a real number which is not rational is *Pi*, the ratio of a circle's circumference to its diameter in Euclidean space. *Pi*, also written as Π, is an infinite decimal; that is, if written out as a decimal, it does not stop. Rounded to five decimal places, it can be written as 3.14159. Other examples of real numbers, which are not rational, are square roots of nonsquare numbers such as 3 or 8. We shall demonstrate a method to show how any real number can be approximated by rational numbers of a special form.

8.4.1 The Setup

We decide in advance

(a) how many decimal points to take computations to and
(b) how long to continue.

We begin with a real number which is not rational. We round off to five decimal places in our examples and we continue computations until $|x - $ approx $| = 0$, where *approx* is a rational approximation of x, up to five decimal places. We consider an example with the real number Π. The target is to represent this as a fraction in a special form combining rational numbers.

Example 8.11 Let $x = \pi = 3.14159\ldots$. We shall compute to five decimal places. Our first approximation is by the integer part: $x_0 = 3$. Since $|x - x_0| \neq 0$ to 5 decimal places, we continue and consider the 0.14159 component.

Write
$$x_1 = 3 + (.14159) = 3 + \frac{14159}{100000}.$$

Since $14159 < 100000$, we cannot really do much with this. However, the trick is to rewrite as follows:
$$x_1 = 3 + \frac{1}{\frac{100000}{14159}}$$

and now we can do a division: $x_1 = 3 + \frac{1}{7.06265} = 3 + \frac{1}{7 + \frac{06265}{100000}}$.

With *Pi*, this procedure continues forever, so in practice we need to limit it. Recalling the setup instructions at this point, we will continue to divide and invert rational fractions until $|x - x_i| = 0$. However, the longer we continue, the closer the right-hand side gets to the actual number that we began with.

Definition 8.2   The representation of a number as in Example 8.11 is called a *continued fraction expansion* of the number [10].

We now consider an example with a square root and then show how the continued fraction expansions of square roots can be used to develop a factoring algorithm.

Example 8.12   We consider an approximation of the square root of 3: $\sqrt{3} \approx 1.73205$. This is:

$$\sqrt{3} = 1 + 73205/100000$$

$$= 1 + \cfrac{1}{100000/73205}$$

$$= 1 + \cfrac{1}{1 + 26795/73205}$$

$$= 1 + \cfrac{1}{1 + \cfrac{1}{73205/26795}}$$

$$= 1 + \cfrac{1}{1 + \cfrac{1}{2 + 19615/26795}}$$

$$= 1 + \cfrac{1}{1 + \cfrac{1}{2 + \cfrac{1}{26796/19615}}}$$

$$= 1 + \cfrac{1}{1 + \cfrac{1}{2 + \cfrac{1}{1 + 7180/19615}}}.$$

Notation

As the numerator on the fractions developed on the right-hand side is always 1, we can use the integer part of each fraction to develop a shortened version of the expansion. So for the expansion of $\sqrt{3}$, we can write the vector $< 1, 1, 2, 1, 2, \ldots >$ to represent the entire expansion. If we have decided in advance how long the expansion will continue, then this length will produce a finite vector. It makes sense to work with such vectors that all have the same length.

Definition 8.3   A vector representation of a real number may repeat after a while. That is, it may look like $< \ldots q_1, q_2, \ldots, q_n, q_1, q_2, \ldots, q_n, q_1, q_2, \ldots, q_n, \cdots >$ where the $q_1, q_2, \ldots, q_n$ component goes on indefinitely. In this case, we say that the *vector and number are periodic of period n.*

If we continue to expand $\sqrt{3}$, we see that it is periodic of period 2. We can then write

$$\sqrt{3} - 1 = \cfrac{1}{1 + \cfrac{1}{2 + \cfrac{1}{1 + \cfrac{1}{2 + \cdots}}}}$$

and

$$\sqrt{3} - 1 = \cfrac{1}{1 + \cfrac{1}{2 + (\sqrt{3} - 1)}}$$

and also rewrite the vector representation of the continued fraction as $\sqrt{3} =<$ $1, 1, 2, \sqrt{3} - 1 >$ with the appropriate interpretation that $\sqrt{3} - 1$ in the right-hand expansion represents its continued fraction.

In general, for a positive nonsquare n, the continued fraction of $\sqrt{n}$ is periodic and we can write

$$\sqrt{n} = \left\langle q_0, q_1, \ldots a_{k-1}, \frac{\sqrt{n} + P_k}{Q_k} \right\rangle \quad \text{for some } k.$$

Where P_k and Q_k are integers. To get more information about Q_k, we consider the vector representation of the continued fraction of $\sqrt{n}$. We argue that the longer we make the continued fraction representation, or equivalently the corresponding vector, the closer we get to the actual number. We thus make the following definition.

Definition 8.4   Let $< q_0, q_1, q_2, \ldots >$ be a continued fraction expansion of $\sqrt{n}$, n a positive integer not a square. Then C_i, $i \geq 0$, represented by $< q_0, q_1, \ldots, q_i >$, is called the *ith convergent of* $\sqrt{n}$. C_i is also considered to be the sum of the first $i + 1$ terms in the continued fraction expansion.

Example 8.13   We determine the first four convergents of each of $\sqrt{3}$ and $\sqrt{5}$. For $\sqrt{3}$, we can use the vector obtained from Example 8.12: $< 1, 1, 2, 1, 2, \ldots >$. The first four convergents are $C_0 = 1$, $C_1 = 1 + (1/1) = 2$, $C_2 = 1 + 1/(1 + 1/2) = 5/3$, and $C_3 = 1 + 1/(1 + 1/(2 + 1/1)) = 7/4$. Checking that each gets closer to $\sqrt{3}$, we compute $\sqrt{3} - 1 = 0.73205$, $\sqrt{3} - 2 = -0.26795$, $\sqrt{3} - 5/3 = 0.06538$ and $\sqrt{3} - 7/4 = -0.01795$. Notice that the sign changes along the way, so the differences alternate above and below the x-axis in Euclidean space, and tend to zero.

We now compute the convergents for $\sqrt{5}$. The vector representation is $<$ $2, 4, 4, 4 \ldots >$ with period 1. The convergents are $C_0 = 2$, $C_1 = 2 + (1/4) = 9/4$, $C_2 = 2 + 1/(4 + 1/4) = 38/17$, and $C_3 = 2 + 1/(4 + 1/(4 + 1/4)) = 161/72$. Again, looking at the differences, we see that $\sqrt{5} - 2 = 0.23607$, $\sqrt{5} - 9/4 = -0.01393$, $\sqrt{5} - 38/17 = 0.00077$, and $\sqrt{5} - 161/72 = -0.00004$.

Example 8.13 shows the general pattern of the convergents. They alternate above and below the x-axis in Euclidean space, tending to zero. Considering the differences of the squares is even more revealing. For 3, we obtain

$$1 - 3 = -2, \quad 2^2 - 3 = 1, \quad \left(\tfrac{5}{3}\right)^2 - 3 = -\tfrac{2}{9}, \quad \left(\tfrac{7}{4}\right)^2 - 3 = \tfrac{1}{16},$$
$$\left(\tfrac{19}{11}\right)^2 - 3 = -\tfrac{2}{121}, \quad \left(\tfrac{26}{15}\right)^2 - 3 = \tfrac{1}{225} \dots.$$

resulting in the sequence

$$-2, \quad 1, \quad -\frac{2}{9}, \quad \frac{1}{16}, \quad -\frac{2}{121}, \quad \frac{1}{225}, \dots$$

There are several points worth noting: the signs alternate, the numerators alternate between 1 and 2 (reflecting the fact that $\sqrt{3}$ is periodic with 1 and 2 repeated), moreover, the denominators are squares. If we separate out the terms with 1 in the numerator from those with 2 in the numerator, we have the two sequences: $-2, -2/9, -2/121, \dots$ and $1, 1/16, 1/225, \dots$. If we break the convergents up into two corresponding sequences: $1, 5/3, \dots$ and $2, 7/4, \dots$, then letting y be the numerator and x the denominator, it can be shown that every element of the first sequence of convergents satisfies the equation

$$y^2 - 3x^2 = -2$$

and every element of the second sequence satisfies

$$y^2 - 3x^2 = 1.$$

8.4.2 Pell's Equation

It turns out that if n is a nonsquare positive integer, then the convergents $C_k = A_k/B_k$ of a continued fraction expansion of $\sqrt{n}$ always satisfy an equation of the form

$$A_k^2 - nB_k^2 = (-1)^{k+1}Q_{k+1},$$

where Q_k is derived from the continued fraction expansion, $< q_0, q_1, \dots, q_i, \dots >$, of $\sqrt{n}$. This equation is known as *Pell's equation*.

8.4.3 Back to Factoring

How do we exploit this information to obtain a general factoring attack on n? If the right-hand side of Pell's equation is a square, then n divides a difference of squares and, once again, we may find a nontrivial greatest common divisor, thus factoring n. If the right-hand side is not a square, we may be able to paste together several equations for various values of k to force a square on the right-hand side. (This is what we did in the quadratic sieve method.)

From Pell's equation, for any prime divisor p of Q_k, we have $A_k^2 \equiv nB_k^2 \pmod{p}$ and so n must be a quadratic residue modulo p. In finding prime divisors of the Q_k's, instead of factoring them, we resort to the well-used method of choosing a base of primes $\mathcal{B} = \{p_1, p_2, \dots, p_k\}$, all less than some bound. In this case, we need only take primes for which n is a quadratic residue. We shall only work with the primes in $\mathcal{B}$ to determine factors of Q_k. There are also shades of the quadratic sieve method here, as we try to patch together squares.

Rather than giving a formal description of the method, we develop a factoring algorithm by means of the next example. Based on the size of the given n to be factored, we also decide in advance how many steps we will try as, in general, the algorithm will be infinite.

A great deal of work goes into computing the convergents. However, there is a general formula that can be applied to compute the q_i instead of the direct computation above. Given q_0 this is

$$q_0, q_i = \left\lfloor \frac{P_i + \sqrt{n}}{Q_i} \right\rfloor \quad \text{for } 1 \le i.$$

Note that if you use the continued fraction directly, the round-off you choose may result in different values from those obtained using this formula. They are not wrong. In general, variations in round-off values or using the formula may result in alternate solutions.

The general formulas for producing the values we need are Set $Q_0 = 1$, $P_0 = 0$, $A_{-2} = 0$, $A_{-1} = 1$, $A_0 = \lfloor \sqrt{n} \rfloor = q_0 = P_1$. Then $A_j = q_j A_{j-1} + A_{j-2}$, $Q_j = \frac{n - P_j^2}{Q_{j-1}}$ and $P_{j+1} = q_j Q_j - P_j$.

Example 8.14 We use the continued fraction method to factor 667. We first choose a base of primes taking only those for which n is a quadratic residue. We can use the Corollary to Euler's criterion to determine the primes we want, up to, say 13 (note that 2 will always be in this set if n is odd): $\mathcal{B} = \{2, 7, 13\}$. We now need the A_i and Q_i for Pell's equation; but we can compute these from the formulas given. The B_i in the equation are unimportant in factoring n.

Set $Q_0 = 1$, $P_0 = 0$, $A_{-2} = 0$, $A_{-1} = 1$, $A_0 = 25 = q_0 = P_1$. We make a table of values, initially with eight rows. At each stage, we test if a prime in the base set divides Q_i.

i	q_i	P_i	Q_i	A_{i-1} (**mod** n)
0	25	0	1	1
1	1	25	$42 = 2 * 3 * 7$	25
2	4	17	9	26
3	1	19	$34 = 2 * 17$	129
4	3	15	13	155
5	7	24	7	594
6	8	25	$6 = 2 * 3$	311
7	2	23	23	414
8	8	23	$6 = 2 * 3$	472

While we now see a potential square using $i = 6$ and $i = 8$, the fact that one of the prime factors is a 3 and is not in the base set, indicates that we will not be successful in factoring 667. We, therefore, add more lines:

i	q_i	P_i	Q_i	A_{i-1} (mod n)
9	7	25	7	188
10				
11				

At row 9, we can stop again, as we now have two 7s appearing (with row 5) and can try to set up a difference of squares. From Pell's equation, $594^2 * 188^2 \equiv (-1)^5 * 7 * (-1)^9 * 7 \pmod{667} \equiv 7^2$. Trying a difference of squares with $594 * 188 \equiv 283 \pmod{667}$, we obtain $\gcd(283 - 7, 667) = 23$ and $\gcd(283 + 7, 667) = 29$. Thus, we have factored 667 as $23 * 29$.

Comment

- If we get a square Q_i with i even, then we can factor directly from this one value.

8.4.4 Computer Examples

1. Use continued fractions to factor 5969.
   Solution. In the setup phase, we choose an integer slightly larger than square root of n; in this case, 77. We also need to put a bound on the continued fraction expansion, so set $J = 8$ as the number of rounds to be computed. (If we fail to factor, we may increase J.) As a factor base, we only need to take primes for which n is a quadratic residue because of Pell's equation. This we can determine without factoring using the square case of Euler's criterion. We choose six primes going just over 77. So $B = \{2, 5, 23, 43, 71, 102\}$. We now expand $\sqrt{5969}$ into a continued fraction using four decimal places.

$$\sqrt{5969} \approx 77.2597 = 77 + \cfrac{1}{\frac{10000}{2593}}$$

$$= 77 + \cfrac{1}{3 + \frac{8565}{10000}} = 77 + \cfrac{1}{3 + \cfrac{1}{1 + \frac{1675}{10000}}}$$

$$= 77 + \cfrac{1}{3 + \cfrac{1}{1 + \cfrac{1}{5 + \frac{9701}{10000}}}} = 77 + \cfrac{1}{3 + \cfrac{1}{1 + \cfrac{1}{5 + \cfrac{1}{1 + \frac{308}{10000}}}}}$$

$$= 77 + \cfrac{1}{3 + \cfrac{1}{1 + \cfrac{1}{5 + \cfrac{1}{1 + \cfrac{1}{32 + \frac{4675}{10000}}}}}} = 77 + \cfrac{1}{3 + \cfrac{1}{1 + \cfrac{1}{5 + \cfrac{1}{1 + \cfrac{1}{32 + \cfrac{1}{2 + \frac{1390}{10000}}}}}}}$$

The continued fraction expansion vector is $\sqrt{5969} = \langle 77, 3, 1, 5, 1, 32, 2, 7, 5, 6, \ldots \rangle$. We use these values as the q_i in the table below. Alternately, the above formula for q_i could have been used.

Our aim is now to use Pell's equation and get the values of the coefficients. We keep track of these values using a table. We begin with some initial values and then use the Euclidean algorithm to obtain the other values:

Set $Q_0 = 1$, $P_0 = 0$, $A_{-2} = 0$, $A_{-1} = 1$, $A_0 = 77 = q_0 = P_1$. Then $A_j = q_j A_{j-1} + A_{j-2}$

$$Q_j = \frac{n - P_j^2}{Q_{j-1}} \quad \text{and} \quad P_{j+1} = q_j Q_j - P_j.$$

i	q_i	P_i	Q_i	A_{i-1} (mod n)
0	77	0	1	1
1	3	77	40	77
2	1	43	103	232
3	5	60	23	309
4	1	55	128	1777
5	32	73	5	2086
6	2	87	-320	2870
7	7	-727	1633	1857
8	5	220	-4336	3931

$A_1 = 3 * A_0 + A_{-1} = 3 * 77 + 1 = 232$
$A_2 = 1 * 232 + 77 = 309$; $A_3 = 5 * 309 + 232 = 1777$
$A_4 = 1 * 1777 + 309 = 2086$; $A_5 = 32 * 2086 + 1777 = 68529$
$A_6 = 2 * 68529 + 2086 = 139144$; $A_7 = 7 * 139144 + 68529 = 1042537$
$Q_1 = \frac{5969 - P_1^2}{Q_0} = \frac{5969 - 77^2}{1} = 40$, so $P_2 = q_1 Q_1 - P_1 = 3 * (40) - 77 = 43$
$Q_2 = \frac{5969 - 43^2}{40} = 103$; $P_3 = q_2 Q_2 - P_2 = 103 - 43 = 60$
$Q_3 = \frac{5969 - 60^2}{103} = 23$; $P_4 = q_3 Q_3 - P_3 = 5 * 23 - 60 = 55$
$Q_4 = \frac{5969 - 55^2}{23} = 128$; $P_5 = q_4 Q_4 - P_4 = 128 - 55 = 73$
$Q_5 = \frac{5969 - 73^2}{128} = 5$; $P_6 = q_5 Q_5 - P_5 = 32 * 5 - 73 = 87$
$Q_6 = \frac{5969 - 87^2}{5} = -320$; $P_7 = q_6 Q_6 - P_6 = 2 * (-320) - 87 = -727$
$Q_7 = \frac{5969 - (727)^2}{-320} = 1633$; $P_8 = q_7 Q_7 - P_7 = 7 * (1633) + 727 = 12158$
$Q_8 = \frac{5969 - (12158)^2}{1633} = -4336$.

We did not obtain any squares in the Q_i, so we try combinations: $A_j^2 \equiv (-1)^j Q_{j+1}$ (mod n) to see if $(A_j * A_k)^2 \equiv (-1)^{j+k} Q_{j+1} * Q_{k+1}$ is a square modulo n.
To do this, we use our factor base to factor the Q_j.
$(-1)^0 Q_1 = 40 = 2^3 * 5$
$(-1)^1 Q_2 = -103$
$(-1)^2 Q_3 = 23$
$(-1)^3 Q_4 = -128 = -2^7$
$(-1)^4 Q_5 = 5$
$(-1)^5 Q_6 = 320 = 2^6 * 5$.

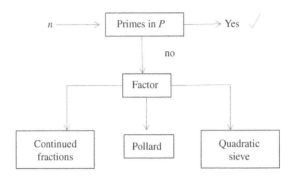

Figure 8.1. Factoring n

We can stop here, since $(-1)^4 Q_5 * (-1)^5 Q_6 = 2^6 * 5^2 = (2^3 * 5)^2 = 40^2$. So $(A_4 * A_5)^2 \equiv (2086 * 2870)^2 \equiv 40^2 \pmod{5969}$ or $5882^2 \equiv 40^2$. It follows that $\gcd(5882 + 40, 5969) = \gcd(5922, 5969) = 47$ is a factor of n. Thus, $5969 = 47 * 127$.

8.4.5 In Summary

There is currently no known polynomial time algorithm for factoring. Figure 8.1 describes the general approach when faced with the challenge of factoring a value n about which nothing is known.

Further Reading. Continued fractions are linked to the Euclidean algorithm which, as we know, is computationally efficient. The direct relationship between them is described in [10], for example. Thus, the use of a Euclidean algorithm-related method for factoring dangles the promise of a polynomial time factoring algorithm. Alas, at this time, such an algorithm is still beyond reach. Chapter 4 of Davenport's book [10] gives a thorough and clear explanation of continued fractions and how they work, and there is also a good historical description of Pell's equation; the notes at the end of that chapter list a number of additional resources on the subject. While not many cryptography texts have ventured into full descriptions of the use of continued fractions in attacks based on factoring, some, such as [31] and [29] mention it. An Internet search, however, should recover a number of documents with examples additional to those in this text.

8.4.6 Problems

1. Start with a real number r and compute a continued fraction expansion for it as in Example 8.11. Suppose the expansion stops after a finite number of steps. That is, somewhere along the way we obtain a fraction $1/1$ that inverts to the same number. Explain why the original number must be a rational number.

2. The vector $< 7, 3, 9, 1 >$ is a continued fraction representation of which number?

3. In Example 8.14, try factoring 667 using rows 6 and 8.

Computer-Assisted Problems

4. Use the general continued fraction method to factor $n = 13290059$. Use the formulas $Q_0 = 1$, $P_0 = 0$, $A_{-2} = 0$, $A_{-1} = 1$, $A_0 = q_0 = P_1 =$ the integer part of the square root of n, $A_j = q_j A_{j-1} + A_{j-2}$,

$$q_j = \left\lfloor \frac{P_j + \sqrt{n}}{Q_j} \right\rfloor, \; Q_j = \frac{n - P_j^2}{Q_{j-1}} \quad \text{and} \quad P_{j+1} = q_j Q_j - P_j$$

to calculate q_i, P_i, Q_i, and A_i. Do this up to $i = 31$ and put the values in a table. Then choose a factor base of primes up to 113 by taking only those primes for which n is a quadratic residue; factor those Q_i which are divisible by the primes in the factor base. Determine which combinations of Q_i's lead to a Fermat-type squares congruence. Check each to find a factor of n, and subsequently, factor n.

TABLE OF PRIMES UP TO 1100 AND SMALLEST PRIMITIVE ROOTS

PRIME	Smallest Primitive Root	PRIME	Smallest Primitive Root	PRIME	Smallest Primitive Root	PRIME	Smallest Primitive Root
2	1	211	2	487	3	797	2
3	2	223	3	491	2	809	3
5	2	227	2	499	7	811	3
7	3	229	6	503	5	821	2
11	2	233	3	509	2	823	3
13	2	239	7	521	3	827	2
17	3	241	7	523	2	829	2
19	2	251	6	541	2	839	11
23	5	257	3	547	2	853	2
29	2	263	5	557	2	857	3
31	3	269	2	563	2	859	2
37	2	271	6	569	3	863	5
41	6	277	5	571	3	877	2
43	3	281	3	577	5	881	3
47	5	283	3	587	2	883	2
53	2	293	2	593	3	887	5
59	2	307	5	599	7	907	2
61	2	311	17	601	7	911	17
67	2	313	10	607	3	919	7
71	7	317	2	613	2	929	3
73	5	331	3	617	3	937	5
79	3	337	10	619	2	941	2
83	2	347	2	631	3	947	2
89	3	349	2	641	3	953	3
97	5	353	3	643	11	967	5
101	2	359	7	647	5	971	6
103	5	367	6	653	2	977	3
107	2	373	2	659	2	983	5
109	6	379	2	661	2	991	6
113	3	383	5	673	5	997	7
127	3	389	2	677	2	1009	11
131	2	397	5	683	5	1013	3
137	3	401	3	691	3	1019	2
139	2	409	21	701	2	1021	10
149	2	419	2	709	2	1031	14
151	6	421	2	719	11	1033	5
157	5	431	7	727	5	1039	3
163	2	433	5	733	6	1049	3
167	5	439	15	739	3	1051	7
173	2	443	2	743	5	1061	2
179	2	449	3	751	3	1063	3
181	2	457	13	757	2	1069	6
191	19	461	2	761	6	1087	3
193	5	463	3	769	11	1091	2
197	2	467	2	773	2	1093	5
199	3	479	13	787	2	1097	3

APPENDIX: SOLUTIONS TO PROBLEMS

Full solutions for the odd-numbered questions are provided here. A full solution set is available from the publisher.

Solutions to 2.1.2

1. (a) n always divides $a - a = 0$.

   (b) If $n|a$, then $n|(a - 0)$ and we get the result. Conversely, if $n|(a - 0)$, then $n|a$.

   (c) This follows from $n|(a - b)$ precisely when $n|(b - a)$.

   (d) If $n|(a - b)$ and $n|(b - c)$, then $n|((a - b) + (b - c))$, so $n|(a - c)$.

3. We test each in turn, as in Example 2.3. Only 1, 3, 7, and 9 have inverses which are, respectively, 1, 7, 3, and 9. Checking each of the 11 possible values, we see that there is only one: 9.

5. The Maple command gcd(65537, 3511); produces output 1.

Solutions to 2.2.2

1. In this case, b divides into a and the gcd is b. You can still write $b = a - (q_1 - 1)b$.

3. $3127 = 2563 * 1 + 564.2563 = 564 * 4 + 307.564 = 307 * 1 + 257.307 = 257 * 1 + 50.257 = 50 * 5 + 7.50 = 7 * 7 + 1$. Thus, 1 is the last non zero remainder and the gcd and so 2563 does have an inverse modulo 3127. To find the inverse, we backtrack the equations to get from Maple $igcdex(2563, 3127,"x," "y")$; x; y; producing 1, 438, -359 so $1 = 2563 * 438 - 3127 * 359$. Now taking this equation modulo 3127, the inverse of 2563 is 438.

5. (a) Any solution x common to the equations must satisfy both the equations $x - 2 = 6k$ for some integer k and $x - 3 = 4m$ for some integer m. The first equation implies that x must be even. If this holds, then the second equation implies that 3 is even, which is false. So there is no solution.

Public Key Cryptography: Applications and Attacks, First Edition. Lynn Margaret Batten.
© 2013 by The Institute of Electrical and Electronics Engineers, Inc. Published 2013 by John Wiley & Sons, Inc.

(b) If we take the same approach as for (a), we obtain simultaneous equations $x - 2 = 6k$ and $x = 4m$ for integers m and k. Combining these gives $2m - 1 = 3k$. If k is even, we get 1 is divisible by 2, which is false. So values of k must be odd. So we check $k = 1, 3, 5$, and so on. These give $m = 2, 5, 8$, and so on. Clearly, we have an infinite number of solutions. The first of these is $x = 8$, then 20, then 32, and so on. We can also have negative values in the list: $k = -1, -3, -5$, and so on, leading to $x = -4, -16$, and so on. So x can be any integer of the form $8 + 12n$, n an integer.

7. We use the Maple command $chrem([11, 12, 13, 14], [101, 201, 301, 401])$; This gives 24503520.

Checking: $24503520 \equiv 11 \pmod{101}$, and so on.

Solutions to 2.3.2

1. Beginning with $x = 0$, we get 1, 2, 4, 8, 5, 10, 9, 7, 3, 6, 1, 2. The solutions have gone through all non zero values modulo 11, so 2 is a primitive root modulo 11. They begin to cycle back after all non zero values have been listed.

3. If n is even, then $n - 1$ is odd. Since $(n - 1)^{n-1} \equiv (-1)^{n-1}$, the fact that $n - 1$ is odd means that this will just be -1, or $n - 1$ modulo n. So $(n - 1)^{n-1} \equiv n - 1$ if n is even.

5. For $a = 4$, $4^{560} \equiv (2^{560})^2$ and so this is 1. For $a = 3$, we have more work to do. We still use the exponents $3^{560} = 3^{512} * 3^{32} * 3^{16}$. Starting with $3^4 = 81$, we have $3^8 \equiv 390$, $3^{16} \equiv 69$, $3^{32} \equiv 273$, $3^{64} \equiv 477$, $3^{128} \equiv 324$, $3^{256} \equiv 69$, and $3^{512} \equiv 273$. And so $3^{560} \equiv 375 \pmod{561}$. Thus, 561 is not a pseudoprime base 3.

7. Take all powers of the values 2 through 6. We see that only 5 leads to all the values 1 though 6 via their powers and so it is the only primitive root: working modulo 7, for 2, $2^2 \equiv 4$, $2^3 \equiv 1$, $2^4 \equiv 2$ and we repeat, only reaching 1, 2, and 4. For 3, we obtain $3^2 \equiv 3$ and all powers simply reduce to 3. But for 5: $5^2 \equiv 4$, $5^3 \equiv 6$, $5^4 \equiv 2$, $5^5 \equiv 3$, $5^6 \equiv 1$ covers all 6 non zero values of the set.

9. The Maple command $2^\wedge 340 \mod 341$; gives 1 and $3^\wedge 340$, $\mod 341$; gives 56. So the composite number 341 is a pseudoprime base 2 but it is not a pseudoprime base 3.

11. By Proposition 2.8, we compute $2511^{(2663-1)/2} \pmod{2663}$ which is $2662 \equiv -1 \pmod{2663}$ and so x is odd.

13. This will have various responses depending on the values chosen.

Solutions to 2.4.6

1. An example is 1, 1, 1, 1 …. in any modulus.

3. An example is 0, 1, 2, 3, 4, 5, 6, 7, 8, 9, 5, 6, 7, 8, 9, 5, 6, 7, 8, 9 … modulo 11.

5. We check $x_1 = f(x_0) = 2x_0 + 7 = 13$, $y_1 = f(2y_0 + 7) = f(13) = 2$. And $2 \neq 13$.

Then $x_2 = f(x_1) = 2x_1 + 7 = 2$, $y_2 = f(f(y_1)) = f(f(2)) = 29$. And $2 \neq 29$.
Then $x_3 = f(x_2) = 2x_2 + 7 = 11$, $y_3 = f(f(y_2)) = f(3) = 13$. And $11 \neq 13$.
Then $x_4 = f(x_3) = 2x_3 + 7 = 29$, $y_4 = f(f(y_3)) = f(2) = 11$. And $29 \neq 11$.
Then $x_5 = f(x_4) = 2x_4 + 7 = 3$, $y_5 = f(f(y_4)) = f(29) = 3$. And $x_5 = 3 = y_5 = x_{10}$ and we have found a match. There is a good chance that the tail length is 5, but this is easy to check. The cycle length must be 5 as any smaller cycle would have size dividing 5, which is impossible.

7. We can adapt the algorithm as follows:
Set $x_i = x_0$, $y_i = x_0$, and $i = 0$.
Repeat $i = i + 1$, $x_i = f(x_{i-1})$, $y_i = f(f(y_{i-1}))$ until $|x_i - y_i| \leq 2$.

9. Setting $x(0) = y(0) = 3$, and computing $x(i)$ and $y(i) = x(2i)$, we obtain
$x(1) = 25 \pmod{111}$
$y(1) = 36 \pmod{111}$

$x(2) = 36 \pmod{111}$
$y(2) = 21 \pmod{111}$

$x(3) = 46 \pmod{111}$
$y(3) = 9 \pmod{111}$

$x(4) = 21 \pmod{111}$
$y(4) = 75 \pmod{111}$

$x(5) = 1 \pmod{111}$
$y(5) = 21 \pmod{111}$

$x(6) = 9 \pmod{111}$
$y(6) = 9 \pmod{111}$

So at this position, we have a collision; it repeats every six values after this.

11. We choose a base prime set $B = \{2, 3, 5, 7, 11, 13, 17, 19, 23, 29, 31\}$. Thus, we need to get 11 equations involving each of these primes to solve for their logarithms. We write a Maple procedure to find powers of three which will get these equations. As we do not know how high the powers of three will need to go (recycling begins at 53046!), we arbitrarily choose 2000 as a bound. If this fails to give us sufficient equations, we will have to increase it.
COMMENT: the variable x in the next line represents the bound on the powers of 3. It is set as a variable since we may need to increase it.
```
indcalc := proc(x) local i, j, b, c, p;
```
COMMENT: We establish a set p of primes so that we can call each prime in a loop below.
```
p := {2, 3, 5, 7, 11, 13, 17, 19, 23, 29, 31};
b[0] := 1;
c[0] := 1;
```
COMMENT: In the next loop, we compute powers of 3 and test the divisors. If a power is only divisible by the primes in the base set p, we print it. The

algorithm only produces values which have no multiple prime divisors. (This is not necessary, but it is easier to write the algorithm to do this.)

```
for i from 1 to x do c[i] := 3&^i mod 53047 : b[i] := c[i] :
            for j from 1 to 11 do if b[i] mod p[j] = 0 then
b[i] := b[i]/p[j] end if : end do :
        if b[i] = 1 then print (i, c[i], ifactor(c[i])) end if :
end do;
end proc;
```

Executing the procedure gave the following output:

indcalc(2000); $3^\wedge 35 = 5 * 29 * 31$; $3^\wedge 206 = 2 * 7 * 23 * 31$; $3^\wedge 307 = 13 * 29$; $3^\wedge 1083 = 5 * 7 * 13 * 19$; $3^\wedge 1104 = 2 * 19 * 29$; $3^\wedge 1266 = 5 * 23 * 29$; $3^\wedge 1277 = 2 * 13 * 31$; $3^\wedge 1484 = 7 * 13$; $3^\wedge 1528 = 2 * 5 * 11 * 13 * 17$; $3^\wedge 1729 = 17 * 19$.

This gives 10 equations for 10 unknowns.

We use msolve in Maple to solve the corresponding system of logarithmic equations: $35 = L(5) + L(29) + L(31)$, and so on. Note that these work modulo phi of 53047, which is 53046.

>

msolve ($\{y + a + b = 35,\ x + z + t + b = 206,\ a + r = 307,\ y + z + r + w = 1083,\ x + r + b = 1277,\ z + r = 1484,\ x + y + u + r + v = 1528,\ v + w = 1729,\ y + t + a = 1266,\ x + w + a = 1104\}$, 53046) ;

There is some redundancy in the result, but we can let the parameter be 0 and we obtain:

The result is $x = L(2) = 4712$, $y = L(5) = 38761$, $z = L(7) = 36731$, $u = L(11) = 5457$, $r = L(13) = 17799$, $v = L(17) = 40891$, $w = L(19) = 13884$, $t = L(23) = 33043$, $a = L(29) = 35554$, $b = L(31) = 31812$.

Adapting the routine to find $8576 * 3^i$ as a product of primes in our base, we find that $8576 * 3^{32} = 5 * 23 * 29$. So we can solve for $L(8576) = L(5) + L(23) + L(29) - 32 = 1234$. This can now be easily verified by computing 3^{1234} and we obtain 8576.

Solutions to 3.1.2

1. Modulo 16, the numbers are: 1, 3, 5, 7, 9, 11, 13, 15; modulo 25, they are 1, 2, 3, 4, 6, 7, 8, 9, 11, 12, 13, 14, 16, 17, 18, 19, 21, 22, 23, 24.

3. The numbers 4 and 8 will also just give powers of 2 as above. $3^2 \equiv 9$, $3^3 \equiv 12$, $3^4 \equiv 6$, $3^5 \equiv 3$, $3^6 \equiv 9$ and we will never get 1. 9 will be the same problem as 3. $5^2 \equiv 10$, $5^3 \equiv 5$, $6^2 \equiv 2^2 * 3^2$, and $12^2 \equiv 4^2 * 3^2$ will give combinations of powers of $2 * 3$; none gives 1. $7^2 \equiv 4$, so $7^4 \equiv 1$ is no good. $14^2 \equiv 2^2 * 7^2$ will only give even numbers. $10^2 \equiv 5^2 * 2^2$ will give products of 5 or 10 with 1,2, 4 or 8 — not 1. $11^2 \equiv (-4)^2 \equiv 1$, no good. $13^2 \equiv (-2)^2$ is no good. So Z_{15} has no primitive root!

5. (a) Working modulo 13, $3^1 \equiv 3$; $3^2 \equiv 9$; $3^3 \equiv 27 \equiv 1$. Further powers of 3 (mod 13) generate only 1, 3, and 9. So 3 is not a primitive root modulo 13.

(b) Working mod 7, $3^1 \equiv 3; 3^2 \equiv 9 \equiv 2; 3^3 \equiv 6; 3^4 \equiv 4; 3^5 \equiv 5; 3^6 \equiv 1$. Thus the powers of 3 (mod 7) generate all of 1, 2, 3, 4, 5, 6. So 3 is a primitive root modulo 7.

7. By definition, we know that s is smaller than or equal to l. Let us assume that s does not divide l. Use the EA to write $l = q * s + r$, where $0 < r < s$. Now $1 \equiv a^l = a^{q*s+r} = [a^s]^q * a^r \equiv 1 * a^r$ (mod n). Now r is smaller than s and $a^r \equiv 1$ (mod n), which is a contradiction.

9. The group is the set $\{1, 7, 11, 13, 17, 19, 23, 29\}$. Any subgroup must contain the multiplicative identity, which is 1. Then the set $\{1\}$ by itself is a subgroup. As soon as we add an additional element, we must include inverses and powers. So if we use 7, then its inverse, 13 must be included, as well as its square, 19. The set $\{1,7,13,19\}$ forms a group in its own right and so is a subgroup. Similarly, $\{1, 17, 19, 23\}, \{1, 11, 19, 29\}, \{1, 11\}, \{1, 19\}, \{1, 29\}$, and the whole set are subgroups.

11. Using Maple, we get the following list of 12 values, which is a permutation of those obtained in question 1: $11, 11^3 \equiv 26, 11^5 \equiv 14, 11^9 \equiv 2, 11^{11} \equiv 10, 11^{13} \equiv 21, 11^{15} \equiv 18, 11^{17} \equiv 3, 11^{19} \equiv 15, 11^{23} \equiv 27, 11^{25} \equiv 19$, and $11^{27} \equiv 8$ (mod 29).

Solutions to 3.2.2

1. Bob computes $c_1 \equiv 3^{26} \equiv 15$ (mod 43), and using the message 14, computes $c_2 \equiv 37^{26} * 14 \equiv 31$ (mod 43). He sends Alice the pair $(15, 31)$.
   To decrypt, Alice computes $31 * 15^{-7}$ (mod 43) $\equiv 31 * 36^{-1} \equiv 14$.

3. The message "meet at 7" can be converted into a number using the method of Example 2 in Section 3.2.1. If we follow that method, we have to decide what to do with the number. We can rewrite 7 as "seven." Or we could leave it as the number $7 = 07$ and see what happens when we try to decipher. Using the latter method, the message becomes 12040419001907. Since the prime is 37, we cannot take message blocks larger than 2. So we encipher in pairs using Gary's secret 3 for each message. The values sent to Amad are $(14; 12 * 6^3, 04 * 6^3, 04 * 6^3, 19 * 6^3, 00 * 6^3, 19 * 6^3, 07 * 6^3) = (14; 2, 13, 13, 34, 00, 34, 32)$.
   Amad receives these, understands that the first value is the primitive root raised to Gary's secret, and computes each component of the message as follows: $(\alpha^b)^{-a} m 1 \alpha^{ab} \equiv (14)^{-a} 2 \equiv m1, (14)^{-a} 13 \equiv m2, (14)^{-a} 13 \equiv m3, (14)^{-a} 34 \equiv m4, (14)^{-a} 00 \equiv m5, (14)^{-a} 34 \equiv m6, (14)^{-a} 32 \equiv m7$ (mod 37). With $a = 9$ being Amad's secret and using $37 - 1 - 9 = 27$ as the exponent rather than -9, we obtain the values 12, 04, 04, 19, 00, 19, 07. Amad converts these back to letters and reads meetath. Since he is expecting a time, he realizes that the last letter must have been a number and changes it back to 7.

5. Serdar knows that $31 * 15^{-a} \equiv 14$ (mod 43), where a in the exponent is Adi's secret. He checks all values of a possible to satisfy this equation. There are 40 possible values and each should take under half a minute to check with a

calculator and should be much faster with Maple or other software. So less than 20 min let us say.

7. You compute $1234 * 512^{-312} \equiv 303 \pmod{2357}$, which is the message.

Solutions to 3.3.2

1. So Eve has $c_1 = (3^b, m_1 3^{ab}) = (15, 31)$ and $c_2 = (\alpha^b, m_2\alpha^{ab}) = (15, 26)$ and knows $14 = m_1$ and $\alpha = 3$. She can now generate m_2 using the above pieces:

$$m_2 = (m_2\alpha^{ab})(m_1)(m_1\alpha^{ab})^{-1} = 26 * 14 * 31^{-1} = 27 \pmod{43}.$$

3. By Proposition 2.8, if 2 is a primitive root, since the exponent 9 is odd, then $(67)^{44}$ must be $-1 \pmod{89}$. But $(67)^{44}$ is $1 \pmod{89}$ and Adam has cheated.

5. Oscar can compute $m = (m\alpha^{ab})(\alpha^{ab})^{-1} = 18 * 40^{-1} \pmod{89}$. He needs to compute the inverse of 40 and can use the EA or a Maple command $40^\wedge(-1) \mod 89$; which gives the answer 69. Then $m = 18 * 69 = 85 \pmod{89}$.

Solutions to 4.1.2

1. Using Maple, a calculator with a modulus function, or fast exponentiation, we have $2^\wedge 390 \mod 391$; 285. By Euler's theorem, $j = \phi(391)$ should work:
   > phi(391);
   352
   > $2^\wedge 352 \mod 391$; yields 1.

3. Recall Theorem 3.2 (The Primitive Root Theorem) which says that $Z/n, n > 1$ has a primitive root if and only if n is of the form $2^a p^b$, where p is an odd prime, $0 \leq a \leq 1$, and $b \geq 0$, or if $n = 4$.
   Let us take $n = 4$, in which case, the only primitive root is 3 (it generates the group of units $\{1, 3\}$). We need different x and y such that $3^x \equiv 3^y \pmod 4$. If we choose $x = 2$, then $y = 4$ will give us equality. Checking, $2 \equiv 4 \pmod 2$ is correct. If we choose $x = 3$, then $y = 5$ will do. Again, $3 \equiv 5 \pmod 2$ is correct.

5. First note that $299520 = \phi(314183)$. Now compute, using Maple for instance, $1573^{299520} \mod 314183$; the answer is 1.

Solutions to 4.2.3

1. Since $n = 3337$ and $\phi(n) = 46 * 70 = 3220$, Joshua uses the EA to find the inverse of 79 modulo 3220 and gets 1019.

3. Emmanuel needs to compute the inverse of 74 modulo $\varphi(229 * 277) = 228 * 276 = 62928$. But $\gcd(74, 62928) > 1$, and so the inverse does not exist.

5. Letting p and q be the unknown primes, we have $p + q = 1050589 - 1048540 + 1 = 2050$. Also $p - q = \sqrt{[2050^2 - 4202356]} = 12$. Thus, the primes are 1031 and 1019.

7. We use the prime number theorem that gives the number as $\pi(10^{200}) - \pi(10^{199})$ or approximately $10^{200}/\ln 10^{200} - 10^{199}/\ln 10^{199}$. Using Maple, this is approximately $1.953233976 * 10^{\wedge}197$.

Solutions to 4.3.2

1. Note that $83 \equiv 3 \pmod 4$ and is prime. Using Proposition 4.5, the principal square root is $40^{\frac{83+1}{4}} = 40^{21} \equiv 17 \pmod{83}$. Confirming, $(17)^2 = 40 \pmod{83}$.

3. The conditions are not satisfied $\gcd(102, 17) = 17$. So we cannot apply this result.

5. Since 103 is prime and $\gcd(102, 11) = 1$, 5 does have an $11th$ root by Theorem 4.6. The Corollary to this theorem then says that $x = 5^r \pmod{103}$ is a solution, where r is the inverse of 11 modulo 102. We use the EA to find r: $1 = 4 * 102 - 37 * 11$. Thus, $r = -37 \equiv 65 \pmod{102}$. Thus, a solution is $5^{65} \equiv 77 \pmod{103}$ and we confirm by checking: $77^{11} \equiv 5 \pmod{103}$.

7. In all cases (Propositions 4.6 and 4.7), the modulus is a prime and so $\gcd(2, \phi(n)) = 1$ will never be satisfied.

9. You might come up with $x^2 \equiv 5 \pmod{247}$ which becomes the pair of equations $x^2 \equiv 5 \pmod{13}$, which has no solutions by Euler's criterion, and $x^2 \equiv 5 \pmod{19}$ that has solutions 9 and 10, found using Proposition 4.5. Overall, there are no solutions.

11. Note that the prime $83987 \equiv 3 \pmod 4$ and so we can use Proposition 4.5.
    > 48382&^(83988/4) mod 83987; 60555
    Checking: > 60555&^2 mod 83987; 35605, which is not 48382, but is in fact the negative of 48382 mod 83987.
    > −48382 mod 83987; 35605
    Therefore, the square roots of $-48382 \pmod{83987}$ are ± 35606.

13. We first factor $527 = 17 * 31$ and then consider the following equations separately: $m^5 \equiv 5 \mod (17)$ and $m^5 \equiv 5 \mod (31)$. We check against each of our relevant theorems. Euler's criterion does not apply to the first equation, but it tells us that the second does have solutions ($5^6 \equiv 1 \pmod{31}$.) Theorem 4.4 can be applied to the first equation, since $\gcd(16, 5) = 1$, but it does not apply to the second equation since 5 divides 30. The corollary to the theorem provides a solution: then $5^{-1} \pmod{16}$ is 13. So $5^{13} \equiv 3 \pmod{17}$ is a solution. For the second equation, we can use Theorem 4.5 since $31 \equiv 1 \pmod 5$ and $\gcd(5, 6) = 1$. In this case, $5^{-1} \pmod 6$ is 5. So $5^5 \equiv 25 \pmod{31}$ is a solution. Combining these two solutions will give us a single common solution. However, Proposition 3.8 indicates that there may be additional solutions. We can easily check all solutions using Maple. > Roots($x^{\wedge}5 - 5$) mod 17; [[3, 1]]
    Means that the first equation has a single root 3.
    > Roots($x^{\wedge}5 - 5$) mod 31; [[7, 1], [14, 1], [19, 1], [25, 1], [28, 1]]
    Means that the second equation has five roots, each occurring once.

We now use the CRT with five combinations to find all solutions to the original equation.

We need an EA equation for 17 and 31: $11 * 17 - 6 * 31 = 1$.

We then get five solutions:

> $3 * (-6 * 31) + 7 * (11 * 17) \mod 527; 224$
> $3 * (-6 * 31) + 14 * (11 * 17) \mod 527; 479$
> $3 * (-6 * 31) + 19 * (11 * 17) \mod 527; 360$
> $3 * (-6 * 31) + 25 * (11 * 17) \mod 527; 428$
> $3 * (-6 * 31) + 28 * (11 * 17) \mod 527; 462$

Check that all are really solutions!

Solutions to 4.4.2

1. Let $c_p \equiv c^d \pmod{p}$ and $c_q \equiv c^d \pmod{q}$. Using $sp + tq = 1$, let $y = c_q sp + c_p tq \pmod{pq}$. Working modulo p, $tp \equiv 1$ and $y \equiv c_p * 1 \equiv c^d \pmod{p}$. Working modulo q, $y \equiv c^d \pmod{q}$. Therefore, $y \equiv c^d \pmod{pq}$ is the desired decryption of c.

3. We can write $c_p = 31^{11} \pmod{17}$ and $c_q = 31^{11} \pmod{19}$. So $c_p \equiv (-3)^{11} \equiv 9^5 * (-3) \equiv 10 \pmod{17}$, and $c_q \equiv (-7)^{11} \equiv 8 \pmod{19}$. Using the same EA equation for 17 and 19 as in Example 4.17 and Problem 2 of Section 4.4.2, the decryption value is $x = 8 * 9 * 17 + 10 * (-8) * 19 \equiv 255 + 95 \pmod{323} \equiv 27$.

5. Anna needs to reduce the order by a factor of 3. she thus need $3^{-1} \pmod{799}$ which is 533. She, therefore, sends $533^{39} * 150^{39} \pmod{799} \equiv 220$ to the company. When the company decrypts, they obtain $220^d \pmod{799}$, where $d = e^{-1} \pmod{\phi(n)}$. Since $n = 17 * 47$, $\phi(n) = 16 * 46$ and so $d = 151$. Then $220^{151} \pmod{799} \equiv 50$. So Anna has successfully reduced Ben's order to 50.

Solutions to 5.1.8

1. Under $+$, it is easy to check that the set is a group with identity 0; under $*$, it is easy to check that the set $\{1, 2, 3, 4\}$ forms a group; in particular, the inverse of 1 is 1, of 2 is 3, of 3 is 2, and of 4 is 4. Distributivity and commutativity hold because they hold in the integers.

3. To determine this, we substitute: on the left, we obtain 2, on the right, 4. So the point is not on the curve.

5. By definition, $-P = (22, -693) = (22, 430)$; it is trivially on the curve. In order to double P, first note that its y co-ordinate is not 0. We, therefore, use Definition 4.1.7: $2P = (s^2 - 2 * 22, -693 + s(22 - x_{2P}))$, where $s = (3 * 22^2 + 322)/2 * 693 = 651 * 263^{-1} = 651 * 427 = 596$. Therefore, $2P = (304, 808)$. Checking that these co-ordinates satisfy the equation, we get $808^2 = 304^3 + 322 * 304 + 964 = 401$.

7. The curve has five points as follows:

```
6 | (2,6)*        *(3,6)
5 |
3 |
2 |
1 | (2,1)*        *(3,1)
0 |                              *(6,0)
  +----------------------------------
    1     2     3     4     5     6
```

9. If $P = Q$ and $y_p = 0$, or if $P = -Q$, then the equation is true immediately from the symmetry of the definition of $+$ for such points. If $P = Q$ and $y_p \neq 0$, examining the definition of addition, Definition 5.7, we see that here also, there is symmetry and the result follows. Thus, we only consider the case where P is neither Q nor $-Q$. In this case, the slope is independent of the order of the points. The x-co-ordinate of the sum is $x_R = s^2 - x_P - x_Q$, which also is independent of the order of the points. What we have to show is that $-y_P + s(x_P - x_R) = -y_Q + s(x_Q - x_R)$. But this is equivalent to $y_Q - y_P + s(x_P - x_R) = s(x_Q - x_R)$ and we know that this is true since $s = (y_P - y_Q)/(x_P - x_Q)$.

11. Do: from $x = 0$ to 280,
    evaluate $x^3 + 200x + 192 \pmod{281}$
    if square root(s) y_j exists, output (x, y_j)
    otherwise, continue
End

This produces the points:

[1, 127],	[1, 154],	[4, 139],	[4, 142],	[6, 22],	[6, 259],	[7, 116],
[7, 165],	[8, 48],	[8, 233],	[10, 35],	[10, 246],	[11, 114],	[11, 167],
[13, 103],	[13, 178],	[14, 39],	[14, 242],	[18, 114],	[18, 167],	[20, 59],
[20, 222],	[21, 100],	[21, 181],	[22, 105],	[22, 176],	[29, 95],	[29, 186],
[30, 92],	[30, 189],	[31, 55],	[31, 226],	[32, 131],	[32, 150],	[33, 110],
[33, 171],	[34, 103],	[34, 178],	[35, 7],	[35, 274],	[37, 42],	[37, 239],
[38, 1],	[38, 280],	[40, 16],	[40, 265],	[42, 105],	[42, 176],	[47, 36],
[47, 245],	[48, 39],	[48, 242],	[50, 84],	[50, 197],	[51, 24],	[51, 257],
[54, 74],	[54, 207],	[55, 16],	[55, 265],	[56, 108],	[56, 173],	[57, 101],
[57, 180],	[59, 57],	[59, 224],	[60, 131],	[60, 150],	[61, 47],	[61, 234],
[66, 80],	[66, 201],	[68, 4],	[68, 277],	[74, 11],	[74, 270],	[75, 127],
[75, 154],	[76, 122],	[76, 159],	[77, 56],	[77, 225],	[78, 53],	[78, 228],
[79, 126],	[79, 155],	[82, 79],	[82, 202],	[83, 100],	[83, 181],	[85, 62],
[85, 219],	[86, 70],	[86, 211],	[87, 3],	[87, 278],	[88, 97],	[88, 184],
[91, 48],	[91, 233],	[93, 10],	[93, 271],	[95, 68],	[95, 213],	[98, 37],
[98, 244],	[100, 64],	[100, 217],	[101, 92],	[101, 189],	[102, 136],	[102, 145],
[104, 93],	[104, 188],	[107, 20],	[107, 261],	[108, 12],	[108, 269],	[112, 130],
[112, 151],	[113, 67],	[113, 214],	[114, 129],	[114, 152],	[115, 134],	[115, 147],
[116, 65],	[116, 216],	[118, 139],	[118, 142],	[119, 59],	[119, 222],	[120, 88],

[120, 193], [123, 46], [123, 235], [126, 38], [126, 243], [127, 40], [127, 241],
[130, 117], [130, 164], [131, 120], [131, 161], [133, 124], [133, 157], [135, 118],
[135, 163], [136, 109], [136, 172], [142, 59], [142, 222], [149, 137], [149, 144],
[150, 92], [150, 189], [151, 78], [151, 203], [152, 26], [152, 255], [153, 26],
[153, 255], [155, 8], [155, 273], [157, 9], [157, 272], [159, 139], [159, 142],
[164, 124], [164, 157], [169, 25], [169, 256], [174, 69], [174, 212], [176, 9],
[176, 272], [177, 100], [177, 181], [179, 49], [179, 232], [180, 120], [180, 161],
[181, 28], [181, 253], [182, 48], [182, 233], [184, 14], [184, 267], [186, 16],
[186, 265], [187, 73], [187, 208], [189, 131], [189, 150], [191, 86], [191, 195],
[192, 118], [192, 163], [193, 23], [193, 258], [195, 82], [195, 199], [198, 93],
[198, 188], [201, 62], [201, 219], [204, 45], [204, 236], [205, 127], [205, 154],
[206, 122], [206, 159], [207, 87], [207, 194], [209, 18], [209, 263], [210, 94],
[210, 187], [211, 129], [211, 152], [212, 66], [212, 215], [217, 105], [217, 176],
[218, 53], [218, 228], [219, 39], [219, 242], [224, 115], [224, 166], [225, 135],
[225, 146], [226, 68], [226, 213], [227, 99], [227, 182], [229, 9], [229, 272],
[231, 51], [231, 230], [232, 6], [232, 275], [234, 103], [234, 178], [235, 118],
[235, 163], [237, 129], [237, 152], [241, 68], [241, 213], [242, 90], [242, 191],
[244, 5], [244, 276], [245, 102], [245, 179], [247, 36], [247, 245], [248, 128],
[248, 153], [250, 13], [250, 268], [251, 120], [251, 161], [252, 114], [252, 167],
[254, 31], [254, 250], [256, 19], [256, 262], [257, 26], [257, 255], [258, 2],
[258, 279], [260, 93], [260, 188], [262, 140], [262, 141], [263, 95], [263, 186],
[264, 77], [264, 204], [265, 124], [265, 157], [266, 53], [266, 228], [268, 36],
[268, 245], [269, 29], [269, 252], [270, 95], [270, 186], [271, 132], [271, 149],
[275, 32], [275, 249], [276, 62], [276, 219], [280, 122], [280, 159].

Solutions to 5.2.5

1. We first choose a prime, say $p = 29$. Then take a point $P = (3, 11)$ which is to go on the curve E. If $y^2 = x^3 + 7x + b$ is the equation of E, choosing the coefficient of x to be 7, then we compute b by substituting the point: $121 = 27 + 21 + b$ (mod 29). Thus, $b = 15$ and E is $y^2 = x^3 + 7x + 15$. To generate my public key, I need a secret value $s = 2$, say. Then my public key is $(29, (3, 11), 2(3, 11))$. To work out the point $2(3, 11)$, we add the point to itself using the formula from Definition 5.7. The slope $s = (3 * 9 + 7)/22 = 5 * 4 = 20$ (mod 29). The co-ordinates of $2P$ are therefore $(17, 28)$. To confirm that this point is on the curve, we can substitute its co-ordinates into the equation to check that they satisfy.

3. Chiara received $(17, 28)$ and $(3, 18)$. She computes $(3, 18) - 3(17, 28) = (12, 0)$. Chiara knows the formula for embedding a message in an elliptic curve point, and so she recovers "1" from 12.

5. Maria knows that Q is a multiple of P, so she computes these multiples: $2P = P + P = (0, 10)$, using slope 11; $3P = P + 2P = (12, 13)$, using slope 8; $4P = 2P + 2P = (8, 13)$, using slope 12. So Binh's secret is 4.

7. We try $x = 230$, 231 and 232 to see if the corresponding y^2 value is a square. These values are 85, 263, and 272. Since $311 = 3$ (mod 4), we try Proposition 4.5 for square roots. In turn 85^{78}, 263^{78}, and 272^{78} (here we use a calculator and work with cubes and squares regularly reducing the modulus) are 256 (which

gives -85), 100—which is a square and so we stop. Thus, we can use the point $(231, 10)$.

9. Sonu receives $((303,325), (167, 203))$ and uses her secret key 2 to decrypt the message. She computes $(167, 203) - 2(303, 325) = (167, 203) - (332, 452)$ (using the slope 455). To obtain the difference, we add the negative point: $(167, 203) + (332, -452) = (167, 203) + (332, 47)$. This sum is $(216, 52)$ (using the slope 117).

Solutions to 5.3.2

1. The first slope is $14/12$ which we cannot compute since 12 and 20 are not relatively prime as shown using the EA: $20 = 12 * 1 + 8, 12 = 8 * 1 + 4, 8 = 4 * 2$. Thus, 4, the last non zero remainder is a factor of 20 and we can write $20 = 4 * 5$.

3. We begin with $y^2 = x^3 + ax + b$, choose a, then a point which will then determine b. Also, note the comments regarding the solution to the previous question. Say we choose $a = 1$ and point $(1, 1)$. Then substituting, we see that b must be $-1 = 17$. Now the slope of 2P is $4/2$ and since we can "cancel" 2s, this is just 2. So we avoid using the EA. Then $2P = (2, 15)$. The next slope, for 4P, is $13/12$. Now we have to invert 12 modulo 18 and the EA tells us that the GCD is 2. So we have factored 18 as $2 * 9$.

5. $multell([105, 1087], 700, 29, 56, 1097)$; gives $[526, 487]$.

Solutions to 6.1.5

1. To check for changes to a message (message authentication); to create a digital signature; to distinguish between messages; to check passwords safely; to have a short form of identifying messages.

3. The input size can be anything but the output varies directly as the input size does. Although this function is easy to compute, it is very easy to find collisions. However, given a hash c, finding an exact value for square root c is not easy except for c an integer which is a square.

5. The probability in succeeding in finding a collision with either hash function is extremely small. For more information, check the papers referred to in the sections on SHA-1 and MD5.

7. Recall that in general, if we have N objects and r people, and the r people choose an object, possibly choosing the same one, then

$$Pr(\text{match}) \approx 1 - \exp(-r^2/2N).$$

So to get a 1 here, we need $\exp(-r^2/2N)$ to be 0. But it is never 0!
Of course, as soon as we have 367 people in a room, two must have the same birthday. The formula is only useful when $N \geq r$.

9. Example 6.2 uses 6-bit blocks. Concatenating m with 001 gives 110100011001 which separates into two blocks $B1 = 110100$ and $B2 = 011001$. Then $H1 =$

$E(B1) = 100111$ and $H2 = E(H1 \ XOR \ B2) = E(111110) = 011111$. Saran receives 011111 along with m. Since Saran knows the encryption scheme and the secret, he can recompute 011111 as above. This confirms that m came from Veelasha and has not been altered.

11. When Jessica receives $d(m) = 425992$ she applies Erik's public key to find m. Thus, (for instance using Maple), she computes $425992^{\wedge}17 \pmod{823091} = 70012$. She reinterprets these numbers alphabetically as $07 = h$, $00 = a$, and $12 = m$. Since she is expecting a time, she rereads it as 7AM. The fact that Erik's public key decrypted the message proves that Erik sent it as only he knows his decryption key. To verify that the message has not been changed, Jessica now checks the hash. She knows that CRC32 was used and so checks both CRC32(70012) which is $0fe9d888$, and CRC32(7am) which is $91806d04$. She sees that the first of these is correct, and so the message is also correct.

Solutions to 6.2.9

1. We check the definition of group in Section 3.1. Since $g^a g^b = g^{a+b}$, the closure property is satisfied. Since additive associativity holds for the exponents, the associative property also holds in the set of all powers of g. As in Example 6.8, we can argue that g has some order a divisor of $p - 1$ and g raised to its order is 1. So the multiplicative identity is a power of g. Finally, consider g^a; we need an inverse which has this same form. Since $g^{ord(g)} = 1$ is its own inverse, without loss of generality, we can assume that $a < ord(g)$. Now $1 = g^{ord(g)} = g^{ord(g)-a+a} = g^{ord(g)-a} g^a$, and so $g^{ord(g)-a}$ is the inverse of g^a in this set. We are done.

3. Bob checks by computing $5^{444} \pmod{5023} \equiv 4678$ and also $y^\beta \beta^\gamma \pmod{p} \equiv 3796^{2294} 2294^{3740} \equiv 728$. So no, Bob should not accept the message as being validly signed by Alice.

5. (i) Since Felicia generates both k and r, and can be trusted, there can be no error in these values. Jeremy computes $m - ar$ and can recompute this for Felicia in case of a dispute. Felicia finally computes s, and so this value can again be trusted.

   (ii) Felicia receives $x = m - ar$ and knows r. Since m alone is never shown to her, she does not know $ar = m - x$, and so cannot compute the inverse of r to find a.

Solutions to 6.3.10

1. The formula is $1 - (1 - 2^{32}/2^{128})^{2^{\wedge}32}$.

3. Bob will do the same verification he did in the Section 6.2.8 problem. He checks by computing $5^{927} \pmod{5023} \equiv 600$ and also $y^\beta \beta^\gamma \pmod{p} \equiv 3796^{1287} 1287^{225} \equiv 600$. Since the two computations match, Bob will assume that Alice signed this message.

5. Lisbeth computes $\gcd(p - 1, \gamma_2 - \gamma_1) = \gcd(3358, 379) = 1$.
   She sets $m_2 - m_1 \equiv r(\gamma_2 - \gamma_1) \pmod{p - 1}$, or $357 \equiv 379r \pmod{3358}$ and is able to solve directly for r as 1011.

7. The probability is $1 - (1 - 16/437)^{16}$ which is approximately 0.4494. We first randomly generate 16 valid messages modulo 437, say
   27, 32, 139, 372, 411, 259, 367 231, 5, 399, 421, 263, 149, 192, 77, 2.
   Now take 16 random values for y and determine each to the 31 modulo 437. We take
   2, 19, 49, 54, 99, 135, 178, 211, 249, 275, 301, 326, 358, 394, 421, 430.
   Computing the powers, we obtain
   98, 171, 87, 423, 199, 212, 7, 174, 79, 367, 328, 128, 233, 363, 337, 31.
   We were lucky enough to have a match with 367. Eve can now send this message to Rex who will think it came from Oscar. (If you did not get a match, four or five tries at these choices should give you one.)

Solutions to 7.1.2

1. The number of trial divisions needed is the number of primes up to about 111111111111111 (15 1s). We can determine this from the Prime Number Theorem, Theorem 4.3, since it is just the number of primes in the range from 2 to 111111111111111; $\pi(111111111111111) \cong$ $111111111111111/\ln(111111111111111) \cong 111111111111111/32.34 \cong$ 3435717721432. This would, therefore, be the number of milliseconds, or about 39765 days; over 65 years!

3. To reduce the computations, we evaluate products of two elements of 12! at a time and reduce modulo 13: $12 * 11 \equiv 2$, $10 * 9 \equiv 12 \equiv -1$, $8 * 7 \equiv 4$, $6 * 5 \equiv 4$ and finally $4 * 3 * 2 \equiv 11 \equiv -2$. The factorial is, therefore, $2 * (-1) * 4 * 4 * (-2) \equiv 12 \equiv -1$ as required.

5. By Definition 7.1, $2^{n-1} \equiv 1 \pmod{n}$ and $3^{n-1} \equiv 1 \pmod{n}$ so, multiplying these, we obtain $6^{n-1} \equiv 1 \pmod{n}$.

7. Clearly, each of these numbers themselves is not prime. There are $9999999 - 8888888 - 1$ numbers between them to check, or 1111110. Half of these, 555555, will be even. Every third one, 370370 of them, will be divisible by 3. Every fifth one, 222222 of them, will be divisible by 5. So we can continue to eliminate on this basis. This is easier to write an algorithm for. Below, we have randomly tested divisibility by all primes less than 200 with a Maple procedure.

```
> findprime := proc() local flag,i, j, p;
p := {2,3,5,7,11,13,17,19,23,29,31,37,39,41,43,47,53,59,61,67,71,73,79,83,
89,97,101,103,107,109,113,127,131,137,139,149,151,157,163,167,173,179,
181,191,193,197,199};
    for i from 8888888 to 9999999 do
       flag := true;
       j := 1;    while (flag = true and j ≤ 47) do
          if (i mod p[j] = 0) then
```

```
         flag := false
      end if:
      j := j + 1:
   end do:
   if flag = true then
        print(i)
   end if:
   end do:
> end proc;
```

The result is still several hundred possible primes, some of which are in fact primes, and others which have prime divisors larger than those in our set. Testing some of the output at random with the command isprime()? or ifactor(); will produce several primes from the output. Some examples are 8888927 and 8888989.

Solutions to 7.2.4

1. Write $13 - 1 = 12 = 2^2 3$. So $s = 2$ and $d = 3$.
   Selecting $a = 7$, we verify that $7^{12} \equiv 1 \pmod{13}$. We proceed to compute:
   - $a^d = 7^3 \pmod{13} = 5 \neq 1$ or -1, and so continue.
   - $a^{2d} = -1 \pmod{13}$ and so again we continue.
   - In the final stage, we check to see if the equation $a^{n-1} = 1 \pmod{13}$ has non trivial solutions found in the previous stage. It does not.

   We try another random a, this time choosing $a = 9$. Now $9^{12} \equiv 1 \pmod{13}$.
   - $a^d = 9^3 \pmod{13} = 1$, so we continue.
   - $a^{2d} = 1 \pmod{13}$ and so again we continue.
   - In the final stage, we check to see if the equation $a^{n-1} = 1 \pmod{13}$ has non trivial solutions found in the previous stage. It does not.

   We conclude that 13 is probably prime.

3. Write $48 = 2^4 3$.

   (a) Compute each value $2^3 \equiv 8, 2^6 \equiv 16, 2^{12} \equiv 11, 2^{24} \equiv 23$ and $5^3 \equiv 27, 5^6 \equiv 43, 5^{12} \equiv 36, 5^{24} \equiv 22 \pmod{49}$. Since we do not get 1 or -1 for any of these values, we would output "49 is probably prime."

   (b) Note that $2^{48} \equiv 39$ and $5^{48} \equiv 43$, so the preliminary test of Miller–Selfridge–Rabin, based on the FLT would have caught this. Also, if we had randomly selected a to be a multiple of 7 (for instance, 7, 14, 21 etc), then squaring would result in 0 and we would have spotted the problem. We try $a = 7$ here: $7^3 \equiv 0$ already indicates that 49 divides 73 which is a product of three small primes and so 7 must divide 49.

5. Factor $n - 1$ as $2^4 * 955022530$. We first choose base 2 and check Fermat with answer 1. (Note that if your computer overflows, you can easily reduce $n - 1$ by factoring out small primes as $16 * 25 * 77 * 1240289$ and then take

$2^\wedge 1240289$ (mod n) followed by the result to the power 77, then to the power 25 and finally to the power 16.) Now try $2^\wedge(955022530) = 1$ and so squaring will also give 1. By the MSR, n is probably prime.

So we choose base 3. Checking Fermat, we obtain $3^{n-1} \equiv 767945134$. Thus, n must be composite.

Solutions to 7.3.4

1. To test the gcd, we divide 3 into 54419 and see that the remainder is 2. Thus the gcd is 1. To verify the exponential equation manually, we write 54418 as a sum of powers of 2 (essentially the binary form) of the number: $54418 = 2^{15} + 2^{14} + 2^{12} + 2^{10} + 2^7 + 2^4 + 2$. Thus, 2 to this power can be written as a product of 2 to each power of 2 separately. We compute them in reverse order: modulo 54419, $2^\wedge 2 = 4$, $2^\wedge 2^4 = 2^\wedge 16 \equiv 11117$, $2^\wedge 2^7 = 2^\wedge(2^4 * 2^3) = (2^\wedge 2^4)^\wedge 2^3 \equiv 11117^\wedge 2^3 = 45773$, $2^\wedge(2^\wedge 10) = (2^\wedge 2^7)^\wedge 2^3 = 45773^\wedge 8 \equiv 45086$, $2^\wedge(2^\wedge 12) = (2^\wedge 2^{10})^\wedge 2^2 \equiv 45086^\wedge 2^2 \equiv 619$, $2^\wedge(2^\wedge 14) = (2^\wedge 2^{12})^\wedge 2^2 \equiv 619^\wedge 4 \equiv 11855$ and $2^\wedge(2^\wedge 15) = (2^\wedge 2^{14})^\wedge 2 \equiv 11855^\wedge 2 \equiv 31167$. If we now take the product of these values, we obtain $2^{54418} \equiv 4 * 11117 * 45773 * 45086 * 619 * 11855 * 31167 \equiv 1$ (mod n).

3. (a) $F_1 = 5$, $F_2 = 17$, $F_3 = 257$, and $F_4 = 65537$.

   (b) Write $257 = 2^8 + 1$. Since $2^8 > 1$, and using 5 as the recommended quadratic residue, by Proth's theorem, F_3 is prime if and only if $5^{(257-1)/2} \equiv -1$ (mod 257), which is true.

5. We can easily factor $n - 1 = 7368 = 2^3 * 3 * 307$. The number 307 is prime (see the Appendix of primes). From Pocklington's theorem, we choose $a = 24$ and $b = 307$ so that b is larger than square root n. We need to look for an integer m such that $\gcd(m^{7368/307} - 1, n) = 1$ and $m^{n-1} \equiv 1$ (mod n). We start with $m = 2$ and check that $2^{7368} \equiv 1$ (mod 7369) and $\gcd(2^{24} - 1, 7369) = 1$. Since both conditions are true, we conclude by Pocklington's theorem, that n is prime.

Solutions to 7.4.3

1. The Mersenne numbers in question are M_4, M_6, M_8, M_9, and M_{10}. Then, without evaluating these, we can use Proposition 7.3 which tells us that, except for M_9, $2^2 - 1 = M_2$, divides each of them. The same proposition tells us that M_3 divides M_9.

3. By Proposition 7.3, both $2^2 - 1 = 3$ and $2^5 - 1 = 31$ divide $M_{10} = 1023$. We can also use a difference of squares formula and see that $2^5 + 1 = 33$ also divides it, which gives us a new prime divisor 11. Thus, $1023 = 3 * 11 * 31$.

5. Computing the values $s_1, s_2, \ldots, s_{16}$, we get the list 4, 14, 194, 37634, 95799, 119121, 66179, 53645, 122218, 126220, 70490, 69559, 99585, 78221, 130559, $s_{16} \equiv 0$ (mod 131071).

Solutions to 7.5.5

1. Many polynomials will not have inverses in this system. For instance, to find an inverse for $3x + 1$, we need to solve $(3x + 1) * p(x) \equiv 1 \pmod 7$ for some polynomial $p(x)$. Since $3x + 1$ is linear, any terms of $p(x)$ greater than linear will necessarily have zero coefficients. So we may assume that $p(x)$ has the form $ax + b$, where a and b are from Z_7. Thus, multiplying out gives $3ax^2 + (a + 3b)x + b \equiv 1 \pmod 7$. Comparing coefficients of each power of x, we obtain the equalities $a \equiv 0$, $a + 3b \equiv 0$ and $b \equiv 1$. However, it is impossible to solve this system of equations modulo 7.

3. It suffices to test each element of $Z/5$ to see if it produces zero from $x^5 + 2x^3 + 1$. So $x = 0$ produces 1; $x = 1$ produces 4; $x = 2$ produces 4; $x = 3$ produces 3 and $x = 4$ produces 3. So the polynomial has no roots.

5. A series of long divisions produces the following equations:
$$x^3 - 6x^2 - 9x + 14 = (x^3 - 1) * 1 + (-6x^2 - 9x + 15)$$
$$x^3 - 1 = (-6x^2 - 9x + 15) * (-x/6) + (-3x^2/2 + 5x/2 - 1)$$
$$-6x^2 - 9x + 15 = (-3x^2/2 + 5x/2 - 1) * 4 - 19(x - 1)$$
$$-3x^2/2 + 5x/2 - 1 = -19(x - 1) * 3x/38 + (x - 1)$$
$$-19(x - 1) = -19(x - 1) + 0.$$
Thus, the gcd is $x - 1$.

7. The polynomial we need to check is $x^{119} + 119x^{118}a +_{119} C_2x^{117}a^2 + \cdots + 119xa^{118} + a^{119} \pmod{119}$. All the coefficients need to be evaluated modulo 119. We do several manually and the rest by computer: $_{119}C_2 = 119 * 118/2$ which is divisible by 119 and so is 0. And $_{119}C_3 = 119 * 118 * 117/6$ which is divisible by 119 and so is 0. The next few terms are also zero until we reach $_{119}C_7 = 119 * 118 * 117 * 116 * 115 * 114 * 113/5040$ is not divisible by 119. Continuing, we see that several other coefficients are not 0. Thus, by the polynomial test, 119 is composite.

Solutions to 8.1.6

1. Squaring each square term and multiplying through by 4 gives $4n = 4rs$ (many terms cancel) and so $n = rs$.

3. We compute the sequence:
$$x_1 = (\lfloor \sqrt{n} \rfloor + 1)^2 - 2079 = 46^2 - 2079 = 37$$
$$x_2 = 47^2 - 2079 = 130$$
$$x_3 = 48^2 - 2079 = 225 = 15^2$$
In the third step, we obtained a square. So $n = 48^2 - 15^2 = (48 - 15)(48 + 15) = 33 * 63$.

5. (a) We start by choosing x and y. We need them to be of different parity as otherwise pn will be even. Try $x = 37$ and $y = 22$. Then $x^2 - y^2$ for $37^2 - 22^2 = 885$. We can, therefore, choose $p = 5$ and $n = 177$.

   (b) Now factor the difference of squares to obtain $15 * 59 = 5 * 177$. We can divide by the prime $p = 5$ to get $177 = 3 * 59$.

7. Problem 4 of Section 7.2.4 suggested using 137 as a base. This gave $137^{220} \equiv 1$, and so we obtain a difference of squares: $(137^{110} - 1) * (137^{110} + 1) \equiv 0 \pmod{221}$. This gives $204 * 206 \equiv 0 \pmod{221}$ and so we test greatest common divisors. Using the EA, we find that $\gcd(204, 221) = 17$ and $\gcd(206, 221) = 1$. The first value allows us to factor 221 as $17 * 13$.

9. We try to find $3 * 1226987$ as a difference of squares starting with values of the difference as close to zero as possible:
$(1917 + 1)^2 - 3 * 1226987 = (1918)^2 - 3680961 = -2237$,
$(1917 + 2)^2 - 3 * 1226987 = (1919)^2 - 3680961 = 1600 = 40^2$.
So $3 * n = (1919)^2 - 40^2 = (1919 - 40) * (1919 + 40) = 1879 * 1959$. And now $n = 1879 * (1959/3) = 1879 * 653$.

Solutions to 8.2.2

1. Since $p - 1 = 2^a$ for some a, we have $p = 2^a + 1$. If a is a power of 2, then this would be a Fermat prime (see question 2 of Section 7.4). Choosing $F_4 = 65537$ satisfies our conditions.

3. We first choose a base $B = \{2, 3, 5, 7, 11, 13, 17, 19, 21, 23, 29, 31\}$. The first integer larger than square root n is 3516. We begin testing squares using an algorithm to produce them modulo 12358397. Here we divide out primes in the base one at a time and produce those squares which have any prime appearing at most 25 times. (25 is a random bound.)

```
quadrsieve := proc(x) local i, j, b, c, k, p;
p := {2, 3, 5, 7, 11, 13, 17, 19, 23, 29, 31, 37};
b[0] := 1;
c[0] := 1;
for i from 3516 to x do c[i] := i&^2 mod 12358397 : b[i] :=
c[i]:
    for j from 1 to 25 do
        for k from 1 to 12 do
if b[i] mod p[k] = 0 then b[i] := b[i]/p[k]
        end if: end do: end do:
    if b[i] = 1 then print(i, c[i], ifactor(c[i])) end if:
end do;
end proc;
> quadrsieve(6000);
```

This produces the following factorizations: $3525^2 = 2^2 * 7^5$; $3692^2 = 7 * 17^3 * 37$; $4972^2 = 2 * 3 * 5 * 7 * 19$; $4982^2 = 2 * 3 * 5 * 7 * 17 * 29$; $4984^2 = 2 * 3^2 * 19^3$; $4988^2 = 2 * 3^3 * 5^2 * 11^2$; $5098^2 = 2 * 3 * 5 * 7 * 11 * 19 * 29$; $5110^2 = 2 * 3^7 * 11 * 29$; $5237^2 = 3 * 5^5 * 17^2$; $5371^2 = 3^2 * 7^2 * 17 * 19 * 29$; $5388^2 = 2 * 5^4 * 7 * 17 * 29$; $5458^2 = 2 * 3 * 5 * 7^3 * 17 * 29$.
A possible combination can be made from $4982^2 = 2 * 3 * 5 * 7 * 17 * 29$ and $5458^2 = 2 * 3 * 5 * 7^3 * 17 * 29$. Multiplying, $(4982 * 5458)^2 = (2474962)^2 \equiv (2 * 3 * 5 * 7^2 * 17 * 29)^2 = (724710)^2$ so we test $\gcd(2474962 - 724710,$

12358397) $= 3677$ and $\gcd(2474962 + 724710, 12358397) = 3361$. It is now easy to confirm that $3361 * 3677 = 12358397$.

Solutions to 8.3.6

1. First set $f(x) = x^2 + 1$ and $x_0 = 2$ and then compute:

$$x_1 = 5, x_2 = 26, x_3 = 12, x_4 = 5, x_5 = 26.$$

So we have hit a cycle. Since $x_1 = x_4 = 5$, we write $f(x_0) = f(x_3)$ and so $2^2 + 1 = 5^2 + 1 \pmod{35}$. This results in checking $\gcd(5 - 2, 35)$ and $\gcd(5 + 2, 35)$. The former is 1 but the latter is 7, and so we have found a divisor of 35.

3. We use the algorithm of question 2 in Section 8.3.5. The output gives a cycle at $i = 6$. The list is $2, 5, 26, 677, 620, 202, 582, 297, 829, 677$, and so on. The tail is $\{2, 5, 26\}$. From the list, we can set $677 \equiv 26^2 + 1 \equiv 829^2 + 1 \pmod{1387}$ and so the gcds to check are $\gcd(829 - 26, 1387) = 73$ and $\gcd(829 + 26, 1387) = 19$. We can easily now verify that $1387 = 73 * 19$.

Solutions to 8.4.6

1. It suffices to suppose that the expansion stops in two steps as the argument is the same if it stops later. Thus, suppose $r = n + 1/(m + 1)$. Then we can write $r = (nm + n + 1)/(m + 1)$, which is rational.

3. Using the corresponding A_{i-1}'s, we obtain the congruence equations $414^2 \equiv (-1)^5 * 6 \pmod{667}$ and $188^2 \equiv (-1)^7 * 6 \pmod{667}$. Multiplying yields $299^2 \equiv 6^2 \pmod{667}$ and so n divides $(299 - 6) * (299 + 6)$. Checking gcds now simply gives us 1 and no proper factor of n.

$\equiv$	14, 146
$a\|b$	14, 146
gcd	18
CRT	22
Z_m	23
Z/m	23
$Z_m \times Z_n$	23
EA	18
DLP	26
FLT	28
DHKE	30
$\phi(n)$	45
$ord_n(a)$	48
SSL	57
PGP	57
$-P$	84
$P + Q$	84
ECDLP	92
ECKE	95
MAC	112
F_i	144
M_i	144
$R[x]$	146
$\deg p(x)$	148
$_nC_m$	149
$\lfloor \sqrt{n} \rfloor$	153
P_i	168

BIBLIOGRAPHY

[1] Agrawal, M., Kayal, N. and Saxena, N. (2004). Primes is in P. *Annals of Mathematics*, 160(2), 781–793.

[2] Bauer, F.L. *Decrypted Secrets*. Springer, Berlin, Heidelberg, New York, 1997.

[3] Blake, I., Seroussi. G. and Smart, N. *Elliptic Curves in Cryptography*. London Mathematical Society Lecture Note Series 265. ISBN 0 521 65374 6, August 1999.

[4] Boyd, C.A. and Mathuria, A. *Protocols for Key Establishment and Authentication*. Springer, Berlin, Heidelberg, New York, 2003.

[5] Brent, R.P. and Pollard, J.M. (1981). Factorization of the eighth Fermat number. *Mathematics of Computation*, 36, 627–630.

[6] Burton, D.M. *Elementary Number Theory*, 6th ed. McGraw-Hill, New York, 2005.

[7] Callegati, F., Cerroni, W. and Ramilli, M. (2009). Man-in-the-middle attack to the HTTPS protocol. *IEEE Security and Privacy*, 7, 78–81.

[8] Cannon, J. and Bosma, W. (2004). *Handbook of Magma Functions*. Version 2.11. Available at http://modular.fas.harvard.edu/docs/magma/ps/hb.ps

[9] Cheng, K., Gao, M. and Guo, M. (2010). Analysis and research on HTTPS hijacking attacks. International Conference on Networks Security. *Wireless Communications and Trusted Computing*, 2, 223–226.

[10] Davenport, H. *The Higher Arithmetic*, 7th ed. Cambridge University Press, Cambridge, New York, 1999.

[11] De Canniere, C. and Rechberger, C. Finding SHA-1 characteristics: general results and applications. In Lai, X. and Chen, K. (eds.), *ASIACRYPT LNCS*, Vol. 4284, Springer, Heidelberg, 2006, pp. 1–20.

[12] Dickson, L.E. *Modern Elementary Theory of Numbers*. The University of Chicago Press, 1965.

[13] Diffie, W. and Hellman, M.E. (1976). New directions in cryptography. *IEEE Transactions on Information Theory*, 22, pp. 644–654.

[14] ElGamal, T. (1985). A public key cryptosystem and a signature scheme based on discrete logarithms. *IEEE Transactions on Information Theory*, 31, pp. 469–472.

[15] Elminaam, D., Kader, H. and Hadhoud, M. (2010). Evaluating the performance of symmetric encryption algorithms. *International Journal of Network Security*, 10(3), pp. 216–222.

[16] Floyd, R.W. (1967). Nondeterministic algorithms. *Journal of the ACM (JACM)*, 14(4), pp. 636–644.

Public Key Cryptography: Applications and Attacks, First Edition. Lynn Margaret Batten.
© 2013 by The Institute of Electrical and Electronics Engineers, Inc. Published 2013 by John Wiley & Sons, Inc.

[17] Garrett, P. *An Introduction to Cryptology*. Prentice Hall, Upper Saddle River, NJ, 2001.

[18] Hankerson, D., Menezes, A. and Vanstone, S. *Guide to Elliptic Curve Cryptography*. Springer, Berlin, New York, 2004.

[19] Hoffstein, J., Pipher, J. and Silverman, J.H. *An Introduction to Mathematical Cryptography*. Springer Science + Business Media, New York, 2008.

[20] Kangsheng, S. (1998). Historical development of the Chinese remainder theorem. *Archive for History of Exact Sciences*, 38(4), pp. 285–305.

[21] Kant, K., Iyer, R. and Mohapatra, P. (2000). Architectural impact of secure socket layer on Internet servers. *Proceedings of Computer Design*, 15, pp. 7–14.

[22] Khan, D. *The Code-Breakers*. Macmillan, 1973.

[23] Knuth, D.E. *The Art of Computer Programming*, Vol. 2. Addison-Wesley, Reading, MA, 1969.

[24] Lenstra, H. (1987). Factoring integers with elliptic curves. *Annals of Mathematics*, 126(2), pp. 649–673.

[25] Lenstra, A. and Verheul, E. (2001). Selecting cryptographic key sizes. *Journal of Cryptology*, 14, pp. 255–293.

[26] Levy, S. *Crypto: How the Code Rebels Beat the Government–Saving Privacy in the Digital Age*. Viking Press, 2001.

[27] Mao, W. *Modern Cryptography: Theory and Practice*. Prentice Hall, Upper Saddle River, NJ, 2004.

[28] McAndrew, A. *Introduction to Cryptography with Open-Source Software*. CRC Press, Florida, 2011.

[29] Menezes, A.J., van Oorschot, P.C. and Vanstone, S.A. *Handbook of Applied Cryptography*. CRC Press, Boca Raton, London, New York, 1997.

[30] Miller, G.L. (1976). Riemann's hypothesis and tests for primality. *Journal of Computer and System Sciences*, 13, pp. 300–317.

[31] Mollin, R.A. *RSA and Public-Key Cryptography*. CRC Press, Florida, 2003.

[32] Mollin, R.A. (2008). On factoring. *International Journal of Contemporary Mathematical Science*, 3(33), pp. 1635–1642.

[33] Montgomery, P.L. (1985). Modular multiplication without trial division. *Maths of Computation*, 44(170), pp. 519–521.

[34] Osvik. D., Bos, J., Stefan. D. and Canright, D. (2010) Fast Software AES Encryption. FSE 2010, *LNCS* 6147, pp. 75–93.

[35] Paar, C. and Pelzl, J. *Understanding Cryptography*. Springer, Berlin, Heidelberg, New York, 2010.

[36] Pincock, S. *Codebreakers—The History of Secret Communication*. Viking Press, 2006.

[37] Pohlig, S.C. and Hellman, M.E. (1978). An improved algorithm for computing logarithms over $GF(p)$ and its cryptographic significance. *IEEE Transactions on Information Theory*. 24, pp. 106–110.

[38] Pollard, J.M. (1974). Theorems on factorization and primality testing. *Proceedings of the Cambridge Philosophical Society*, 76, pp. 521–528.

[39] Pollard, J.M. (1978). A Monte Carlo method for factorization. *Tidskrift för Informationsbehandling (BIT)*, 15, pp. 331–334.

[40] Pollard, J.M. (1978). Monte Carlo methods for index computation (mod p). *Mathematics Computations*, 32, pp. 918–924.

[41] Pomerance, C. Analysis and comparison of some integer factoring algorithms. In Lenstra, H.W. and Tijdeman, R. (eds.), *Computational Methods in Number Theory*, Part 1, Mathematisch Centrum, Amsterdam, 1982, pp. 89–139.

[42] Pomerance, C. (1985). The quadratic sieve factoring algorithm. In Eurocrypt'84. *LNCS* 209, pp. 169–182.

[43] Potlapally, N.R., Ravi, S., Raghunathan, A. and Jha. N.K., (2003). Analyzing the Energy Consumption of Security Protocols. ISLPED'03, August 25–27, ACM 2003, Seoul, Korea.

[44] Rabah, K. (2003). Secure online content management using EC ElGamal cryptosystems. *A Global Open Versity Technical Research Publication*, 1(2). Available at www.globalopenversity.org

[45] Rabin, M.O. (1980). Probabilistic algorithm for testing primality. *Journal of Number Theory*, 12, pp. 128–138.

[46] Rivest, R.A., Shamir, A. and Adleman, L. (1978). A method for obtaining digital signatures and public-key cryptosystems. *Communications of the ACM*, 21, pp. 120–126.

[47] Rosen, K.H. *Discrete Mathematics and its Applications*, 4th ed. McGraw-Hill International Editions, Boston, New York, London, 1999.

[48] Shannon, C.E. (1949). Communication theory of secrecy systems. *Bell System Technical Journal*, 28, pp. 656–715.

[49] Stallings, W. and Brown, L. *Computer Security; Principles and Practice*. Pearson Prentice Hall, Upper Saddle River, NJ, 2008.

[50] Stewart, J. *Calculus: Concepts and Contexts*, 3rd ed. Brooks/Cole, 2005.

[51] Tan, W., Wang X., Lou, X. and Pan. M. (2011). Analysis of RSA based on quantitating key security strength. *Advances in Control Engineering and Information Science*, 15, pp. 1340–1344.

[52] Trappe, W. and Washington, L. *Introduction to Cryptography with Coding Theory*, 2nd ed. Pearson International, 2006.

[53] Verma, S. and Garg, D. (2011). Improvement in RSA cryptosystem. *Journal of Advances in Information Technology*, 2(3), pp. 146–151.

[54] Wander, A., Gura, N., Eberle, H., Gupta, V. and Shantz, S. (2005). Energy analysis of public-key cryptography on small wireless devices. *Pervasive Computing, IEEE*, pp. 324–328.

[55] Wiener, M. (1990). Cryptanalysis of short RSA secret exponents. *IEEE Transactions on Information Theory*, 36, pp. 553–558.

[56] Williams, H.C. and Shallit, J.O. Factoring integers before computers. Mathematics of computation 1943–1993, fifty years of computational mathematics In Gautschi, W. (ed.), *Proceedings of Symposium in Applied Mathematics*, Vol. 48, AMS, Providence, RI, 1994, pp. 481–531.

References to Websites

[57] CISSP: https://www.isc2.org/cissp/default.aspx

[58] ECC: http://www.certicom.com/index.php/10-introduction

[59] ECRYPT II Yearly Report on Algorithms and Keysizes. European Network of Excellence in Cryptology II. ICT-2007-216676. Available at `http://www.ecrypt.eu.org/documents/D.SPA.17.pdf`.

[60] ElGamal: `http://en.wikipedia.org/wiki/Taher_Elgamal`

[61] Fermat number divisors: `http://wwwfermatsearch.org`

[62] Hash Functions: `http://ehash.iaik.tugraz.at/wiki/The_eHash_Main_Page`

[63] ISO (hash functions): `http://www.iso.org/iso/iso_catalogue/catalogue_tc/catalogue_detail.htm?csnumber=39876`

[64] Magma: `http://modular.fas.harvard.edu/docs/magma/ps/hb.ps`

[65] Maple: `http://www.maplesoft.com`

[66] Mersenne prime search: `http://www.mersenne.org/prime.htm`

[67] NIST: `http://www.nist.gov` and `http://csrc.nist.gov/publications/fips/fips180-2/fips180-2withchangenotice.pdf`

INDEX

Public Key Cryptography: Applications and Attacks, First Edition. Lynn Margaret Batten.
© 2013 by the Institute of Electrical and Electronics Engineers. Published 2013 by John Wiley & Sons, Inc.

Books in the IEEE Press Series on
Information and Communication Networks Security

Series Editor, **Stamatios V. Kartalopoulos**

The focus of this series is to introduce current and emerging security technologies to electrical and computer engineering practitioners, researchers, and students, particularly those who specialize in information processing and secure transport, or in security of communication networks. This series seeks to foster interdisciplinary engineering education to satisfy the needs of industry and academia, and it challenges engineers, computer scientists, mathematicians, and physicists to develop security problems that may be unsolvable, or to solve problems that have been claimed as unsolvable.

1. *Security of Information and Communication Networks*
   Stamatios V. Kartalopoulos

2. *Engineering Information Security: The Application of Systems Engineering Concepts to Achieve Information Assurance w/CD*
   Stuart Jacobs

3. *Public Key Cryptography: Applications and Attacks*
   Lynn Batten

Printed in the USA
K040759SCI121216   01S290530000000001654